the four gosp

M000021988

with introductions by

a.n. wilson

A.N. Wilson is an award-winning novelist and biographer. His most recent book, *Our Times* (2009), concludes his acclaimed trilogy on British history from Queen Victoria's accession to the present day. His biographies include studies of John Betjeman, Sir Walter Scott, John Milton, Tolstoy, C.S. Lewis and Hillaire Belloc. He lives in North London.

nick cave

The lead singer of The Birthday Party, The Bad Seeds and Grinderman, Nick Cave has been performing music for more than thirty years. He has written two novels, *And the Ass Saw the Angel* (1989) and *The Death of Bunny Munro* (2009). He lives in Brighton.

richard holloway

Richard Holloway is a well-known writer and broadcaster. A former Bishop of Edinburgh and Gresham Professor of Divinity, he is now a fellow of the Royal Society of Edinburgh. His most recent book, *Between the Monster and the Saint*, was published in 2008. He lives in Edinburgh.

blake morrison

Blake Morrison has written fiction, poetry, journalism, literary criticism and libretti. His award-winning memoir, *And When Did You Last See Your Father?*, was made into a feature film. Morrison lives in London, where he is Professor of Creative and Life Writing at Goldsmiths College.

the four gospels

matthew
mark
luke
john

with introductions by

a.n. wilson
nick cave
richard holloway
blake morrison

authorised king james version

printed by authority

CANONGATE
Edinburgh · London · New York · Melbourne

Published by Canongate Books in 2010

1

The *Pocket Canons* were first published in Great Britain in 1998 by Canongate Books
Ltd, 14 High Street, Edinburgh EH1 1TE

www.meetatthegate.com

British Library Cataloguing-in-Publication Data
A catalogue record for this book is available on
request from the British Library

ISBN 978 1 84767 835 5

Typeset by Palimpsest Book Production Ltd,
Grangemouth, Stirlingshire

Printed and bound in Great Britain by Clays Ltd, St Ives plc

When an old friend rang me out of the blue in the summer of 1997, I had no idea that the call was going to set a ball rolling that still hasn't stopped. Matt Darby had two simple questions that he wanted me to answer: had anyone ever published the Bible in its constituent parts and if not, why not?

I was immediately intrigued by the questions. It was clear even to me with my scant knowledge of its publishing history that the Bible was not one book but a series of books. And yes, the Bible's daunting length only added to its inaccessibility. And yes, the publishers of the Bible tended to make their editions look as unappealing as possible. But however we jazzed the Good Book up would anyone actually buy such editions? Matt thought so and his evangelical fervour for the project was infectious.

Having recently persuaded someone famous (the rapper Ice T) to introduce an old text (Iceberg Slim's memoir, *Pimp*) in order to bring it to a new audience, I had seen the impact that such unholy alliances can make and dropped this idea into the mix. Why don't we commission introductions from a diverse and interesting group of people? From people who don't have a religious drum to beat. Fifteen hundred words. Make them personal not prescriptive. This will help us enormously when we publish the series and make people want to buy our editions. Won't it?

This discussion about the Bible's format and how the individual books could be re-presented to a modern audience in a modern way was to be the first of many. By the time we launched the series, fifteen months later, it had blossomed into something beautiful, not least because of Angus Hyland's award-winning and stunning jacket designs but also because we had persuaded twelve good men and women to write introductions and they had excelled themselves. We licensed our editions around the world. The series generated an enormous amount of press ink and radio chatter. We sold a lot of copies and we were doing God's work.

Or were we? Paul Slenert, self-appointed leader of the 'Jesus is Alive ministry', took umbrage at our hijacking of his Bible and tried to do everything in his power to stop the series being published. He tried to take us to court on a charge of blasphemy and when this failed he proceeded to send letters to every parish in the UK, warning them about the series and urging them to write and ask me *personally* to withdraw the series. I must have received over 2000 letters in the following month, half of which simply regurgitated his outrage and repeated his belief that we would burn in hell. The other half were letters of support, encouraging us to ignore this deluded fool and saying that the Pocket Canons were the best thing to happen to the Bible in decades. It was fascinating to witness these diametrically opposed reactions and a fine reminder of how the Bible is still used to justify extremely dubious and dangerous attitudes (the Christian Right in America have since taken such abuse to new levels).

The Bible is, above all, a work of literature and we approached people who we felt would read it as such. It was in response to the King James version that they wrote the introductions that follow and the range of ideas expressed and experiences recounted is broader than any church that I know of. Some of the pieces are extremely personal but all of them are heartfelt and the wonderful array seems to me to epitomise what the whole project was about – celebrating language, encouraging dialogue and respecting the individual.

Jamie Byng
Publisher

contents

matthew

introduction by a. n. wilson

You are holding in your hands a tiny book which has changed more human lives than *The Communist Manifesto* or Freud's *Interpretation of Dreams*: a book which has shaped whole civilizations: a book which, for many people, has been not a gospel but The Gospel.

And you are bound to ask, because you are born out of time in a post-Christian age, into a world of newspapers and investigative reporting and science – 'Is it true?'

Did a Virgin really conceive (1:23) and give birth to a boy-child in Bethlehem (2:1)? Did wise men, guided by a star, come to worship him (2:2)? Did he grow up to be able to walk on water (14:26), to perform miracles, to found the Church (16:26), to rise from the dead?

Stop, stop. Don't ask. They are all questions which seem reasonable enough, but they will lead you into the most pointless, arid negativism. Your educated, scientific, modern mind will decide that no one ever walked on water; no Virgin ever conceived; that corpses do not come to life. And by rejecting this Gospel, you will reject one of the most disturbing and extraordinary books ever written; not, as you might think, on intelligent grounds, but because you (and I, alas) are too hemmed in by our imaginative limitations to see the sort of things this book is doing.

3

Before you apply to it the supposedly rational tests which you would apply to a newspaper report or a television documentary, imagine the chapters which describe the trial and Crucifixion of Christ set to music in Bach's *Saint Matthew Passion*. Consider the millions of people who, for the last 1900 years have recited the prayer (6:9–13) which begins 'Our Father'. Think of the old women in Stalin's Russia, when the men were too cowardly to profess their loyalty to the Church, who stubbornly continued to chant the opening verses of the Sermon on the Mount in defiance of the KGB. 'Blessed are they that mourn for they shall be comforted' (5:4).

This is a book, not of easily-dismissed fairy tales but of power and passion; more arresting, disturbing and truthful than most reading-matter which you could buy for the price of a magazine on a station bookstall or in the paperback store. This is the Gospel of Christ, in all its terribleness, its wonder, its awe-inspiring truth and its self-contradictions.

Nor should you think that the contradictory emotions which assail and trouble you as you read it – as trouble you they must – are all storms and tempest inside *you*. For this book itself was born out of conflict and struggle and contradiction.

Matthew's Gospel reflects the tension which saw the new religion – what we call Christianity – being fashioned from the old – Judaism. It is by paradox an intensely Jewish, and an intensely anti-Jewish work – indeed it is the great Ur-text of anti-semitism. The historical Jesus is not to be found in this book, nor in any book. He eludes our search. Matthew's Jesus is seen through the prism of a particular faith, of a particular group, somewhere in the Mediterranean world. Rome? 85–100 AD?

By the time the book reached something like its present form (50 years after Jesus had left the scene?) Christianity was emerging as something which, if not distinct from Judaism, was at least repellent to most Jews. Paul's Letter to the Galatians (of *circa* 50 AD) describes a rift between the first Christians of Asia Minor, converts of Paul, and the followers of Peter and James in Jerusalem who had known the earthly Jesus. It seems like an angry and irreconcilable quarrel. Paul, though, or because, a Jew, had decided that those who followed the Jewish Law (*Torah*), the Law given by God on Mount Sinai to his people, were living in bonds from which Christ came to set them free. For Peter and his friends, the dietary laws of Judaism, the requirement of circumcision, and so forth, were 'not bonds but wings'; they were symbols of lives dedicated to God.

No compromise, surely, was possible, between these two ways? Either you circumcise your son or you don't. Either it is sinful to eat pork, or it isn't.

But to another generation, Matthew's, the problems were different. The irreconcilables, rather than being fudged, are held together in self-contradiction. Peter and Paul, who in earlier New Testament texts were the leaders of opposing Ways, emerge in this text as co-partners (though, of course, Paul's ideas, rather than his name, are what we find here).

It is Jesus himself, in this legendary reconstruction, who speaks lines which, in an earlier generation of Christianity, had been assigned to protagonists in the quarrel. On the one hand, with the followers of Paul, he wants to leave the syna-gogue. See chapter 12, a key moment, when the Pharisees accuse Jesus of breaking the Law by healing a man on the Sabbath. His reaction is to lead his people away from the mainstream of Jewry, but he does so, as Paul had done, by quoting the Jewish Scriptures. 'I will put my spirit upon him, and he shall shew judgment to the Gentiles' (12:18). On the other hand, Matthew's Jesus is not simply a libertarian like Paul. He wishes to reassure the Jewish conservatives: 'Think not that I am come to destroy the law, or the prophets: I am not come to destroy, but to fulfil' (5:17).

How is the miracle accomplished? It is done by seeing the new congregation or synagogue, or gathering-together of the Elect as the New Israel: the Church.

So Matthew constructs his book as a miniature *Torah*. Like Moses, Matthew's Jesus goes up to a mountain (5:1) and delivers a New Law to his followers. At the end of the tale, in a gesture which could never have taken place in his-tory but which is heavy with religious paradox, a pagan, Roman Governor performs a Jewish purification ritual – he washes his hands – to demonstrate his innocence of Christ's murder. It is the Jewish mob who cry out, 'His blood be on us, and on our children' (27:25). A terrible text which would have profound consequences in Europe during the centuries that it penetrated the collective consciousness. It was not just a few Jews in this Gospel who are responsible for the torture and death of Jesus. It is 'all the people' (27:25).

Matthew's Gospel is not just the product of the embryo-Church. It is, really, a book about the Church, and it shapes what the Church, both in East and West, was destined to become.

The Church is a house founded upon a rock; and that rock is, primarily, the teaching of Christ. 'Therefore, whosoever heareth these sayings of mine, and doeth them, I will liken him unto a wise man, which built his house upon a rock: and the rain descended, and the floods came, and the winds blew, and beat upon that house; and it fell not: for it was founded upon a rock' (7:24–5).

The teachings, of course, are the exact reverse of worldly-wise notions of security. Our obsessions with security – financial, military, domestic – are blown sky high by Jesus's teaching: not to lay up treasure, not to resist evil with violence. Yet a detachment from what we would call security seems like a prerequisite here for church membership. And the Church, for Matthew, is the ante-chamber of the Kingdom of God.

And notice the extraordinary emphasis on the superiority of the poor over the rich. When John the Baptist asks (chapter 11) whether Jesus is the One who is to come, the message comes back, 'Go and shew John again those things which ye do hear and see'. A list follows, reaching a rhetorical *crescendo*. 'The blind receive their sight, and the lame walk, the lepers are cleansed, and the deaf hear, the dead are raised up' … Each thing is more remarkable than the last. But what is more remarkable even than the resurrection of the dead? The final item in the list: 'The poor have the gospel preached to them' (11:4–5).

That is not because Jesus was a sentimentalist or a socialist. It is because only the detached and the dispossessed, that is the poor, can hear his gospel. When a rich young man tried to follow Jesus, he 'went away sorrowful' (19:22) because the message was too simple, and too stern. Only those who live as though there is no tomorrow, and who do not store up treasure, can enter the kingdom.

This is the rock on which the Church is founded. It is founded on a rock in another sense: it is founded on Simon whose title or nickname, given to him by Jesus in one of the most dramatic scenes in the Gospel, is Peter. There is no name 'Peter' in the ancient world. You find it on no ossuary or tomb. It is a word meaning 'Rock'. It is a Gospel word. In chapter 16, Jesus asks his friends who do men say that he is? And they tell him – some say he is a prophet, or Elijah come back to earth. But you? Who do you say that he is?

The fisherman from Galilee blurts out, '"Thou art the Christ, the Son of the Living God." And Jesus answered and said unto him, "Blessed art thou, Simon Bar-Jona: for flesh and blood hath not revealed it unto thee, but my Father which is in heaven. And I say unto thee, that thou art Peter, and upon this rock I will build my church;' (16:16–18).

This is the Simon who, only a little while earlier (14:27–31) has attempted to walk with Jesus on the water of the stormy lake of Galilee and who has sunk because he had no faith. This is the Simon Peter who, as Jesus had predicted, has no courage at the last. As Jesus had predicted, when his Master had been arrested, Peter denies even knowing him; and, when he confronts his own cowardice and weakness, 'he went out and wept bitterly' (26:75).

Here we see how the Christian community which shaped

this Gospel has reconciled the early conflicts between Paul – for whom the Gospel was the acceptance of Grace – and Peter for whom it had been an observance of Law. For the Rock on which the Church is founded is not a rock of success, or moral strength, but of doubt, weakness, failure. The boat (another metaphor for the Church throughout this book) runs into storms and its crew panics. Only Jesus, apparently asleep, can calm the storms. 'And he hath said unto me, "My grace is sufficient for thee, for my strength is made perfect in weakness".' (2 *Corinthians* 12:9).

The attempt to follow the new *Torah*, the Sermon on the Mount, will not lead to a new legalism. Nor will anyone be able to follow Jesus's command to be perfect, even as God is perfect (5:48). Instead, it will lead to an understanding that, though we might abstain from murder, we shall still be angry; though we might avoid adultery, that is nothing to be proud of: for we shall still feel lust. It is Matthew the sinner and tax gatherer who is accepted in the Beloved. Christ the physician comes to heal sinners, not the righteous.

The author of this book did not attempt to write a realistic narrative of the kind we might expect from a post-enlightenment historian. For instance, judging from the earliest Christian writings and the *Letters of Paul*, it seems fairly likely that the Church began in Jerusalem. But *Matthew* has it beginning on a hillside in Galilee. *Mark*, the Gospel on which this book relies so heavily, says nothing about a miraculous conception, or a birth in Bethlehem. But the tale of a Virgin-birth and the recognition of the child by the wise men from the east perfectly illustrates the double-sided purpose of this book. On the one hand, the child is born to fulfil the Messianic prophecies of Judaism. On the other hand, he is recognised, not by the king of the Jews, but by wise Gentiles. Just so, at the end, he tells his followers to go into the ends of the earth, baptizing and teaching all people.

The sceptical mind will find these 28 chapters to be a catalogue of improbabilities. To any student of ethics, who has studied Aristotle or John Stuart Mill, or Dewey or Rawls, here is no morality at all but what Chesterton called 'The Ethics of Elfland'.

At the centre-stage is Jesus, calling the rich to discard their wealth and offering the kingdom to the poor. He offers not peace but a sword (10:34). Yet he says (11:28), 'Come unto me, all ye that labour and are heavy laden, and I will give you rest.'

Perhaps the most distinctive and haunting of all Matthew's stories – perhaps the most haunting passage in the entire New Testament – is that parable in the final discourse (25:31–46) when Jesus predicts that the King will welcome the chosen into his kingdom. They are those who have seen him, not in his glory, but as poor, naked, hungry, in prison and in need. Neither the blessed, nor the damned, in this tale, understand during their lifetimes, that in so far as they responded to the depths of human need in others, they had responded to God. It is in the context of this story that we begin to understand the sense in which this book is true. By the stern test of that parable and of this Gospel, most of us will feel like that rich young man. We will go away sorrowful, deeply conscious of our inability either to understand the Gospel, or to live up to its precepts or to have the humility to accept Divine Grace. Yet, though we are sorrowful, and though we go away, we shall never read this text without being, in some small degree, changed.

the gospel according to st matthew

The book of the generation of Jesus Christ, the son of David, the son of Abraham.

²Abraham begat Isaac; and Isaac begat Jacob; and Jacob begat Judas and his brethren. ³And Judas begat Phares and Zara of Thamar; and Phares begat Esrom; and Esrom begat Aram. ⁴And Aram begat Aminadab; and Aminadab begat Naasson; and Naasson begat Salmon. ⁵And Salmon begat Booz of Rachab; and Booz begat Obed of Ruth; and Obed begat Jesse. ⁶And Jesse begat David the king; and David the king begat Solomon of her that had been the wife of Urias. ⁷And Solomon begat Roboam; and Roboam begat Abia; and Abia begat Asa. ⁸And Asa begat Josaphat; and Josaphat begat Joram; and Joram begat Ozias. ⁹And Ozias begat Joatham; and Joatham begat Achaz; and Achaz begat Ezekias. ¹⁰And Ezekias begat Manasses; and Manasses begat Amon; and Amon begat Josias. ¹¹And Josias begat Jechonias and his brethren, about the time they were carried away to Babylon. ¹²And after they were brought to Babylon, Jechonias begat Salathiel; and Salathiel begat Zorobabel. ¹³And Zorobabel begat Abiud; and Abiud begat Eliakim; and Eliakim begat Azor. ¹⁴And Azor begat Sadoc; and Sadoc begat Achim; and Achim begat Eliud. ¹⁵And Eliud begat Eleazar; and Eleazar begat Matthan; and Matthan begat Jacob. ¹⁶And Jacob begat Joseph the

husband of Mary, of whom was born Jesus, who is called Christ. ¹⁷ So all the generations from Abraham to David are fourteen generations; and from David until the carrying away into Babylon are fourteen generations; and from the carrying away into Babylon unto Christ are fourteen generations.

¹⁸ Now the birth of Jesus Christ was on this wise. When as his mother Mary was espoused to Joseph, before they came together, she was found with child of the Holy Ghost. ¹⁹ Then Joseph her husband, being a just man, and not willing to make her a publick example, was minded to put her away privily. ²⁰ But while he thought on these things, behold, the angel of the Lord appeared unto him in a dream, saying, 'Joseph, thou son of David, fear not to take unto thee Mary thy wife, for that which is conceived in her is of the Holy Ghost. ²¹ And she shall bring forth a son, and thou shalt call his name "Jesus": for he shall save his people from their sins.' ²² Now all this was done, that it might be fulfilled which was spoken of the Lord by the prophet, saying, ²³ 'Behold, a virgin shall be with child, and shall bring forth a son, and they shall call his name "Emmanuel", which being interpreted is, "God with us". ²⁴ Then Joseph being raised from sleep did as the angel of the Lord had bidden him, and took unto him his wife; ²⁵ and knew her not till she had brought forth her firstborn son, and he called his name 'Jesus'.

2 Now when Jesus was born in Bethlehem of Judæa in the days of Herod the king, behold, there came wise men from the east to Jerusalem, ² saying, 'Where is he that is born King of the Jews? For we have seen his star in the east, and

are come to worship him.' ³ When Herod the king had heard these things, he was troubled, and all Jerusalem with him. ⁴And when he had gathered all the chief priests and scribes of the people together, he demanded of them where Christ should be born. ⁵And they said unto him, 'In Bethlehem of Judæa, for thus it is written by the prophet, ⁶ "And thou Bethlehem, in the land of Juda, art not the least among the princes of Juda, for out of thee shall come a Governor, that shall rule my people Israel."' ⁷ Then Herod, when he had privily called the wise men, enquired of them diligently what time the star appeared. ⁸And he sent them to Bethlehem, and said, 'Go and search diligently for the young child; and when ye have found him, bring me word again, that I may come and worship him also.' ⁹ When they had heard the king, they departed; and, lo, the star, which they saw in the east, went before them, till it came and stood over where the young child was. ¹⁰ When they saw the star, they rejoiced with exceeding great joy.

¹¹And when they were come into the house, they saw the young child with Mary his mother, and fell down, and worshipped him, and when they had opened their treasures, they presented unto him gifts: gold, and frankincense, and myrrh. ¹²And being warned of God in a dream that they should not return to Herod, they departed into their own country another way. ¹³And when they were departed, behold, the angel of the Lord appeareth to Joseph in a dream, saying, 'Arise, and take the young child and his mother, and flee into Egypt, and be thou there until I bring thee word, for Herod will seek the young child to destroy him.' ¹⁴ When he arose, he

took the young child and his mother by night, and departed into Egypt, [15] and was there until the death of Herod, that it might be fulfilled which was spoken of the Lord by the prophet, saying, 'Out of Egypt have I called my son.'

[16] Then Herod, when he saw that he was mocked of the wise men, was exceeding wroth, and sent forth, and slew all the children that were in Bethlehem, and in all the coasts thereof, from two years old and under, according to the time which he had diligently enquired of the wise men. [17] Then was fulfilled that which was spoken by Jeremy the prophet, saying, [18] 'In Rama was there a voice heard, lamentation, and weeping, and great mourning, Rachel weeping for her children, and would not be comforted, because they are not.'

[19] But when Herod was dead, behold, an angel of the Lord appeareth in a dream to Joseph in Egypt, [20] saying, 'Arise, and take the young child and his mother, and go into the land of Israel, for they are dead which sought the young child's life.' [21] And he arose, and took the young child and his mother, and came into the land of Israel. [22] But when he heard that Archelaus did reign in Judæa in the room of his father Herod, he was afraid to go thither; notwithstanding, being warned of God in a dream, he turned aside into the parts of Galilee. [23] And he came and dwelt in a city called Nazareth, that it might be fulfilled which was spoken by the prophets, 'He shall be called a Nazarene.'

3 In those days came John the Baptist, preaching in the wilderness of Judæa, [2] and saying, 'Repent ye, for the kingdom of heaven is at hand.' [3] For this is he that was spoken

of by the prophet Esaias, saying, 'The voice of one crying in the wilderness, "Prepare ye the way of the Lord, make his paths straight."' ⁴And the same John had his raiment of camel's hair, and a leathern girdle about his loins; and his meat was locusts and wild honey. ⁵Then went out to him Jerusalem, and all Judæa, and all the region round about Jordan, ⁶and were baptized of him in Jordan, confessing their sins.

⁷But when he saw many of the Pharisees and Sadducees come to his baptism, he said unto them, 'O generation of vipers, who hath warned you to flee from the wrath to come? ⁸Bring forth therefore fruits meet for repentance, ⁹and think not to say within yourselves, "We have Abraham to our father," for I say unto you that God is able of these stones to raise up children unto Abraham. ¹⁰And now also the axe is laid unto the root of the trees: therefore every tree which bringeth not forth good fruit is hewn down, and cast into the fire. ¹¹I indeed baptize you with water unto repentance, but he that cometh after me is mightier than I, whose shoes I am not worthy to bear. He shall baptize you with the Holy Ghost, and with fire, ¹²whose fan is in his hand, and he will throughly purge his floor, and gather his wheat into the garner; but he will burn up the chaff with unquenchable fire.'

¹³Then cometh Jesus from Galilee to Jordan unto John, to be baptized of him. ¹⁴But John forbad him, saying, 'I have need to be baptized of thee, and comest thou to me?' ¹⁵And Jesus answering said unto him, 'Suffer it to be so now, for thus it becometh us to fulfil all righteousness.' Then he suffered him. ¹⁶And Jesus, when he was baptized, went up straightway out of the water, and, lo, the heavens were opened unto

him, and he saw the Spirit of God descending like a dove, and lighting upon him: [17]and lo a voice from heaven, saying, 'This is my beloved Son, in whom I am well pleased.'

4 Then was Jesus led up of the Spirit into the wilderness to be tempted of the devil. [2]And when he had fasted forty days and forty nights, he was afterward an hungred. [3]And when the tempter came to him, he said, 'If thou be the Son of God, command that these stones be made bread.' [4]But he answered and said, 'It is written, "Man shall not live by bread alone, but by every word that proceedeth out of the mouth of God."' [5]Then the devil taketh him up into the holy city, and setteth him on a pinnacle of the temple, [6]and saith unto him, 'If thou be the Son of God, cast thyself down, for it is written, "He shall give his angels charge concerning thee, and in their hands they shall bear thee up, lest at any time thou dash thy foot against a stone."' [7]Jesus said unto him, 'It is written again, "Thou shalt not tempt the Lord thy God."' [8]Again, the devil taketh him up into an exceeding high mountain, and sheweth him all the kingdoms of the world, and the glory of them; [9]and saith unto him, 'All these things will I give thee, if thou wilt fall down and worship me.' [10]Then saith Jesus unto him, 'Get thee hence, Satan: for it is written, "Thou shalt worship the Lord thy God, and him only shalt thou serve."' [11]Then the devil leaveth him, and, behold, angels came and ministered unto him.

[12]Now when Jesus had heard that John was cast into prison, he departed into Galilee; [13]and leaving Nazareth, he came and dwelt in Capernaum, which is upon the sea coast,

in the borders of Zabulon and Nephthalim, ¹⁴ that it might be fulfilled which was spoken by Esaias the prophet, saying, ¹⁵ 'The land of Zabulon, and the land of Nephthalim, by the way of the sea, beyond Jordan, Galilee of the Gentiles; ¹⁶ the people which sat in darkness saw great light; and to them which sat in the region and shadow of death light is sprung up.'

¹⁷ From that time Jesus began to preach, and to say, 'Repent, for the kingdom of heaven is at hand.'

¹⁸ And Jesus, walking by the sea of Galilee, saw two brethren, Simon called Peter, and Andrew his brother, casting a net into the sea, for they were fishers. ¹⁹ And he saith unto them, 'Follow me, and I will make you fishers of men.' ²⁰ And they straightway left their nets, and followed him. ²¹ And going on from thence, he saw other two brethren, James the son of Zebedee, and John his brother, in a ship with Zebedee their father, mending their nets; and he called them. ²² And they immediately left the ship and their father, and followed him.

²³ And Jesus went about all Galilee, teaching in their synagogues, and preaching the gospel of the kingdom, and healing all manner of sickness and all manner of disease among the people. ²⁴ And his fame went throughout all Syria, and they brought unto him all sick people that were taken with divers diseases and torments, and those which were possessed with devils, and those which were lunatick, and those that had the palsy; and he healed them. ²⁵ And there followed him great multitudes of people from Galilee, and from Decapolis, and from Jerusalem, and from Judæa, and from beyond Jordan.

5 And seeing the multitudes, he went up into a mountain, and when he was set, his disciples came unto him, ²and he opened his mouth, and taught them, saying,

³ Blessed are the poor in spirit,
for theirs is the kingdom of heaven.
⁴ Blessed are they that mourn,
for they shall be comforted.
⁵ Blessed are the meek,
for they shall inherit the earth.
⁶ Blessed are they which do hunger
and thirst after righteousness,
for they shall be filled.
⁷ Blessed are the merciful,
for they shall obtain mercy.
⁸ Blessed are the pure in heart,
for they shall see God.
⁹ Blessed are the peacemakers,
for they shall be called the children of God.
¹⁰ Blessed are they which are persecuted
for righteousness' sake,
for theirs is the kingdom of heaven.
¹¹ Blessed are ye, when men shall revile you,
and persecute you, and shall say all manner
of evil against you falsely, for my sake.

¹²'Rejoice, and be exceeding glad, for great is your reward in heaven, for so persecuted they the prophets which were before you.

¹³ 'Ye are the salt of the earth: but if the salt have lost his

savour, wherewith shall it be salted? It is thenceforth good for nothing, but to be cast out, and to be trodden under foot of men. ¹⁴ Ye are the light of the world. A city that is set on an hill cannot be hid. ¹⁵ Neither do men light a candle, and put it under a bushel, but on a candlestick; and it giveth light unto all that are in the house. ¹⁶ Let your light so shine before men, that they may see your good works, and glorify your Father which is in heaven.

¹⁷ 'Think not that I am come to destroy the law, or the prophets; I am not come to destroy, but to fulfil. ¹⁸ For verily I say unto you, till heaven and earth pass, one jot or one tittle shall in no wise pass from the law, till all be fulfilled. ¹⁹ Whosoever therefore shall break one of these least commandments, and shall teach men so, he shall be called the least in the kingdom of heaven: but whosoever shall do and teach them, the same shall be called great in the kingdom of heaven. ²⁰ For I say unto you that, except your righteousness shall exceed the righteousness of the scribes and Pharisees, ye shall in no case enter into the kingdom of heaven.

²¹ 'Ye have heard that it was said by them of old time, "Thou shalt not kill", and whosoever shall kill shall be in danger of the judgment: ²² but I say unto you that whosoever is angry with his brother without a cause shall be in danger of the judgment, and whosoever shall say to his brother, "Raca," shall be in danger of the council, but whosoever shall say, "Thou fool," shall be in danger of hell fire. ²³ Therefore if thou bring thy gift to the altar, and there rememberest that thy brother hath ought against thee, ²⁴ leave there thy gift before the altar, and go thy way; first be reconciled to

thy brother, and then come and offer thy gift. ²⁵Agree with thine adversary quickly, whiles thou art in the way with him; lest at any time the adversary deliver thee to the judge, and the judge deliver thee to the officer, and thou be cast into prison. ²⁶Verily I say unto thee, thou shalt by no means come out thence, till thou hast paid the uttermost farthing.

²⁷'Ye have heard that it was said by them of old time, "Thou shalt not commit adultery," ²⁸but I say unto you that whosoever looketh on a woman to lust after her hath committed adultery with her already in his heart. ²⁹And if thy right eye offend thee, pluck it out, and cast it from thee: for it is profitable for thee that one of thy members should perish, and not that thy whole body should be cast into hell. ³⁰And if thy right hand offend thee, cut it off, and cast it from thee: for it is profitable for thee that one of thy members should perish, and not that thy whole body should be cast into hell. ³¹It hath been said, "Whosoever shall put away his wife, let him give her a writing of divorcement." ³²But I say unto you that whosoever shall put away his wife, saving for the cause of fornication, causeth her to commit adultery, and whosoever shall marry her that is divorced committeth adultery.

³³'Again, ye have heard that it hath been said by them of old time, "Thou shalt not forswear thyself, but shalt perform unto the Lord thine oaths." ³⁴But I say unto you, "Swear not at all; neither by heaven, for it is God's throne, ³⁵nor by the earth, for it is his footstool, neither by Jerusalem, for it is the city of the great King." ³⁶Neither shalt thou swear by thy head, because thou canst not make one hair white or black. ³⁷But let your communication be "Yea, yea", "Nay, nay", for

whatsoever is more than these cometh of evil.

³⁸ 'Ye have heard that it hath been said, "An eye for an eye, and a tooth for a tooth": ³⁹ but I say unto you that ye resist not evil, but whosoever shall smite thee on thy right cheek, turn to him the other also. ⁴⁰And if any man will sue thee at the law, and take away thy coat, let him have thy cloke also. ⁴¹And whosoever shall compel thee to go a mile, go with him twain. ⁴²Give to him that asketh thee, and from him that would borrow of thee turn not thou away.

⁴³ 'Ye have heard that it hath been said, "Thou shalt love thy neighbour, and hate thine enemy." ⁴⁴But I say unto you, "Love your enemies, bless them that curse you, do good to them that hate you, and pray for them which despitefully use you, and persecute you"; ⁴⁵ that ye may be the children of your Father which is in heaven, for he maketh his sun to rise on the evil and on the good, and sendeth rain on the just and on the unjust. ⁴⁶For if ye love them which love you, what reward have ye? Do not even the publicans the same? ⁴⁷And if ye salute your brethren only, what do ye more than others? Do not even the publicans so? ⁴⁸Be ye therefore perfect, even as your Father which is in heaven is perfect.

6 'Take heed that ye do not your alms before men, to be seen of them; otherwise ye have no reward of your Father which is in heaven. ²Therefore when thou doest thine alms, do not sound a trumpet before thee, as the hypocrites do in the synagogues and in the streets, that they may have glory of men. Verily I say unto you, "They have their reward." ³But when thou doest alms, let not thy left hand know what thy

right hand doeth, [4] that thine alms may be in secret, and thy Father which seeth in secret himself shall reward thee openly.

[5] 'And when thou prayest, thou shalt not be as the hypocrites are, for they love to pray standing in the synagogues and in the corners of the streets, that they may be seen of men. Verily I say unto you, "They have their reward." [6] But thou, when thou prayest, enter into thy closet, and when thou hast shut thy door, pray to thy Father which is in secret; and thy Father which seeth in secret shall reward thee openly. [7] But when ye pray, use not vain repetitions, as the heathen do, for they think that they shall be heard for their much speaking. [8] Be not ye therefore like unto them, for your Father knoweth what things ye have need of, before ye ask him. [9] After this manner therefore pray ye:

> Our Father which art in heaven,
>> Hallowed be thy name.
> [10] Thy kingdom come.
>> Thy will be done in earth, as it is in heaven.
> [11] Give us this day our daily bread.
> [12] And forgive us our debts,
>> as we forgive our debtors.
> [13] And lead us not into temptation,
>> but deliver us from evil:
>>> for thine is the kingdom,
>> and the power, and the glory,
>>> for ever. Amen.

[14] 'For if ye forgive men their trespasses, your heavenly Father will also forgive you, [15] but if ye forgive not men their

trespasses, neither will your Father forgive your trespasses.

[16] 'Moreover when ye fast, be not, as the hypocrites, of a sad countenance: for they disfigure their faces, that they may appear unto men to fast. Verily I say unto you, "They have their reward." [17] But thou, when thou fastest, anoint thine head, and wash thy face, [18] that thou appear not unto men to fast, but unto thy Father which is in secret: and thy Father, which seeth in secret, shall reward thee openly.

[19] 'Lay not up for yourselves treasures upon earth, where moth and rust doth corrupt, and where thieves break through and steal, [20] but lay up for yourselves treasures in heaven, where neither moth nor rust doth corrupt, and where thieves do not break through nor steal: [21] for where your treasure is, there will your heart be also. [22] The light of the body is the eye: if therefore thine eye be single, thy whole body shall be full of light. [23] But if thine eye be evil, thy whole body shall be full of darkness. If therefore the light that is in thee be darkness, how great is that darkness!

[24] 'No man can serve two masters: for either he will hate the one, and love the other; or else he will hold to the one, and despise the other. Ye cannot serve God and mammon. [25] Therefore I say unto you, take no thought for your life, what ye shall eat, or what ye shall drink; nor yet for your body, what ye shall put on. Is not the life more than meat, and the body than raiment? [26] Behold the fowls of the air, for they sow not, neither do they reap, nor gather into barns; yet your heavenly Father feedeth them. Are ye not much better than they? [27] Which of you by taking thought can add one cubit unto his stature? [28] And why take ye thought for

raiment? Consider the lilies of the field, how they grow; they toil not, neither do they spin, ²⁹ and yet I say unto you that even Solomon in all his glory was not arrayed like one of these. ³⁰ Wherefore, if God so clothe the grass of the field, which today is, and tomorrow is cast into the oven, shall he not much more clothe you, O ye of little faith? ³¹ Therefore take no thought, saying, "What shall we eat?" or, "What shall we drink?" or, "Wherewithal shall we be clothed?" ³²(For after all these things do the Gentiles seek) for your heavenly Father knoweth that ye have need of all these things. ³³ But seek ye first the kingdom of God, and his righteousness; and all these things shall be added unto you. ³⁴ Take therefore no thought for the morrow, for the morrow shall take thought for the things of itself. Sufficient unto the day is the evil thereof.

7 ¹Judge not, that ye be not judged. ² For with what judgment ye judge, ye shall be judged, and with what measure ye mete, it shall be measured to you again. ³And why beholdest thou the mote that is in thy brother's eye, but considerest not the beam that is in thine own eye? ⁴Or how wilt thou say to thy brother, "Let me pull out the mote out of thine eye," and, behold, a beam is in thine own eye? ⁵Thou hypocrite, first cast out the beam out of thine own eye; and then shalt thou see clearly to cast out the mote out of thy brother's eye.

⁶'Give not that which is holy unto the dogs, neither cast ye your pearls before swine, lest they trample them under their feet, and turn again and rend you.

⁷'Ask, and it shall be given you; seek, and ye shall find;

knock, and it shall be opened unto you: ⁸ for every one that asketh receiveth; and he that seeketh findeth; and to him that knocketh it shall be opened. ⁹ Or what man is there of you, whom if his son ask bread, will he give him a stone? ¹⁰ Or if he ask a fish, will he give him a serpent? ¹¹ If ye then, being evil, know how to give good gifts unto your children, how much more shall your Father which is in heaven give good things to them that ask him? ¹² Therefore all things whatsoever ye would that men should do to you, do ye even so to them: for this is the law and the prophets.

¹³ 'Enter ye in at the strait gate, for wide is the gate, and broad is the way, that leadeth to destruction, and many there be which go in thereat. ¹⁴ Because strait is the gate, and narrow is the way, which leadeth unto life, and few there be that find it.

¹⁵ 'Beware of false prophets, which come to you in sheep's clothing, but inwardly they are ravening wolves. ¹⁶ Ye shall know them by their fruits. Do men gather grapes of thorns, or figs of thistles? ¹⁷ Even so every good tree bringeth forth good fruit; but a corrupt tree bringeth forth evil fruit. ¹⁸ A good tree cannot bring forth evil fruit, neither can a corrupt tree bring forth good fruit. ¹⁹ Every tree that bringeth not forth good fruit is hewn down, and cast into the fire. ²⁰ Wherefore by their fruits ye shall know them.

²¹ 'Not every one that saith unto me, "Lord, Lord," shall enter into the kingdom of heaven; but he that doeth the will of my Father which is in heaven. ²² Many will say to me in that day, "Lord, Lord, have we not prophesied in thy name? And in thy name have cast out devils? And in thy name done

many wonderful works?" ²³And then will I profess unto them, "I never knew you: depart from me, ye that work iniquity."

²⁴ 'Therefore whosoever heareth these sayings of mine, and doeth them, I will liken him unto a wise man, which built his house upon a rock: ²⁵and the rain descended, and the floods came, and the winds blew, and beat upon that house; and it fell not: for it was founded upon a rock. ²⁶And every one that heareth these sayings of mine, and doeth them not, shall be likened unto a foolish man, which built his house upon the sand, ²⁷and the rain descended, and the floods came, and the winds blew, and beat upon that house; and it fell, and great was the fall of it.' ²⁸And it came to pass, when Jesus had ended these sayings, the people were astonished at his doctrine: ²⁹for he taught them as one having authority, and not as the scribes.

8 When he was come down from the mountain, great multitudes followed him. ²And, behold, there came a leper and worshipped him, saying, 'Lord, if thou wilt, thou canst make me clean.' ³And Jesus put forth his hand, and touched him, saying, 'I will; be thou clean.' And immediately his leprosy was cleansed. ⁴And Jesus saith unto him, 'See thou tell no man; but go thy way, shew thyself to the priest, and offer the gift that Moses commanded, for a testimony unto them.'

⁵And when Jesus was entered into Capernaum, there came unto him a centurion, beseeching him, ⁶and saying, 'Lord, my servant lieth at home sick of the palsy, grievously tormented.' ⁷And Jesus saith unto him, 'I will come and heal

him.' ⁸ The centurion answered and said, 'Lord, I am not worthy that thou shouldest come under my roof: but speak the word only, and my servant shall be healed. ⁹ For I am a man under authority, having soldiers under me, and I say to this man, "Go," and he goeth; and to another, "Come," and he cometh; and to my servant, "Do this," and he doeth it.' ¹⁰ When Jesus heard it, he marvelled, and said to them that followed, 'Verily I say unto you, I have not found so great faith, no, not in Israel. ¹¹ And I say unto you that many shall come from the east and west, and shall sit down with Abraham, and Isaac, and Jacob, in the kingdom of heaven. ¹² But the children of the kingdom shall be cast out into outer darkness: there shall be weeping and gnashing of teeth.' ¹³ And Jesus said unto the centurion, 'Go thy way; and as thou hast believed, so be it done unto thee.' And his servant was healed in the selfsame hour.

¹⁴ And when Jesus was come into Peter's house, he saw his wife's mother laid, and sick of a fever. ¹⁵ And he touched her hand, and the fever left her, and she arose, and ministered unto them.

¹⁶ When the even was come, they brought unto him many that were possessed with devils, and he cast out the spirits with his word, and healed all that were sick, ¹⁷ that it might be fulfilled which was spoken by Esaias the prophet, saying, 'Himself took our infirmities, and bare our sicknesses.'

¹⁸ Now when Jesus saw great multitudes about him, he gave commandment to depart unto the other side. ¹⁹ And a certain scribe came, and said unto him, 'Master, I will follow thee whithersoever thou goest.' ²⁰ And Jesus saith unto him,

'The foxes have holes, and the birds of the air have nests; but the Son of man hath not where to lay his head.' ²¹And another of his disciples said unto him, 'Lord, suffer me first to go and bury my father.' ²²But Jesus said unto him, 'Follow me; and let the dead bury their dead.'

²³And when he was entered into a ship, his disciples followed him. ²⁴And, behold, there arose a great tempest in the sea, insomuch that the ship was covered with the waves; but he was asleep. ²⁵And his disciples came to him, and awoke him, saying, 'Lord, save us. We perish.' ²⁶And he saith unto them, 'Why are ye fearful, O ye of little faith?' Then he arose, and rebuked the winds and the sea; and there was a great calm. ²⁷But the men marvelled, saying, 'What manner of man is this, that even the winds and the sea obey him!'

²⁸And when he was come to the other side into the country of the Gergesenes, there met him two possessed with devils, coming out of the tombs, exceeding fierce, so that no man might pass by that way. ²⁹And, behold, they cried out, saying, 'What have we to do with thee, Jesus, thou Son of God? Art thou come hither to torment us before the time?' ³⁰And there was a good way off from them an herd of many swine feeding. ³¹So the devils besought him, saying, 'If thou cast us out, suffer us to go away into the herd of swine.' ³²And he said unto them, 'Go.' And when they were come out, they went into the herd of swine, and, behold, the whole herd of swine ran violently down a steep place into the sea, and perished in the waters. ³³And they that kept them fled, and went their ways into the city, and told every thing, and what was befallen to the possessed of the devils. ³⁴And,

behold, the whole city came out to meet Jesus, and when they saw him, they besought him that he would depart out of their coasts.

9 And he entered into a ship, and passed over, and came into his own city. ²And, behold, they brought to him a man sick of the palsy, lying on a bed: and Jesus seeing their faith said unto the sick of the palsy, 'Son, be of good cheer; thy sins be forgiven thee.' ³And, behold, certain of the scribes said within themselves, 'This man blasphemeth.' ⁴And Jesus knowing their thoughts said, 'Wherefore think ye evil in your hearts? ⁵For whether is easier, to say, "Thy sins be forgiven thee," or to say, "Arise, and walk"? ⁶But that ye may know that the Son of man hath power on earth to forgive sins,' then saith he to the sick of the palsy, 'Arise, take up thy bed, and go unto thine house.' ⁷And he arose, and departed to his house. ⁸But when the multitudes saw it, they marvelled, and glorified God, which had given such power unto men.

⁹And as Jesus passed forth from thence, he saw a man, named Matthew, sitting at the receipt of custom, and he saith unto him, 'Follow me.' And he arose, and followed him.

¹⁰And it came to pass, as Jesus sat at meat in the house, behold, many publicans and sinners came and sat down with him and his disciples. ¹¹And when the Pharisees saw it, they said unto his disciples, 'Why eateth your Master with publicans and sinners?' ¹²But when Jesus heard that, he said unto them, 'They that be whole need not a physician, but they that are sick. ¹³But go ye and learn what that meaneth, "I will have mercy, and not sacrifice," for I am not come to

call the righteous, but sinners to repentance.'

¹⁴ Then came to him the disciples of John, saying, 'Why do we and the Pharisees fast oft, but thy disciples fast not?' ¹⁵ And Jesus said unto them, 'Can the children of the bride-chamber mourn, as long as the bridegroom is with them? But the days will come, when the bridegroom shall be taken from them, and then shall they fast. ¹⁶ No man putteth a piece of new cloth unto an old garment, for that which is put in to fill it up taketh from the garment, and the rent is made worse. ¹⁷ Neither do men put new wine into old bottles: else the bottles break, and the wine runneth out, and the bottles perish; but they put new wine into new bottles, and both are preserved.'

¹⁸ While he spake these things unto them, behold, there came a certain ruler, and worshipped him, saying, 'My daughter is even now dead, but come and lay thy hand upon her, and she shall live.' ¹⁹ And Jesus arose, and followed him, and so did his disciples.

²⁰ And, behold, a woman, which was diseased with an issue of blood twelve years, came behind him, and touched the hem of his garment, ²¹ for she said within herself, 'If I may but touch his garment, I shall be whole.' ²² But Jesus turned him about, and when he saw her, he said, 'Daughter, be of good comfort; thy faith hath made thee whole.' And the woman was made whole from that hour. ²³ And when Jesus came into the ruler's house, and saw the minstrels and the people making a noise, ²⁴ he said unto them, 'Give place, for the maid is not dead, but sleepeth.' And they laughed him to scorn. ²⁵ But when the people were put forth, he went in, and took her by the hand, and the maid arose. ²⁶ And the fame

hereof went abroad into all that land.

²⁷And when Jesus departed thence, two blind men followed him, crying, and saying, 'Thou Son of David, have mercy on us.' ²⁸And when he was come into the house, the blind men came to him, and Jesus saith unto them, 'Believe ye that I am able to do this?' They said unto him, 'Yea, Lord.' ²⁹Then touched he their eyes, saying, 'According to your faith be it unto you.' ³⁰And their eyes were opened; and Jesus straitly charged them, saying, 'See that no man know it.' ³¹But they, when they were departed, spread abroad his fame in all that country.

³²As they went out, behold, they brought to him a dumb man possessed with a devil. ³³And when the devil was cast out, the dumb spake, and the multitudes marvelled, saying, 'It was never so seen in Israel.' ³⁴But the Pharisees said, 'He casteth out devils through the prince of the devils.' ³⁵And Jesus went about all the cities and villages, teaching in their synagogues, and preaching the gospel of the kingdom, and healing every sickness and every disease among the people.

³⁶But when he saw the multitudes, he was moved with compassion on them, because they fainted, and were scattered abroad, as sheep having no shepherd. ³⁷Then saith he unto his disciples, 'The harvest truly is plenteous, but the labourers are few; ³⁸pray ye therefore the Lord of the harvest, that he will send forth labourers into his harvest.'

10 And when he had called unto him his twelve disciples, he gave them power against unclean spirits, to cast them out, and to heal all manner of sickness and all manner

of disease. ²Now the names of the twelve apostles are these: the first, Simon, who is called Peter, and Andrew his brother; James the son of Zebedee, and John his brother; ³Philip, and Bartholomew; Thomas, and Matthew the publican; James the son of Alphæus, and Lebbæus, whose surname was Thaddæus; ⁴Simon the Canaanite, and Judas Iscariot, who also betrayed him. ⁵These twelve Jesus sent forth, and commanded them, saying, 'Go not into the way of the Gentiles, and into any city of the Samaritans enter ye not: ⁶but go rather to the lost sheep of the house of Israel. ⁷And as ye go, preach, saying, "The kingdom of heaven is at hand." ⁸Heal the sick, cleanse the lepers, raise the dead, cast out devils: freely ye have received, freely give. ⁹Provide neither gold, nor silver, nor brass in your purses, ¹⁰nor scrip for your journey, neither two coats, neither shoes, nor yet staves, for the workman is worthy of his meat. ¹¹And into whatsoever city or town ye shall enter, enquire who in it is worthy; and there abide till ye go thence. ¹²And when ye come into an house, salute it. ¹³And if the house be worthy, let your peace come upon it: but if it be not worthy, let your peace return to you. ¹⁴And whosoever shall not receive you, nor hear your words, when ye depart out of that house or city, shake off the dust of your feet. ¹⁵Verily I say unto you, it shall be more tolerable for the land of Sodom and Gomorrha in the day of judgment, than for that city.

¹⁶'Behold, I send you forth as sheep in the midst of wolves: be ye therefore wise as serpents, and harmless as doves. ¹⁷But beware of men, for they will deliver you up to the councils, and they will scourge you in their synagogues; ¹⁸and ye shall

be brought before governors and kings for my sake, for a testimony against them and the Gentiles. ¹⁹But when they deliver you up, take no thought how or what ye shall speak, for it shall be given you in that same hour what ye shall speak. ²⁰For it is not ye that speak, but the Spirit of your Father which speaketh in you. ²¹And the brother shall deliver up the brother to death, and the father the child, and the children shall rise up against their parents, and cause them to be put to death. ²²And ye shall be hated of all men for my name's sake: but he that endureth to the end shall be saved. ²³But when they persecute you in this city, flee ye into another, for verily I say unto you, ye shall not have gone over the cities of Israel, till the Son of man be come. ²⁴The disciple is not above his master, nor the servant above his lord. ²⁵It is enough for the disciple that he be as his master, and the servant as his lord. If they have called the master of the house Beelzebub, how much more shall they call them of his household? ²⁶Fear them not therefore, for there is nothing covered, that shall not be revealed; and hid, that shall not be known. ²⁷What I tell you in darkness, that speak ye in light: and what ye hear in the ear, that preach ye upon the housetops. ²⁸And fear not them which kill the body, but are not able to kill the soul, but rather fear him which is able to destroy both soul and body in hell. ²⁹Are not two sparrows sold for a farthing? And one of them shall not fall on the ground without your Father. ³⁰But the very hairs of your head are all numbered. ³¹Fear ye not therefore, ye are of more value than many sparrows. ³²Whosoever therefore shall confess me before men, him will I confess also before my Father which is in heaven.

[33] But whosoever shall deny me before men, him will I also deny before my Father which is in heaven. [34] Think not that I am come to send peace on earth; I came not to send peace, but a sword. [35] For I am come to set a man at variance against his father, and the daughter against her mother, and the daughter-in-law against her mother-in-law. [36] And a man's foes shall be they of his own household. [37] He that loveth father or mother more than me is not worthy of me: and he that loveth son or daughter more than me is not worthy of me. [38] And he that taketh not his cross, and followeth after me, is not worthy of me. [39] He that findeth his life shall lose it: and he that loseth his life for my sake shall find it.

[40] 'He that receiveth you receiveth me, and he that receiveth me receiveth him that sent me. [41] He that receiveth a prophet in the name of a prophet shall receive a prophet's reward; and he that receiveth a righteous man in the name of a righteous man shall receive a righteous man's reward. [42] And whosoever shall give to drink unto one of these little ones a cup of cold water only in the name of a disciple, verily I say unto you, he shall in no wise lose his reward.'

11 And it came to pass, when Jesus had made an end of commanding his twelve disciples, he departed thence to teach and to preach in their cities. [2] Now when John had heard in the prison the works of Christ, he sent two of his disciples, [3] and said unto him, 'Art thou he that should come, or do we look for another?' [4] Jesus answered and said unto them, 'Go and shew John again those things which ye do hear and see: [5] the blind receive their sight, and the lame

walk, the lepers are cleansed, and the deaf hear, the dead are raised up, and the poor have the gospel preached to them. ⁶And blessed is he, whosoever shall not be offended in me.'

⁷And as they departed, Jesus began to say unto the multitudes concerning John, 'What went ye out into the wilderness to see? A reed shaken with the wind? ⁸But what went ye out for to see? A man clothed in soft raiment? Behold, they that wear soft clothing are in kings' houses. ⁹But what went ye out for to see? A prophet? Yea, I say unto you, and more than a prophet. ¹⁰For this is he, of whom it is written, "Behold, I send my messenger before thy face, which shall prepare thy way before thee." ¹¹Verily I say unto you, among them that are born of women there hath not risen a greater than John the Baptist; notwithstanding he that is least in the kingdom of heaven is greater than he. ¹²And from the days of John the Baptist until now the kingdom of heaven suffereth violence, and the violent take it by force. ¹³For all the prophets and the law prophesied until John. ¹⁴And if ye will receive it, this is Elias, which was for to come. ¹⁵He that hath ears to hear, let him hear.

¹⁶'But whereunto shall I liken this generation? It is like unto children sitting in the markets, and calling unto their fellows, ¹⁷and saying, "We have piped unto you, and ye have not danced; we have mourned unto you, and ye have not lamented." ¹⁸For John came neither eating nor drinking, and they say, "He hath a devil." ¹⁹The Son of man came eating and drinking, and they say, "Behold a man gluttonous, and a winebibber, a friend of publicans and sinners." But wisdom is justified of her children.'

²⁰ Then began he to upbraid the cities wherein most of his mighty works were done, because they repented not. ²¹ 'Woe unto thee, Chorazin! Woe unto thee, Bethsaida! For if the mighty works, which were done in you, had been done in Tyre and Sidon, they would have repented long ago in sackcloth and ashes. ²² But I say unto you, it shall be more tolerable for Tyre and Sidon at the day of judgment, than for you. ²³ And thou, Capernaum, which art exalted unto heaven, shalt be brought down to hell: for if the mighty works, which have been done in thee, had been done in Sodom, it would have remained until this day. ²⁴ But I say unto you, that it shall be more tolerable for the land of Sodom in the day of judgment, than for thee.'

²⁵ At that time Jesus answered and said, 'I thank thee, O Father, Lord of heaven and earth, because thou hast hid these things from the wise and prudent, and hast revealed them unto babes. ²⁶ Even so, Father, for so it seemed good in thy sight. ²⁷ All things are delivered unto me of my Father, and no man knoweth the Son, but the Father; neither knoweth any man the Father, save the Son, and he to whomsoever the Son will reveal him.

²⁸ 'Come unto me, all ye that labour and are heavy laden, and I will give you rest. ²⁹ Take my yoke upon you, and learn of me; for I am meek and lowly in heart: and ye shall find rest unto your souls. ³⁰ For my yoke is easy, and my burden is light.'

12 At that time Jesus went on the sabbath day through the corn; and his disciples were an hungred, and began to pluck the ears of corn, and to eat. ² But when the Pharisees

saw it, they said unto him, 'Behold, thy disciples do that which is not lawful to do upon the sabbath day.' ³But he said unto them, 'Have ye not read what David did, when he was an hungred, and they that were with him; ⁴how he entered into the house of God, and did eat the shewbread, which was not lawful for him to eat, neither for them which were with him, but only for the priests? ⁵Or have ye not read in the law, how that on the sabbath days the priests in the temple profane the sabbath, and are blameless? ⁶But I say unto you that in this place is one greater than the temple. ⁷But if ye had known what this meaneth, I will have mercy, and not sacrifice, ye would not have condemned the guiltless. ⁸For the Son of man is Lord even of the sabbath day.' ⁹And when he was departed thence, he went into their synagogue.

¹⁰And, behold, there was a man which had his hand withered. And they asked him, saying, 'Is it lawful to heal on the sabbath days?' that they might accuse him. ¹¹And he said unto them, 'What man shall there be among you, that shall have one sheep, and if it fall into a pit on the sabbath day, will he not lay hold on it, and lift it out? ¹²How much then is a man better than a sheep? Wherefore it is lawful to do well on the sabbath days.' ¹³Then saith he to the man, 'Stretch forth thine hand.' And he stretched it forth; and it was restored whole, like as the other.

¹⁴Then the Pharisees went out, and held a council against him, how they might destroy him. ¹⁵But when Jesus knew it, he withdrew himself from thence, and great multitudes followed him, and he healed them all; ¹⁶and charged them that they should not make him known, ¹⁷that it might be fulfilled

which was spoken by Esaias the prophet, saying, ¹⁸'Behold my servant, whom I have chosen; my beloved, in whom my soul is well pleased: I will put my spirit upon him, and he shall shew judgment to the Gentiles. ¹⁹He shall not strive, nor cry; neither shall any man hear his voice in the streets. ²⁰A bruised reed shall he not break, and smoking flax shall he not quench, till he send forth judgment unto victory. ²¹And in his name shall the Gentiles trust.'

²²Then was brought unto him one possessed with a devil, blind, and dumb: and he healed him, insomuch that the blind and dumb both spake and saw. ²³And all the people were amazed, and said, 'Is not this the son of David?' ²⁴But when the Pharisees heard it, they said, 'This fellow doth not cast out devils, but by Beelzebub the prince of the devils.' ²⁵And Jesus knew their thoughts, and said unto them, 'Every kingdom divided against itself is brought to desolation; and every city or house divided against itself shall not stand. ²⁶And if Satan cast out Satan, he is divided against himself; how shall then his kingdom stand? ²⁷And if I by Beelzebub cast out devils, by whom do your children cast them out? Therefore they shall be your judges. ²⁸But if I cast out devils by the Spirit of God, then the kingdom of God is come unto you. ²⁹Or else how can one enter into a strong man's house, and spoil his goods, except he first bind the strong man? And then he will spoil his house. ³⁰He that is not with me is against me; and he that gathereth not with me scattereth abroad.

³¹'Wherefore I say unto you, all manner of sin and blasphemy shall be forgiven unto men: but the blasphemy against the Holy Ghost shall not be forgiven unto men. ³²And who-

soever speaketh a word against the Son of man, it shall be forgiven him: but whosoever speaketh against the Holy Ghost, it shall not be forgiven him, neither in this world, neither in the world to come. ³³ Either make the tree good, and his fruit good, or else make the tree corrupt, and his fruit corrupt: for the tree is known by his fruit. ³⁴ O generation of vipers, how can ye, being evil, speak good things? For out of the abundance of the heart the mouth speaketh. ³⁵ A good man out of the good treasure of the heart bringeth forth good things: and an evil man out of the evil treasure bringeth forth evil things. ³⁶ But I say unto you that every idle word that men shall speak, they shall give account thereof in the day of judgment. ³⁷ For by thy words thou shalt be justified, and by thy words thou shalt be condemned.'

³⁸ Then certain of the scribes and of the Pharisees answered, saying, 'Master, we would see a sign from thee.' ³⁹ But he answered and said unto them, 'An evil and adulterous generation seeketh after a sign; and there shall no sign be given to it, but the sign of the prophet Jonas: ⁴⁰ for as Jonas was three days and three nights in the whale's belly; so shall the Son of man be three days and three nights in the heart of the earth. ⁴¹ The men of Nineveh shall rise in judgment with this generation, and shall condemn it: because they repented at the preaching of Jonas; and, behold, a greater than Jonas is here. ⁴² The queen of the south shall rise up in the judgment with this generation, and shall condemn it: for she came from the uttermost parts of the earth to hear the wisdom of Solomon; and, behold, a greater than Solomon is here. ⁴³ When the unclean spirit is gone out of a man, he walketh through

dry places, seeking rest, and findeth none. ⁴⁴ Then he saith, "I will return into my house from whence I came out"; and when he is come, he findeth it empty, swept, and garnished. ⁴⁵ Then goeth he, and taketh with himself seven other spirits more wicked than himself, and they enter in and dwell there, and the last state of that man is worse than the first. Even so shall it be also unto this wicked generation.'

⁴⁶ While he yet talked to the people, behold, his mother and his brethren stood without, desiring to speak with him. ⁴⁷ Then one said unto him, 'Behold, thy mother and thy brethren stand without, desiring to speak with thee.' ⁴⁸ But he answered and said unto him that told him, 'Who is my mother? And who are my brethren?' ⁴⁹ And he stretched forth his hand toward his disciples, and said, 'Behold my mother and my brethren! ⁵⁰ For whosoever shall do the will of my Father which is in heaven, the same is my brother, and sister, and mother.'

13 The same day went Jesus out of the house, and sat by the sea side. ²And great multitudes were gathered together unto him, so that he went into a ship, and sat; and the whole multitude stood on the shore. ³And he spake many things unto them in parables, saying, 'Behold, a sower went forth to sow; ⁴and when he sowed, some seeds fell by the way side, and the fowls came and devoured them up. ⁵Some fell upon stony places, where they had not much earth: and forthwith they sprung up, because they had no deepness of earth. ⁶And when the sun was up, they were scorched; and because they had no root, they withered away.

⁷And some fell among thorns; and the thorns sprung up, and choked them. ⁸But other fell into good ground, and brought forth fruit, some an hundredfold, some sixtyfold, some thirty-fold. ⁹Who hath ears to hear, let him hear.' ¹⁰And the disciples came, and said unto him, 'Why speakest thou unto them in parables?' ¹¹He answered and said unto them, 'Because it is given unto you to know the mysteries of the kingdom of heaven, but to them it is not given. ¹²For whosoever hath, to him shall be given, and he shall have more abundance: but whosoever hath not, from him shall be taken away even that he hath. ¹³Therefore speak I to them in parables: because they seeing see not; and hearing they hear not, neither do they understand. ¹⁴And in them is fulfilled the prophecy of Esaias, which saith, "By hearing ye shall hear, and shall not under-stand; and seeing ye shall see, and shall not perceive: ¹⁵for this people's heart is waxed gross, and their ears are dull of hearing, and their eyes they have closed, lest at any time they should see with their eyes, and hear with their ears, and should understand with their heart, and should be con-verted, and I should heal them." ¹⁶But blessed are your eyes, for they see, and your ears, for they hear. ¹⁷For verily I say unto you that many prophets and righteous men have desired to see those things which ye see, and have not seen them; and to hear those things which ye hear, and have not heard them.

¹⁸'Hear ye therefore the parable of the sower. ¹⁹When any one heareth the word of the kingdom, and understandeth it not, then cometh the wicked one, and catcheth away that which was sown in his heart. This is he which received seed by the way side. ²⁰But he that received the seed into stony

places, the same is he that heareth the word, and anon with joy receiveth it; ²¹ yet hath he not root in himself, but dureth for a while: for when tribulation or persecution ariseth because of the word, by and by he is offended. ²² He also that received seed among the thorns is he that heareth the word; and the care of this world, and the deceitfulness of riches, choke the word, and he becometh unfruitful. ²³ But he that received seed into the good ground is he that heareth the word, and understandeth it; which also beareth fruit, and bringeth forth, some an hundredfold, some sixty, some thirty.'

²⁴Another parable put he forth unto them, saying, 'The kingdom of heaven is likened unto a man which sowed good seed in his field: ²⁵ but while men slept, his enemy came and sowed tares among the wheat, and went his way. ²⁶ But when the blade was sprung up, and brought forth fruit, then appeared the tares also. ²⁷ So the servants of the householder came and said unto him, "Sir, didst not thou sow good seed in thy field? From whence then hath it tares?" ²⁸ He said unto them, "An enemy hath done this." The servants said unto him, "Wilt thou then that we go and gather them up?" ²⁹ But he said, "Nay, lest while ye gather up the tares, ye root up also the wheat with them. ³⁰ Let both grow together until the harvest: and in the time of harvest I will say to the reapers, 'Gather ye together first the tares, and bind them in bundles to burn them, but gather the wheat into my barn.'"'

³¹Another parable put he forth unto them, saying, 'The kingdom of heaven is like to a grain of mustard seed, which a man took, and sowed in his field, ³² which indeed is the least of all seeds: but when it is grown, it is the greatest among

herbs, and becometh a tree, so that the birds of the air come and lodge in the branches thereof.'

³³Another parable spake he unto them. 'The kingdom of heaven is like unto leaven, which a woman took, and hid in three measures of meal, till the whole was leavened.' ³⁴All these things spake Jesus unto the multitude in parables; and without a parable spake he not unto them, ³⁵that it might be fulfilled which was spoken by the prophet, saying, 'I will open my mouth in parables; I will utter things which have been kept secret from the foundation of the world.' ³⁶Then Jesus sent the multitude away, and went into the house, and his disciples came unto him, saying, 'Declare unto us the parable of the tares of the field.' ³⁷He answered and said unto them, 'He that soweth the good seed is the Son of man; ³⁸the field is the world; the good seed are the children of the kingdom; but the tares are the children of the wicked one; ³⁹the enemy that sowed them is the devil; the harvest is the end of the world; and the reapers are the angels. ⁴⁰As therefore the tares are gathered and burned in the fire, so shall it be in the end of this world. ⁴¹The Son of man shall send forth his angels, and they shall gather out of his kingdom all things that offend, and them which do iniquity, ⁴²and shall cast them into a furnace of fire: there shall be wailing and gnashing of teeth. ⁴³Then shall the righteous shine forth as the sun in the kingdom of their Father. Who hath ears to hear, let him hear.

⁴⁴'Again, the kingdom of heaven is like unto treasure hid in a field; the which when a man hath found, he hideth, and for joy thereof goeth and selleth all that he hath, and buyeth that field.

⁴⁵ 'Again, the kingdom of heaven is like unto a merchant man, seeking goodly pearls, ⁴⁶ who, when he had found one pearl of great price, went and sold all that he had, and bought it.

⁴⁷ 'Again, the kingdom of heaven is like unto a net, that was cast into the sea, and gathered of every kind: ⁴⁸ which, when it was full, they drew to shore, and sat down, and gathered the good into vessels, but cast the bad away. ⁴⁹ So shall it be at the end of the world. The angels shall come forth, and sever the wicked from among the just, ⁵⁰ and shall cast them into the furnace of fire: there shall be wailing and gnashing of teeth.' ⁵¹ Jesus saith unto them, 'Have ye understood all these things?' They say unto him, 'Yea, Lord.' ⁵² Then said he unto them, 'Therefore every scribe which is instructed unto the kingdom of heaven is like unto a man that is an householder, which bringeth forth out of his treasure things new and old.'

⁵³ And it came to pass, that when Jesus had finished these parables, he departed thence. ⁵⁴ And when he was come into his own country, he taught them in their synagogue, insomuch that they were astonished, and said, 'Whence hath this man this wisdom, and these mighty works? ⁵⁵ Is not this the carpenter's son? Is not his mother called Mary? And his brethren, James, and Joses, and Simon, and Judas? ⁵⁶ And his sisters, are they not all with us? Whence then hath this man all these things?' ⁵⁷ And they were offended in him. But Jesus said unto them, 'A prophet is not without honour, save in his own country, and in his own house.' ⁵⁸ And he did not many mighty works there because of their unbelief.

14 At that time Herod the tetrarch heard of the fame of Jesus, ²and said unto his servants, 'This is John the Baptist; he is risen from the dead; and therefore mighty works do shew forth themselves in him.'

³For Herod had laid hold on John, and bound him, and put him in prison for Herodias' sake, his brother Philip's wife. ⁴For John said unto him, 'It is not lawful for thee to have her.' ⁵And when he would have put him to death, he feared the multitude, because they counted him as a prophet. ⁶But when Herod's birthday was kept, the daughter of Herodias danced before them, and pleased Herod. ⁷Whereupon he promised with an oath to give her whatsoever she would ask. ⁸And she, being before instructed of her mother, said, 'Give me here John Baptist's head in a charger.' ⁹And the king was sorry; nevertheless for the oath's sake, and them which sat with him at meat, he commanded it to be given her. ¹⁰And he sent, and beheaded John in the prison. ¹¹And his head was brought in a charger, and given to the damsel, and she brought it to her mother. ¹²And his disciples came, and took up the body, and buried it, and went and told Jesus.

¹³When Jesus heard of it, he departed thence by ship into a desert place apart, and when the people had heard thereof, they followed him on foot out of the cities. ¹⁴And Jesus went forth, and saw a great multitude, and was moved with compassion toward them, and he healed their sick.

¹⁵And when it was evening, his disciples came to him, saying, 'This is a desert place, and the time is now past; send the multitude away, that they may go into the villages, and buy themselves victuals.' ¹⁶But Jesus said unto them, 'They

need not depart; give ye them to eat.' ¹⁷And they say unto him, 'We have here but five loaves, and two fishes.' ¹⁸He said, 'Bring them hither to me.' ¹⁹And he commanded the multitude to sit down on the grass, and took the five loaves, and the two fishes, and looking up to heaven, he blessed, and brake, and gave the loaves to his disciples, and the disciples to the multitude. ²⁰And they did all eat, and were filled: and they took up of the fragments that remained twelve baskets full. ²¹And they that had eaten were about five thousand men, beside women and children.

²²And straightway Jesus constrained his disciples to get into a ship, and to go before him unto the other side, while he sent the multitudes away. ²³And when he had sent the multitudes away, he went up into a mountain apart to pray: and when the evening was come, he was there alone. ²⁴But the ship was now in the midst of the sea, tossed with waves: for the wind was contrary. ²⁵And in the fourth watch of the night Jesus went unto them, walking on the sea. ²⁶And when the disciples saw him walking on the sea, they were troubled, saying, 'It is a spirit' and they cried out for fear. ²⁷But straightway Jesus spake unto them, saying, 'Be of good cheer; it is I; be not afraid.' ²⁸And Peter answered him and said, 'Lord, if it be thou, bid me come unto thee on the water.' ²⁹And he said, 'Come.' And when Peter was come down out of the ship, he walked on the water, to go to Jesus. ³⁰But when he saw the wind boisterous, he was afraid; and beginning to sink, he cried, saying, 'Lord, save me.' ³¹And immediately Jesus stretched forth his hand, and caught him, and said unto him, 'O thou of little faith, wherefore didst thou doubt?' ³²And when

they were come into the ship, the wind ceased. ³³ Then they that were in the ship came and worshipped him, saying, 'Of a truth thou art the Son of God.'

³⁴And when they were gone over, they came into the land of Gennesaret. ³⁵And when the men of that place had knowledge of him, they sent out into all that country round about, and brought unto him all that were diseased; ³⁶and besought him that they might only touch the hem of his garment: and as many as touched were made perfectly whole.

15 Then came to Jesus scribes and Pharisees, which were of Jerusalem, saying, ²'Why do thy disciples transgress the tradition of the elders? For they wash not their hands when they eat bread.' ³But he answered and said unto them, 'Why do ye also transgress the commandment of God by your tradition? ⁴For God commanded, saying, "Honour thy father and mother," and, "He that curseth father or mother, let him die the death." ⁵But ye say, "Whosoever shall say to his father or his mother, 'It is a gift, by whatsoever thou mightest be profited by me' ⁶and honour not his father or his mother, he shall be free." Thus have ye made the commandment of God of none effect by your tradition. ⁷Ye hypocrites, well did Esaias prophesy of you, saying, ⁸"This people draweth nigh unto me with their mouth, and honoureth me with their lips; but their heart is far from me. ⁹But in vain they do worship me, teaching for doctrines the commandments of men."'

¹⁰And he called the multitude, and said unto them, 'Hear, and understand: ¹¹not that which goeth into the mouth defileth a man; but that which cometh out of the mouth, this

defileth a man.' ¹² Then came his disciples, and said unto him, 'Knowest thou that the Pharisees were offended, after they heard this saying?' ¹³ But he answered and said, 'Every plant, which my heavenly Father hath not planted, shall be rooted up. ¹⁴ Let them alone: they be blind leaders of the blind. And if the blind lead the blind, both shall fall into the ditch.' ¹⁵ Then answered Peter and said unto him, 'Declare unto us this parable.' ¹⁶ And Jesus said, 'Are ye also yet without understanding? ¹⁷ Do not ye yet understand, that whatsoever entereth in at the mouth goeth into the belly, and is cast out into the draught? ¹⁸ But those things which proceed out of the mouth come forth from the heart; and they defile the man. ¹⁹ For out of the heart proceed evil thoughts, murders, adulteries, fornications, thefts, false witness, blasphemies. ²⁰ These are the things which defile a man: but to eat with unwashen hands defileth not a man.'

²¹ Then Jesus went thence, and departed into the coasts of Tyre and Sidon. ²² And, behold, a woman of Canaan came out of the same coasts, and cried unto him, saying, 'Have mercy on me, O Lord, thou Son of David; my daughter is grievously vexed with a devil.' ²³ But he answered her not a word. And his disciples came and besought him, saying, 'Send her away; for she crieth after us.' ²⁴ But he answered and said, 'I am not sent but unto the lost sheep of the house of Israel.' ²⁵ Then came she and worshipped him, saying, 'Lord, help me.' ²⁶ But he answered and said, 'It is not meet to take the children's bread, and to cast it to dogs.' ²⁷ And she said, 'Truth, Lord, yet the dogs eat of the crumbs which fall from their masters' table.' ²⁸ Then Jesus answered and said unto

her, 'O woman, great is thy faith. Be it unto thee even as thou wilt.' And her daughter was made whole from that very hour. ²⁹And Jesus departed from thence, and came nigh unto the sea of Galilee; and went up into a mountain, and sat down there. ³⁰And great multitudes came unto him, having with them those that were lame, blind, dumb, maimed, and many others, and cast them down at Jesus' feet; and he healed them, ³¹insomuch that the multitude wondered, when they saw the dumb to speak, the maimed to be whole, the lame to walk, and the blind to see, and they glorified the God of Israel.

³²Then Jesus called his disciples unto him, and said, 'I have compassion on the multitude, because they continue with me now three days, and have nothing to eat, and I will not send them away fasting, lest they faint in the way.' ³³And his disciples say unto him, 'Whence should we have so much bread in the wilderness, as to fill so great a multitude?' ³⁴And Jesus saith unto them, 'How many loaves have ye?' And they said, 'Seven, and a few little fishes.' ³⁵And he commanded the multitude to sit down on the ground. ³⁶And he took the seven loaves and the fishes, and gave thanks, and brake them, and gave to his disciples, and the disciples to the multitude. ³⁷And they did all eat, and were filled, and they took up of the broken meat that was left seven baskets full. ³⁸And they that did eat were four thousand men, beside women and children. ³⁹And he sent away the multitude, and took ship, and came into the coasts of Magdala.

16 The Pharisees also with the Sadducees came, and tempting desired him that he would shew them a sign from

heaven. ² He answered and said unto them, 'When it is evening, ye say, "It will be fair weather, for the sky is red." ³And in the morning, "It will be foul weather today, for the sky is red and lowring." O ye hypocrites, ye can discern the face of the sky; but can ye not discern the signs of the times? ⁴A wicked and adulterous generation seeketh after a sign; and there shall no sign be given unto it, but the sign of the prophet Jonas.' And he left them, and departed. ⁵And when his disciples were come to the other side, they had forgotten to take bread.

⁶ Then Jesus said unto them, 'Take heed and beware of the leaven of the Pharisees and of the Sadducees.' ⁷And they reasoned among themselves, saying, 'It is because we have taken no bread,' ⁸ which when Jesus perceived, he said unto them, 'O ye of little faith, why reason ye among yourselves, because ye have brought no bread? ⁹Do ye not yet understand, neither remember the five loaves of the five thousand, and how many baskets ye took up?¹⁰Neither the seven loaves of the four thousand, and how many baskets ye took up? ¹¹How is it that ye do not understand that I spake it not to you concerning bread, that ye should beware of the leaven of the Pharisees and of the Sadducees?' ¹²Then understood they how that he bade them not beware of the leaven of bread, but of the doctrine of the Pharisees and of the Sadducees.

¹³ When Jesus came into the coasts of Cæsarea Philippi, he asked his disciples, saying, 'Whom do men say that I the Son of man am?' ¹⁴And they said, 'Some say that thou art John the Baptist: some, Elias; and others, Jeremias, or one of the prophets.' ¹⁵ He saith unto them, 'But whom say ye that I

am?' ¹⁶And Simon Peter answered and said, 'Thou art the Christ, the Son of the living God.' ¹⁷And Jesus answered and said unto him, 'Blessed art thou, Simon Bar-jona, for flesh and blood hath not revealed it unto thee, but my Father which is in heaven. ¹⁸And I say also unto thee that thou art Peter, and upon this rock I will build my church; and the gates of hell shall not prevail against it. ¹⁹And I will give unto thee the keys of the kingdom of heaven, and whatsoever thou shalt bind on earth shall be bound in heaven, and whatsoever thou shalt loose on earth shall be loosed in heaven.' ²⁰Then charged he his disciples that they should tell no man that he was Jesus the Christ.

²¹From that time forth began Jesus to shew unto his disciples, how that he must go unto Jerusalem, and suffer many things of the elders and chief priests and scribes, and be killed, and be raised again the third day. ²²Then Peter took him, and began to rebuke him, saying, 'Be it far from thee, Lord: this shall not be unto thee.' ²³But he turned, and said unto Peter, 'Get thee behind me, Satan. Thou art an offence unto me, for thou savourest not the things that be of God, but those that be of men.'

²⁴Then said Jesus unto his disciples, 'If any man will come after me, let him deny himself, and take up his cross, and follow me. ²⁵For whosoever will save his life shall lose it, and whosoever will lose his life for my sake shall find it. ²⁶For what is a man profited, if he shall gain the whole world, and lose his own soul? Or what shall a man give in exchange for his soul? ²⁷For the Son of man shall come in the glory of his Father with his angels; and then he shall reward every

man according to his works. ²⁸ Verily I say unto you, there be some standing here, which shall not taste of death, till they see the Son of man coming in his kingdom.'

17 And after six days Jesus taketh Peter, James, and John his brother, and bringeth them up into an high mountain apart, ² and was transfigured before them, and his face did shine as the sun, and his raiment was white as the light. ³And, behold, there appeared unto them Moses and Elias talking with him. ⁴Then answered Peter, and said unto Jesus, 'Lord, it is good for us to be here: if thou wilt, let us make here three tabernacles; one for thee, and one for Moses, and one for Elias.' ⁵While he yet spake, behold, a bright cloud overshadowed them, and behold a voice out of the cloud, which said, 'This is my beloved Son, in whom I am well pleased; hear ye him.' ⁶And when the disciples heard it, they fell on their face, and were sore afraid. ⁷And Jesus came and touched them, and said, 'Arise, and be not afraid.' ⁸And when they had lifted up their eyes, they saw no man, save Jesus only. ⁹And as they came down from the mountain, Jesus charged them, saying, 'Tell the vision to no man, until the Son of man be risen again from the dead.' ¹⁰And his disciples asked him, saying, 'Why then say the scribes that Elias must first come?' ¹¹And Jesus answered and said unto them, 'Elias truly shall first come, and restore all things. ¹²But I say unto you that Elias is come already, and they knew him not, but have done unto him whatsoever they listed. Likewise shall also the Son of man suffer of them.' ¹³Then the disciples understood that he spake unto them of John the Baptist.

¹⁴And when they were come to the multitude, there came to him a certain man, kneeling down to him, and saying, ¹⁵'Lord, have mercy on my son, for he is lunatick, and sore vexed, for ofttimes he falleth into the fire, and oft into the water. ¹⁶And I brought him to thy disciples, and they could not cure him.' ¹⁷Then Jesus answered and said, 'O faithless and perverse generation, how long shall I be with you? How long shall I suffer you? Bring him hither to me.' ¹⁸And Jesus rebuked the devil; and he departed out of him, and the child was cured from that very hour. ¹⁹Then came the disciples to Jesus apart, and said, 'Why could not we cast him out?' ²⁰And Jesus said unto them, 'Because of your unbelief: for verily I say unto you, if ye have faith as a grain of mustard seed, ye shall say unto this mountain, "Remove hence to yonder place," and it shall remove; and nothing shall be impossible unto you. ²¹Howbeit this kind goeth not out but by prayer and fasting.'

²²And while they abode in Galilee, Jesus said unto them, 'The Son of man shall be betrayed into the hands of men: ²³and they shall kill him, and the third day he shall be raised again.' And they were exceeding sorry.

²⁴And when they were come to Capernaum, they that received tribute money came to Peter, and said, 'Doth not your master pay tribute?' ²⁵He saith, 'Yes.' And when he was come into the house, Jesus prevented him, saying, 'What thinkest thou, Simon? Of whom do the kings of the earth take custom or tribute? Of their own children, or of strangers?' ²⁶Peter saith unto him, 'Of strangers.' Jesus saith unto him, 'Then are the children free. ²⁷Notwithstanding, lest we should

offend them, go thou to the sea, and cast an hook, and take up the fish that first cometh up; and when thou hast opened his mouth, thou shalt find a piece of money; that take, and give unto them for me and thee.'

18 At the same time came the disciples unto Jesus, saying, 'Who is the greatest in the kingdom of heaven?' ²And Jesus called a little child unto him, and set him in the midst of them, ³and said, 'Verily I say unto you, except ye be converted, and become as little children, ye shall not enter into the kingdom of heaven. ⁴Whosoever therefore shall humble himself as this little child, the same is greatest in the kingdom of heaven. ⁵And whoso shall receive one such little child in my name receiveth me. ⁶But whoso shall offend one of these little ones which believe in me, it were better for him that a millstone were hanged about his neck, and that he were drowned in the depth of the sea.

⁷'Woe unto the world because of offences! For it must needs be that offences come; but woe to that man by whom the offence cometh! ⁸Wherefore if thy hand or thy foot offend thee, cut them off, and cast them from thee: it is better for thee to enter into life halt or maimed, rather than having two hands or two feet to be cast into everlasting fire. ⁹And if thine eye offend thee, pluck it out, and cast it from thee: it is better for thee to enter into life with one eye, rather than having two eyes to be cast into hell fire. ¹⁰Take heed that ye despise not one of these little ones; for I say unto you, that in heaven their angels do always behold the face of my Father which is in heaven. ¹¹For the Son of man is come to save that

which was lost. ¹² How think ye? If a man have an hundred sheep, and one of them be gone astray, doth he not leave the ninety and nine, and goeth into the mountains, and seeketh that which is gone astray? ¹³And if so be that he find it, verily I say unto you, he rejoiceth more of that sheep, than of the ninety and nine which went not astray. ¹⁴ Even so it is not the will of your Father which is in heaven, that one of these little ones should perish.

¹⁵ 'Moreover if thy brother shall trespass against thee, go and tell him his fault between thee and him alone: if he shall hear thee, thou hast gained thy brother. ¹⁶ But if he will not hear thee, then take with thee one or two more, that in the mouth of two or three witnesses every word may be established. ¹⁷And if he shall neglect to hear them, tell it unto the church: but if he neglect to hear the church, let him be unto thee as an heathen man and a publican. ¹⁸ Verily I say unto you, whatsoever ye shall bind on earth shall be bound in heaven, and whatsoever ye shall loose on earth shall be loosed in heaven. ¹⁹Again I say unto you that if two of you shall agree on earth as touching any thing that they shall ask, it shall be done for them of my Father which is in heaven. ²⁰ For where two or three are gathered together in my name, there am I in the midst of them.'

²¹ Then came Peter to him, and said, 'Lord, how oft shall my brother sin against me, and I forgive him? Till seven times?' ²² Jesus saith unto him, 'I say not unto thee, "Until seven times," but, "Until seventy times seven."

²³ 'Therefore is the kingdom of heaven likened unto a certain king, which would take account of his servants. ²⁴And

when he had begun to reckon, one was brought unto him, which owed him ten thousand talents. ²⁵But forasmuch as he had not to pay, his lord commanded him to be sold, and his wife, and children, and all that he had, and payment to be made. ²⁶The servant therefore fell down, and worshipped him, saying, "Lord, have patience with me, and I will pay thee all." ²⁷Then the lord of that servant was moved with compassion, and loosed him, and forgave him the debt. ²⁸But the same servant went out, and found one of his fellowservants, which owed him an hundred pence, and he laid hands on him, and took him by the throat, saying, "Pay me that thou owest." ²⁹And his fellowservant fell down at his feet, and besought him, saying, "Have patience with me, and I will pay thee all." ³⁰And he would not, but went and cast him into prison, till he should pay the debt. ³¹So when his fellowservants saw what was done, they were very sorry, and came and told unto their lord all that was done. ³²Then his lord, after that he had called him, said unto him, "O thou wicked servant, I forgave thee all that debt, because thou desiredst me. ³³Shouldest not thou also have had compassion on thy fellowservant, even as I had pity on thee?" ³⁴And his lord was wroth, and delivered him to the tormentors, till he should pay all that was due unto him. ³⁵So likewise shall my heavenly Father do also unto you, if ye from your hearts forgive not every one his brother their trespasses.'

19 And it came to pass, that when Jesus had finished these sayings, he departed from Galilee, and came into the coasts of Judæa beyond Jordan; ²and great multitudes

followed him; and he healed them there.

³ The Pharisees also came unto him, tempting him, and saying unto him, 'Is it lawful for a man to put away his wife for every cause?' ⁴And he answered and said unto them, 'Have ye not read, that he which made them at the beginning made them male and female, ⁵and said, "For this cause shall a man leave father and mother, and shall cleave to his wife, and they twain shall be one flesh"? ⁶Wherefore they are no more twain, but one flesh. What therefore God hath joined together, let not man put asunder.' ⁷They say unto him, 'Why did Moses then command to give a writing of divorcement, and to put her away?' ⁸He saith unto them, 'Moses, because of the hardness of your hearts suffered you to put away your wives: but from the beginning it was not so. ⁹And I say unto you, whosoever shall put away his wife, except it be for fornication, and shall marry another, committeth adultery: and whoso marrieth her which is put away doth commit adultery.'

¹⁰ His disciples say unto him, 'If the case of the man be so with his wife, it is not good to marry.' ¹¹But he said unto them, 'All men cannot receive this saying, save they to whom it is given. ¹² For there are some eunuchs, which were so born from their mother's womb, and there are some eunuchs, which were made eunuchs of men, and there be eunuchs, which have made themselves eunuchs for the kingdom of heaven's sake. He that is able to receive it, let him receive it.'

¹³ Then were there brought unto him little children, that he should put his hands on them, and pray, and the disciples rebuked them. ¹⁴But Jesus said, 'Suffer little children, and

forbid them not, to come unto me, for of such is the kingdom of heaven.' ¹⁵And he laid his hands on them, and departed thence.

¹⁶And, behold, one came and said unto him, 'Good Master, what good thing shall I do, that I may have eternal life?' ¹⁷And he said unto him, 'Why callest thou me good? There is none good but one, that is, God: but if thou wilt enter into life, keep the commandments.' ¹⁸He saith unto him, 'Which?' Jesus said, 'Thou shalt do no murder, thou shalt not commit adultery, thou shalt not steal, thou shalt not bear false witness, ¹⁹honour thy father and thy mother, and thou shalt love thy neighbour as thyself.' ²⁰The young man saith unto him, 'All these things have I kept from my youth up; what lack I yet?' ²¹Jesus said unto him, 'If thou wilt be perfect, go and sell that thou hast, and give to the poor, and thou shalt have treasure in heaven, and come and follow me.' ²²But when the young man heard that saying, he went away sorrowful, for he had great possessions.

²³Then said Jesus unto his disciples, 'Verily I say unto you, that a rich man shall hardly enter into the kingdom of heaven. ²⁴And again I say unto you, it is easier for a camel to go through the eye of a needle, than for a rich man to enter into the kingdom of God.' ²⁵When his disciples heard it, they were exceedingly amazed, saying, 'Who then can be saved?' ²⁶But Jesus beheld them, and said unto them, 'With men this is impossible; but with God all things are possible.'

²⁷Then answered Peter and said unto him, 'Behold, we have forsaken all, and followed thee; what shall we have therefore?' ²⁸And Jesus said unto them, 'Verily I say unto you that ye which have followed me, in the regeneration

when the Son of man shall sit in the throne of his glory, ye also shall sit upon twelve thrones, judging the twelve tribes of Israel. ²⁹And every one that hath forsaken houses, or brethren, or sisters, or father, or mother, or wife, or children, or lands, for my name's sake, shall receive an hundredfold, and shall inherit everlasting life. ³⁰But many that are first shall be last; and the last shall be first.

20 ¹For the kingdom of heaven is like unto a man that is an householder, which went out early in the morning to hire labourers into his vineyard. ²And when he had agreed with the labourers for a penny a day, he sent them into his vineyard. ³And he went out about the third hour, and saw others standing idle in the marketplace, ⁴and said unto them, "Go ye also into the vineyard, and whatsoever is right I will give you." And they went their way. ⁵Again he went out about the sixth and ninth hour, and did likewise. ⁶And about the eleventh hour he went out, and found others standing idle, and saith unto them, "Why stand ye here all the day idle?" ⁷They say unto him, "Because no man hath hired us." He saith unto them, "Go ye also into the vineyard; and whatsoever is right, that shall ye receive." ⁸So when even was come, the lord of the vineyard saith unto his steward, "Call the labourers, and give them their hire, beginning from the last unto the first." ⁹And when they came that were hired about the eleventh hour, they received every man a penny. ¹⁰But when the first came, they supposed that they should have received more; and they likewise received every man a penny. ¹¹And when they had received it, they

murmured against the goodman of the house, ¹²saying, "These last have wrought but one hour, and thou hast made them equal unto us, which have borne the burden and heat of the day." ¹³But he answered one of them, and said, "Friend, I do thee no wrong; didst not thou agree with me for a penny? ¹⁴Take that thine is, and go thy way: I will give unto this last, even as unto thee. ¹⁵Is it not lawful for me to do what I will with mine own? Is thine eye evil, because I am good?" ¹⁶So the last shall be first, and the first last: for many be called, but few chosen.'

¹⁷And Jesus going up to Jerusalem took the twelve disciples apart in the way, and said unto them, ¹⁸'Behold, we go up to Jerusalem; and the Son of man shall be betrayed unto the chief priests and unto the scribes, and they shall condemn him to death, ¹⁹and shall deliver him to the Gentiles to mock, and to scourge, and to crucify him, and the third day he shall rise again.'

²⁰Then came to him the mother of Zebedee's children with her sons, worshipping him, and desiring a certain thing of him. ²¹And he said unto her, 'What wilt thou?' She saith unto him, 'Grant that these my two sons may sit, the one on thy right hand, and the other on the left, in thy kingdom.' ²²But Jesus answered and said, 'Ye know not what ye ask. Are ye able to drink of the cup that I shall drink of, and to be baptized with the baptism that I am baptized with?' They say unto him, 'We are able.' ²³And he saith unto them, 'Ye shall drink indeed of my cup, and be baptized with the baptism that I am baptized with: but to sit on my right hand, and on my left, is not mine to give, but it shall be given to

them for whom it is prepared of my Father.' ²⁴And when the ten heard it, they were moved with indignation against the two brethren. ²⁵But Jesus called them unto him, and said, 'Ye know that the princes of the Gentiles exercise dominion over them, and they that are great exercise authority upon them. ²⁶But it shall not be so among you: but whosoever will be great among you, let him be your minister; ²⁷and whosoever will be chief among you, let him be your servant. ²⁸Even as the Son of man came not to be ministered unto, but to minister, and to give his life a ransom for many. ²⁹And as they departed from Jericho, a great multitude followed him.

³⁰And, behold, two blind men sitting by the way side, when they heard that Jesus passed by, cried out, saying, 'Have mercy on us, O Lord, thou Son of David.' ³¹And the multitude rebuked them, because they should hold their peace: but they cried the more, saying, 'Have mercy on us, O Lord, thou Son of David.' ³²And Jesus stood still, and called them, and said, 'What will ye that I shall do unto you?' ³³They say unto him, 'Lord, that our eyes may be opened.' ³⁴So Jesus had compassion on them, and touched their eyes, and immediately their eyes received sight, and they followed him.

21 And when they drew nigh unto Jerusalem, and were come to Bethphage, unto the mount of Olives, then sent Jesus two disciples, ²saying unto them, 'Go into the village over against you, and straightway ye shall find an ass tied, and a colt with her; loose them, and bring them unto me. ³And if any man say ought unto you, ye shall say, "The Lord hath need of them," and straightway he will send them.'

⁴All this was done, that it might be fulfilled which was spoken by the prophet, saying, ⁵'Tell ye the daughter of Sion, "Behold, thy King cometh unto thee, meek, and sitting upon an ass, and a colt the foal of an ass."' ⁶And the disciples went, and did as Jesus commanded them, ⁷and brought the ass, and the colt, and put on them their clothes, and they set him thereon. ⁸And a very great multitude spread their garments in the way; others cut down branches from the trees, and strawed them in the way. ⁹And the multitudes that went before, and that followed, cried, saying, 'Hosanna to the Son of David. Blessed is he that cometh in the name of the Lord. Hosanna in the highest.' ¹⁰And when he was come into Jerusalem, all the city was moved, saying, 'Who is this?' ¹¹And the multitude said, 'This is Jesus the prophet of Nazareth of Galilee.'

¹²And Jesus went into the temple of God, and cast out all them that sold and bought in the temple, and overthrew the tables of the moneychangers, and the seats of them that sold doves, ¹³and said unto them, 'It is written, "My house shall be called the house of prayer," but ye have made it a den of thieves.' ¹⁴And the blind and the lame came to him in the temple; and he healed them. ¹⁵And when the chief priests and scribes saw the wonderful things that he did, and the children crying in the temple, and saying, 'Hosanna to the Son of David,' they were sore displeased, ¹⁶and said unto him, 'Hearest thou what these say?' And Jesus saith unto them, 'Yea; have ye never read, "Out of the mouth of babes and sucklings thou hast perfected praise"?'

¹⁷And he left them, and went out of the city into Bethany; and he lodged there. ¹⁸Now in the morning as he returned

into the city, he hungered. [19]And when he saw a fig tree in the way, he came to it, and found nothing thereon, but leaves only, and said unto it, 'Let no fruit grow on thee henceforward for ever.' And presently the fig tree withered away. [20]And when the disciples saw it, they marvelled, saying, 'How soon is the fig tree withered away!' [21]Jesus answered and said unto them, 'Verily I say unto you, if ye have faith, and doubt not, ye shall not only do this which is done to the fig tree, but also if ye shall say unto this mountain, "Be thou removed, and be thou cast into the sea," it shall be done. [22]And all things, whatsoever ye shall ask in prayer, believing, ye shall receive.'

[23]And when he was come into the temple, the chief priests and the elders of the people came unto him as he was teaching, and said, 'By what authority doest thou these things? And who gave thee this authority?' [24]And Jesus answered and said unto them, 'I also will ask you one thing, which if ye tell me, I in like wise will tell you by what authority I do these things. [25]The baptism of John, whence was it? From heaven, or of men?' And they reasoned with themselves, saying, 'If we shall say, "From heaven," he will say unto us, "Why did ye not then believe him?" [26]But if we shall say, "Of men," we fear the people, for all hold John as a prophet.' [27]And they answered Jesus, and said, 'We cannot tell.' And he said unto them, 'Neither tell I you by what authority I do these things.

[28]'But what think ye? A certain man had two sons; and he came to the first, and said, "Son, go work to day in my vineyard." [29]He answered and said, "I will not," but afterward he

repented, and went. [30]And he came to the second, and said likewise. And he answered and said, "I go, sir," and went not. [31]Whether of them twain did the will of his father?' They say unto him, 'The first.' Jesus saith unto them, 'Verily I say unto you that the publicans and the harlots go into the kingdom of God before you. [32]For John came unto you in the way of righteousness, and ye believed him not: but the publicans and the harlots believed him, and ye, when ye had seen it, repented not afterward, that ye might believe him.

[33]'Hear another parable. There was a certain householder, which planted a vineyard, and hedged it round about, and digged a winepress in it, and built a tower, and let it out to husbandmen, and went into a far country. [34]And when the time of the fruit drew near, he sent his servants to the husbandmen, that they might receive the fruits of it. [35]And the husbandmen took his servants, and beat one, and killed another, and stoned another. [36]Again, he sent other servants more than the first, and they did unto them likewise. [37]But last of all he sent unto them his son, saying, "They will reverence my son." [38]But when the husbandmen saw the son, they said among themselves, "This is the heir; come, let us kill him, and let us seize on his inheritance." [39]And they caught him, and cast him out of the vineyard, and slew him. [40]When the lord therefore of the vineyard cometh, what will he do unto those husbandmen?' [41]They say unto him, 'He will miserably destroy those wicked men, and will let out his vineyard unto other husbandmen, which shall render him the fruits in their seasons.' [42]Jesus saith unto them, 'Did ye never read in the scriptures, "The stone which the builders rejected,

the same is become the head of the corner: this is the Lord's doing, and it is marvellous in our eyes"? ⁴³Therefore say I unto you, the kingdom of God shall be taken from you, and given to a nation bringing forth the fruits thereof. ⁴⁴And whosoever shall fall on this stone shall be broken, but on whomsoever it shall fall, it will grind him to powder.' ⁴⁵And when the chief priests and Pharisees had heard his parables, they perceived that he spake of them. ⁴⁶But when they sought to lay hands on him, they feared the multitude, because they took him for a prophet.

22 And Jesus answered and spake unto them again by parables, and said, ²'The kingdom of heaven is like unto a certain king, which made a marriage for his son, ³and sent forth his servants to call them that were bidden to the wedding, and they would not come. ⁴Again, he sent forth other servants, saying, "Tell them which are bidden, 'Behold, I have prepared my dinner: my oxen and my fatlings are killed, and all things are ready; come unto the marriage.'" ⁵But they made light of it, and went their ways, one to his farm, another to his merchandise, ⁶and the remnant took his servants, and entreated them spitefully, and slew them. ⁷But when the king heard thereof, he was wroth, and he sent forth his armies, and destroyed those murderers, and burned up their city. ⁸Then saith he to his servants, "The wedding is ready, but they which were bidden were not worthy. ⁹Go ye therefore into the highways, and as many as ye shall find, bid to the marriage." ¹⁰So those servants went out into the highways, and gathered together all as many as they found, both

bad and good, and the wedding was furnished with guests.

¹¹ 'And when the king came in to see the guests, he saw there a man which had not on a wedding garment, ¹² and he saith unto him, "Friend, how camest thou in hither not having a wedding garment?" And he was speechless. ¹³ Then said the king to the servants, "Bind him hand and foot, and take him away, and cast him into outer darkness: there shall be weeping and gnashing of teeth." ¹⁴ For many are called, but few are chosen.'

¹⁵ Then went the Pharisees, and took counsel how they might entangle him in his talk. ¹⁶ And they sent out unto him their disciples with the Herodians, saying, 'Master, we know that thou art true, and teachest the way of God in truth, neither carest thou for any man, for thou regardest not the person of men. ¹⁷ Tell us therefore, what thinkest thou? Is it lawful to give tribute unto Caesar, or not?' ¹⁸ But Jesus perceived their wickedness, and said, 'Why tempt ye me, ye hypocrites? ¹⁹ Shew me the tribute money.' And they brought unto him a penny. ²⁰ And he saith unto them, 'Whose is this image and superscription?' ²¹ They say unto him, 'Caesar's.' Then saith he unto them, 'Render therefore unto Caesar the things which are Caesar's; and unto God the things that are God's.' ²² When they had heard these words, they marvelled, and left him, and went their way.

²³ The same day came to him the Sadducees, which say that there is no resurrection, and asked him, ²⁴ saying, 'Master, Moses said, "If a man die, having no children, his brother shall marry his wife, and raise up seed unto his brother." ²⁵ Now there were with us seven brethren, and the first,

when he had married a wife, deceased, and, having no issue, left his wife unto his brother: ²⁶ likewise the second also, and the third, unto the seventh. ²⁷ And last of all the woman died also. ²⁸ Therefore in the resurrection whose wife shall she be of the seven? For they all had her.' ²⁹ Jesus answered and said unto them, 'Ye do err, not knowing the scriptures, nor the power of God. ³⁰ For in the resurrection they neither marry, nor are given in marriage, but are as the angels of God in heaven. ³¹ But as touching the resurrection of the dead, have ye not read that which was spoken unto you by God, saying, ³² "I am the God of Abraham, and the God of Isaac, and the God of Jacob?" God is not the God of the dead, but of the living.' ³³ And when the multitude heard this, they were astonished at his doctrine.

³⁴ But when the Pharisees had heard that he had put the Sadducees to silence, they were gathered together. ³⁵ Then one of them, which was a lawyer, asked him a question, tempting him, and saying, ³⁶ 'Master, which is the great commandment in the law?' ³⁷ Jesus said unto him, '"Thou shalt love the Lord thy God with all thy heart, and with all thy soul, and with all thy mind." ³⁸ This is the first and great commandment. ³⁹ And the second is like unto it, "Thou shalt love thy neighbour as thyself." ⁴⁰ On these two commandments hang all the law and the prophets.'

⁴¹ While the Pharisees were gathered together, Jesus asked them, ⁴² saying, 'What think ye of Christ? Whose son is he?' They say unto him, 'The Son of David.' ⁴³ He saith unto them, 'How then doth David in spirit call him "Lord", saying, ⁴⁴ "The Lord said unto my Lord, 'Sit thou on my right hand,

till I make thine enemies thy footstool'?" ⁴⁵If David then call him "Lord", how is he his son?' ⁴⁶And no man was able to answer him a word, neither durst any man from that day forth ask him any more questions.

23 Then spake Jesus to the multitude, and to his disciples, ²saying, 'The scribes and the Pharisees sit in Moses' seat; ³all therefore whatsoever they bid you observe, that observe and do; but do not ye after their works, for they say, and do not. ⁴For they bind heavy burdens and grievous to be borne, and lay them on men's shoulders; but they themselves will not move them with one of their fingers. ⁵But all their works they do for to be seen of men; they make broad their phylacteries, and enlarge the borders of their garments, ⁶and love the uppermost rooms at feasts, and the chief seats in the synagogues, ⁷and greetings in the markets, and to be called of men, "Rabbi, Rabbi". ⁸But be not ye called Rabbi: for one is your Master, even Christ; and all ye are brethren. ⁹And call no man your father upon the earth: for one is your Father, which is in heaven. ¹⁰Neither be ye called masters: for one is your Master, even Christ. ¹¹But he that is greatest among you shall be your servant. ¹²And whosoever shall exalt himself shall be abased; and he that shall humble himself shall be exalted.

¹³'But woe unto you, scribes and Pharisees, hypocrites! For ye shut up the kingdom of heaven against men, for ye neither go in yourselves, neither suffer ye them that are entering to go in. ¹⁴Woe unto you, scribes and Pharisees, hypocrites! For ye devour widows' houses, and for a pretence

make long prayer: therefore ye shall receive the greater damnation. ¹⁵ Woe unto you, scribes and Pharisees, hypocrites! For ye compass sea and land to make one proselyte, and when he is made, ye make him twofold more the child of hell than yourselves. ¹⁶ Woe unto you, ye blind guides, which say, "Whosoever shall swear by the temple, it is nothing; but whosoever shall swear by the gold of the temple, he is a debtor!" ¹⁷ Ye fools and blind: for whether is greater, the gold, or the temple that sanctifieth the gold? ¹⁸ And, "Whosoever shall swear by the altar, it is nothing; but whosoever sweareth by the gift that is upon it, he is guilty." ¹⁹ Ye fools and blind: for whether is greater, the gift, or the altar that sanctifieth the gift? ²⁰ Whoso therefore shall swear by the altar, sweareth by it, and by all things thereon. ²¹ And whoso shall swear by the temple, sweareth by it, and by him that dwelleth therein. ²² And he that shall swear by heaven, sweareth by the throne of God, and by him that sitteth thereon. ²³ Woe unto you, scribes and Pharisees, hypocrites! For ye pay tithe of mint and anise and cummin, and have omitted the weightier matters of the law, judgment, mercy, and faith. These ought ye to have done, and not to leave the other undone. ²⁴ Ye blind guides, which strain at a gnat, and swallow a camel. ²⁵ Woe unto you, scribes and Pharisees, hypocrites! For ye make clean the outside of the cup and of the platter, but within they are full of extortion and excess. ²⁶ Thou blind Pharisee, cleanse first that which is within the cup and platter, that the outside of them may be clean also. ²⁷ Woe unto you, scribes and Pharisees, hypocrites! For ye are like unto whited sepulchres, which indeed appear beautiful outward, but are within full of dead men's bones, and of all uncleanness. [28] Even so ye also outwardly appear righteous unto men, but within ye are full of hypocrisy and iniquity. [29] Woe unto you, scribes and Pharisees, hypocrites! Because ye build the tombs of the prophets, and garnish the sepulchres of the righteous, [30] and say, "If we had been in the days of our fathers, we would not have been partakers with them in the blood of the prophets." [31] Wherefore ye be witnesses unto yourselves, that ye are the children of them which killed the prophets. [32] Fill ye up then the measure of your fathers. [33] Ye serpents, ye generation of vipers, how can ye escape the damnation of hell?

[34] 'Wherefore, behold, I send unto you prophets, and wise men, and scribes: and some of them ye shall kill and crucify; and some of them shall ye scourge in your synagogues, and persecute them from city to city: [35] that upon you may come all the righteous blood shed upon the earth, from the blood of righteous Abel unto the blood of Zacharias son of Barachias, whom ye slew between the temple and the altar. [36] Verily I say unto you, all these things shall come upon this generation. [37] O Jerusalem, Jerusalem, thou that killest the prophets, and stonest them which are sent unto thee, how often would I have gathered thy children together, even as a hen gathereth her chickens under her wings, and ye would not! [38] Behold, your house is left unto you desolate. [39] For I say unto you, ye shall not see me henceforth, till ye shall say, "Blessed is he that cometh in the name of the Lord."'

24 And Jesus went out, and departed from the temple, and his disciples came to him for to shew him the

buildings of the temple. ²And Jesus said unto them, 'See ye not all these things? Verily I say unto you, there shall not be left here one stone upon another, that shall not be thrown down.'

³And as he sat upon the mount of Olives, the disciples came unto him privately, saying, 'Tell us, when shall these things be? And what shall be the sign of thy coming, and of the end of the world?' ⁴And Jesus answered and said unto them, 'Take heed that no man deceive you. ⁵For many shall come in my name, saying, "I am Christ," and shall deceive many. ⁶And ye shall hear of wars and rumours of wars; see that ye be not troubled, for all these things must come to pass, but the end is not yet. ⁷For nation shall rise against nation, and kingdom against kingdom, and there shall be famines, and pestilences, and earthquakes, in diverse places. ⁸All these are the beginning of sorrows. ⁹Then shall they deliver you up to be afflicted, and shall kill you, and ye shall be hated of all nations for my name's sake. ¹⁰And then shall many be offended, and shall betray one another, and shall hate one another. ¹¹And many false prophets shall rise, and shall deceive many. ¹²And because iniquity shall abound, the love of many shall wax cold. ¹³But he that shall endure unto the end, the same shall be saved. ¹⁴And this gospel of the kingdom shall be preached in all the world for a witness unto all nations; and then shall the end come. ¹⁵When ye therefore shall see the abomination of desolation, spoken of by Daniel the prophet, stand in the holy place (whoso readeth, let him understand), ¹⁶then let them which be in Judæa flee into the mountains; ¹⁷let him which is on the housetop not come down to take any thing out of his house: ¹⁸neither let him

which is in the field return back to take his clothes. ¹⁹And woe unto them that are with child, and to them that give suck in those days! ²⁰But pray ye that your flight be not in the winter, neither on the sabbath day. ²¹For then shall be great tribulation, such as was not since the beginning of the world to this time, no, nor ever shall be. ²²And except those days should be shortened, there should no flesh be saved, but for the elect's sake those days shall be shortened. ²³Then if any man shall say unto you, "Lo, here is Christ," or "There," believe it not. ²⁴For there shall arise false Christs, and false prophets, and shall shew great signs and wonders; insomuch that, if it were possible, they shall deceive the very elect. ²⁵Behold, I have told you before. ²⁶Wherefore if they shall say unto you, "Behold, he is in the desert," go not forth; "Behold, he is in the secret chambers," believe it not. ²⁷For as the lightning cometh out of the east, and shineth even unto the west; so shall also the coming of the Son of man be. ²⁸For wheresoever the carcase is, there will the eagles be gathered together.

²⁹'Immediately after the tribulation of those days shall the sun be darkened, and the moon shall not give her light, and the stars shall fall from heaven, and the powers of the heavens shall be shaken. ³⁰And then shall appear the sign of the Son of man in heaven, and then shall all the tribes of the earth mourn, and they shall see the Son of man coming in the clouds of heaven with power and great glory. ³¹And he shall send his angels with a great sound of a trumpet, and they shall gather together his elect from the four winds, from one end of heaven to the other. ³²Now learn a parable of the fig tree. When his branch is yet tender, and putteth

forth leaves, ye know that summer is nigh: ³³ so likewise ye, when ye shall see all these things, know that it is near, even at the doors. ³⁴ Verily I say unto you, this generation shall not pass, till all these things be fulfilled. ³⁵ Heaven and earth shall pass away, but my words shall not pass away.

³⁶ 'But of that day and hour knoweth no man, no, not the angels of heaven, but my Father only. ³⁷ But as the days of Noe were, so shall also the coming of the Son of man be. ³⁸ For as in the days that were before the flood they were eating and drinking, marrying and giving in marriage, until the day that Noe entered into the ark, ³⁹ and knew not until the flood came, and took them all away; so shall also the coming of the Son of man be. ⁴⁰ Then shall two be in the field; the one shall be taken, and the other left. ⁴¹ Two women shall be grinding at the mill; the one shall be taken, and the other left.

⁴² 'Watch therefore: for ye know not what hour your Lord doth come. ⁴³ But know this, that if the goodman of the house had known in what watch the thief would come, he would have watched, and would not have suffered his house to be broken up. ⁴⁴ Therefore be ye also ready: for in such an hour as ye think not the Son of man cometh. ⁴⁵ Who then is a faithful and wise servant, whom his lord hath made ruler over his household, to give them meat in due season? ⁴⁶ Blessed is that servant, whom his lord when he cometh shall find so doing. ⁴⁷ Verily I say unto you that he shall make him ruler over all his goods. ⁴⁸ But and if that evil servant shall say in his heart, "My lord delayeth his coming," ⁴⁹ and shall begin to smite his fellow-servants, and to eat and drink with the drunken; ⁵⁰ the lord of that servant shall come in a day when

he looketh not for him, and in an hour that he is not aware of, [51] and shall cut him asunder, and appoint him his portion with the hypocrites: there shall be weeping and gnashing of teeth.

25 'Then shall the kingdom of heaven be likened unto ten virgins, which took their lamps, and went forth to meet the bridegroom. [2] And five of them were wise, and five were foolish. [3] They that were foolish took their lamps, and took no oil with them, [4] but the wise took oil in their vessels with their lamps. [5] While the bridegroom tarried, they all slumbered and slept. [6] And at midnight there was a cry made, "Behold, the bridegroom cometh; go ye out to meet him." [7] Then all those virgins arose, and trimmed their lamps. [8] And the foolish said unto the wise, "Give us of your oil; for our lamps are gone out." [9] But the wise answered, saying, "Not so, lest there be not enough for us and you, but go ye rather to them that sell, and buy for yourselves." [10] And while they went to buy, the bridegroom came; and they that were ready went in with him to the marriage; and the door was shut. [11] Afterward came also the other virgins, saying, "Lord, Lord, open to us." [12] But he answered and said, "Verily I say unto you, I know you not." [13] Watch therefore, for ye know neither the day nor the hour wherein the Son of man cometh.

[14] 'For the kingdom of heaven is as a man travelling into a far country, who called his own servants, and delivered unto them his goods, [15] and unto one he gave five talents, to another two, and to another one; to every man according to his several ability; and straightway took his journey. [16] Then he that had received the five talents went and traded with the same,

and made them other five talents. ¹⁷And likewise he that had received two, he also gained other two. ¹⁸But he that had received one went and digged in the earth, and hid his lord's money. ¹⁹After a long time the lord of those servants cometh, and reckoneth with them. ²⁰And so he that had received five talents came and brought other five talents, saying, "Lord, thou deliveredst unto me five talents; behold, I have gained beside them five talents more." ²¹His lord said unto him, "Well done, thou good and faithful servant: thou hast been faithful over a few things; I will make thee ruler over many things; enter thou into the joy of thy lord." ²²He also that had received two talents came and said, "Lord, thou deliveredst unto me two talents; behold, I have gained two other talents beside them." ²³His lord said unto him, "Well done, good and faithful servant; thou hast been faithful over a few things, I will make thee ruler over many things; enter thou into the joy of thy lord." ²⁴Then he which had received the one talent came and said, "Lord, I knew thee that thou art an hard man, reaping where thou hast not sown, and gathering where thou hast not strawed, ²⁵and I was afraid, and went and hid thy talent in the earth: lo, there thou hast that is thine." ²⁶His lord answered and said unto him, "Thou wicked and slothful servant, thou knewest that I reap where I sowed not, and gather where I have not strawed. ²⁷Thou oughtest therefore to have put my money to the exchangers, and then at my coming I should have received mine own with usury. ²⁸Take therefore the talent from him, and give it unto him which hath ten talents. ²⁹For unto every one that hath shall be given, and he shall have abundance: but from him that hath not shall be taken away even that which he hath. ³⁰And cast ye the unprofitable servant into outer darkness: there shall be weeping and gnashing of teeth."

³¹'When the Son of man shall come in his glory, and all the holy angels with him, then shall he sit upon the throne of his glory, ³²and before him shall be gathered all nations, and he shall separate them one from another, as a shepherd divideth his sheep from the goats, ³³and he shall set the sheep on his right hand, but the goats on the left. ³⁴Then shall the King say unto them on his right hand, "Come, ye blessed of my Father, inherit the kingdom prepared for you from the foundation of the world; ³⁵for I was an hungred, and ye gave me meat; I was thirsty, and ye gave me drink; I was a stranger, and ye took me in; ³⁶naked, and ye clothed me; I was sick, and ye visited me; I was in prison, and ye came unto me." ³⁷Then shall the righteous answer him, saying, "Lord, when saw we thee an hungred, and fed thee? Or thirsty, and gave thee drink? ³⁸When saw we thee a stranger, and took thee in? Or naked, and clothed thee? ³⁹Or when saw we thee sick, or in prison, and came unto thee?" ⁴⁰And the King shall answer and say unto them, "Verily I say unto you, inasmuch as ye have done it unto one of the least of these my brethren, ye have done it unto me." ⁴¹Then shall he say also unto them on the left hand, "Depart from me, ye cursed, into everlasting fire, prepared for the devil and his angels: ⁴²for I was an hungred, and ye gave me no meat; I was thirsty, and ye gave me no drink; ⁴³I was a stranger, and ye took me not in; naked, and ye clothed me not; sick, and in prison, and ye visited me not." ⁴⁴Then shall they also answer him, saying, "Lord, when

saw we thee an hungred, or athirst, or a stranger, or naked, or sick, or in prison, and did not minister unto thee?" [45] Then shall he answer them, saying, "Verily I say unto you, inasmuch as ye did it not to one of the least of these, ye did it not to me." [46] And these shall go away into everlasting punishment, but the righteous into life eternal.'

26 And it came to pass, when Jesus had finished all these sayings, he said unto his disciples, [2] 'Ye know that after two days is the feast of the passover, and the Son of man is betrayed to be crucified.' [3] Then assembled together the chief priests, and the scribes, and the elders of the people, unto the palace of the high priest, who was called Caiaphas, [4] and consulted that they might take Jesus by subtilty, and kill him. [5] But they said, 'Not on the feast day, lest there be an uproar among the people.'

[6] Now when Jesus was in Bethany, in the house of Simon the leper, [7] there came unto him a woman having an alabaster box of very precious ointment, and poured it on his head, as he sat at meat. [8] But when his disciples saw it, they had indignation, saying, 'To what purpose is this waste? [9] For this ointment might have been sold for much, and given to the poor.' [10] When Jesus understood it, he said unto them, 'Why trouble ye the woman? For she hath wrought a good work upon me. [11] For ye have the poor always with you; but me ye have not always. [12] For in that she hath poured this ointment on my body, she did it for my burial. [13] Verily I say unto you, wheresoever this gospel shall be preached in the whole world, there shall also this, that this woman hath

done, be told for a memorial of her.'

¹⁴ Then one of the twelve, called Judas Iscariot, went unto the chief priests, ¹⁵ and said unto them, 'What will ye give me, and I will deliver him unto you?' And they covenanted with him for thirty pieces of silver. ¹⁶ And from that time he sought opportunity to betray him.

¹⁷ Now the first day of the feast of unleavened bread the disciples came to Jesus, saying unto him, 'Where wilt thou that we prepare for thee to eat the passover?' ¹⁸ And he said, 'Go into the city to such a man, and say unto him, "The Master saith, 'My time is at hand; I will keep the passover at thy house with my disciples.'"' ¹⁹ And the disciples did as Jesus had appointed them; and they made ready the passover. ²⁰ Now when the even was come, he sat down with the twelve. ²¹ And as they did eat, he said, 'Verily I say unto you that one of you shall betray me.' ²² And they were exceeding sorrowful, and began every one of them to say unto him, 'Lord, is it I?' ²³ And he answered and said, 'He that dippeth his hand with me in the dish, the same shall betray me. ²⁴ The Son of man goeth as it is written of him, but woe unto that man by whom the Son of man is betrayed! It had been good for that man if he had not been born.' ²⁵ Then Judas, which betrayed him, answered and said, 'Master, is it I?' He said unto him, 'Thou hast said.'

²⁶ And as they were eating, Jesus took bread, and blessed it, and brake it, and gave it to the disciples, and said, 'Take, eat; this is my body.' ²⁷ And he took the cup, and gave thanks, and gave it to them, saying, 'Drink ye all of it, ²⁸ for this is my blood of the new testament, which is shed for many for the

remission of sins. [29] But I say unto you, I will not drink henceforth of this fruit of the vine, until that day when I drink it new with you in my Father's kingdom.' [30] And when they had sung an hymn, they went out into the mount of Olives. [31] Then saith Jesus unto them, 'All ye shall be offended because of me this night, for it is written, "I will smite the shepherd, and the sheep of the flock shall be scattered abroad." [32] But after I am risen again, I will go before you into Galilee.' [33] Peter answered and said unto him, 'Though all men shall be offended because of thee, yet will I never be offended.' [34] Jesus said unto him, 'Verily I say unto thee that this night, before the cock crow, thou shalt deny me thrice.' [35] Peter said unto him, 'Though I should die with thee, yet will I not deny thee.' Likewise also said all the disciples.

[36] Then cometh Jesus with them unto a place called Gethsemane, and saith unto the disciples, 'Sit ye here, while I go and pray yonder.' [37] And he took with him Peter and the two sons of Zebedee, and began to be sorrowful and very heavy. [38] Then saith he unto them, 'My soul is exceeding sorrowful, even unto death; tarry ye here, and watch with me.' [39] And he went a little farther, and fell on his face, and prayed, saying, 'O my Father, if it be possible, let this cup pass from me: nevertheless not as I will, but as thou wilt.' [40] And he cometh unto the disciples, and findeth them asleep, and saith unto Peter, 'What, could ye not watch with me one hour? [41] Watch and pray, that ye enter not into temptation: the spirit indeed is willing, but the flesh is weak.' [42] He went away again the second time, and prayed, saying, 'O my Father, if this cup may not pass away from me, except I drink it, thy will be

done.' ⁴³And he came and found them asleep again: for their eyes were heavy. ⁴⁴And he left them, and went away again, and prayed the third time, saying the same words. ⁴⁵Then cometh he to his disciples, and saith unto them, 'Sleep on now, and take your rest: behold, the hour is at hand, and the Son of man is betrayed into the hands of sinners. ⁴⁶Rise, let us be going: behold, he is at hand that doth betray me.'

⁴⁷And while he yet spake, lo, Judas, one of the twelve, came, and with him a great multitude with swords and staves, from the chief priests and elders of the people. ⁴⁸Now he that betrayed him gave them a sign, saying, 'Whomsoever I shall kiss, that same is he; hold him fast.' ⁴⁹And forthwith he came to Jesus, and said, 'Hail, master,' and kissed him. ⁵⁰And Jesus said unto him, 'Friend, wherefore art thou come?' Then came they, and laid hands on Jesus, and took him. ⁵¹And, behold, one of them which were with Jesus stretched out his hand, and drew his sword, and struck a servant of the high priest's, and smote off his ear. ⁵²Then said Jesus unto him, 'Put up again thy sword into his place: for all they that take the sword shall perish with the sword. ⁵³Thinkest thou that I cannot now pray to my Father, and he shall presently give me more than twelve legions of angels? ⁵⁴But how then shall the scriptures be fulfilled, that thus it must be?' ⁵⁵In that same hour said Jesus to the multitudes, 'Are ye come out as against a thief with swords and staves for to take me? I sat daily with you teaching in the temple, and ye laid no hold on me. ⁵⁶But all this was done, that the scriptures of the prophets might be fulfilled.' Then all the disciples forsook him, and fled.

⁵⁷And they that had laid hold on Jesus led him away to Caiaphas the high priest, where the scribes and the elders were assembled. ⁵⁸But Peter followed him afar off unto the high priest's palace, and went in, and sat with the servants, to see the end. ⁵⁹Now the chief priests, and elders, and all the council, sought false witness against Jesus, to put him to death, ⁶⁰but found none; yea, though many false witnesses came, yet found they none. At the last came two false witnesses, ⁶¹and said, 'This fellow said, "I am able to destroy the temple of God, and to build it in three days."' ⁶²And the high priest arose, and said unto him, 'Answerest thou nothing? What is it which these witness against thee?' ⁶³But Jesus held his peace. And the high priest answered and said unto him, 'I adjure thee by the living God, that thou tell us whether thou be the Christ, the Son of God.' ⁶⁴Jesus saith unto him, 'Thou hast said: nevertheless I say unto you, hereafter shall ye see the Son of man sitting on the right hand of power, and coming in the clouds of heaven.' ⁶⁵Then the high priest rent his clothes, saying, 'He hath spoken blasphemy; what further need have we of witnesses? Behold, now ye have heard his blasphemy. ⁶⁶What think ye?' They answered and said, 'He is guilty of death.' ⁶⁷Then did they spit in his face, and buffeted him; and others smote him with the palms of their hands, ⁶⁸saying, 'Prophesy unto us, thou Christ. Who is he that smote thee?'

⁶⁹Now Peter sat without in the palace, and a damsel came unto him, saying, 'Thou also wast with Jesus of Galilee.' ⁷⁰But he denied before them all, saying, 'I know not what thou sayest.' ⁷¹And when he was gone out into the porch,

another maid saw him, and said unto them that were there, 'This fellow was also with Jesus of Nazareth.' [72]And again he denied with an oath: 'I do not know the man.' [73]And after a while came unto him they that stood by, and said to Peter, 'Surely thou also art one of them; for thy speech bewrayeth thee.' [74]Then began he to curse and to swear, saying, 'I know not the man.' And immediately the cock crew. [75]And Peter remembered the word of Jesus, which said unto him, 'Before the cock crow, thou shalt deny me thrice.' And he went out, and wept bitterly.

27 When the morning was come, all the chief priests and elders of the people took counsel against Jesus to put him to death: [2]and when they had bound him, they led him away, and delivered him to Pontius Pilate the governor.

[3]Then Judas, which had betrayed him, when he saw that he was condemned, repented himself, and brought again the thirty pieces of silver to the chief priests and elders, [4]saying, 'I have sinned in that I have betrayed the innocent blood.' And they said, 'What is that to us? See thou to that.' [5]And he cast down the pieces of silver in the temple, and departed, and went and hanged himself. [6]And the chief priests took the silver pieces, and said, 'It is not lawful for to put them into the treasury, because it is the price of blood.' [7]And they took counsel, and bought with them the potter's field, to bury strangers in. [8]Wherefore that field was called 'the field of blood' unto this day. [9]Then was fulfilled that which was spoken by Jeremy the prophet, saying, 'And they took the thirty pieces of silver, the price of him that was valued,

whom they of the children of Israel did value, [10] and gave them for the potter's field, as the Lord appointed me.' [11] And Jesus stood before the governor, and the governor asked him, saying, 'Art thou the King of the Jews?' And Jesus said unto him, 'Thou sayest.' [12] And when he was accused of the chief priests and elders, he answered nothing. [13] Then said Pilate unto him, 'Hearest thou not how many things they witness against thee?' [14] And he answered him to never a word; insomuch that the governor marvelled greatly. [15] Now at that feast the governor was wont to release unto the people a prisoner, whom they would. [16] And they had then a notable prisoner, called Barabbas. [17] Therefore when they were gathered together, Pilate said unto them, 'Whom will ye that I release unto you? Barabbas, or Jesus which is called Christ?' [18] For he knew that for envy they had delivered him.

[19] When he was set down on the judgment seat, his wife sent unto him, saying, 'Have thou nothing to do with that just man: for I have suffered many things this day in a dream because of him.' [20] But the chief priests and elders persuaded the multitude that they should ask Barabbas, and destroy Jesus. [21] The governor answered and said unto them, 'Whether of the twain will ye that I release unto you?' They said, 'Barabbas.' [22] Pilate saith unto them, 'What shall I do then with Jesus which is called Christ?' They all say unto him, 'Let him be crucified.' [23] And the governor said, 'Why, what evil hath he done?' But they cried out the more, saying, 'Let him be crucified.'

[24] When Pilate saw that he could prevail nothing, but that rather a tumult was made, he took water, and washed his

hands before the multitude, saying, 'I am innocent of the blood of this just person: see ye to it.' ²⁵ Then answered all the people, and said, 'His blood be on us, and on our children.'

²⁶ Then released he Barabbas unto them, and when he had scourged Jesus, he delivered him to be crucified. ²⁷ Then the soldiers of the governor took Jesus into the common hall, and gathered unto him the whole band of soldiers. ²⁸ And they stripped him, and put on him a scarlet robe.

²⁹ And when they had platted a crown of thorns, they put it upon his head, and a reed in his right hand, and they bowed the knee before him, and mocked him, saying, 'Hail, King of the Jews!' ³⁰ And they spit upon him, and took the reed, and smote him on the head. ³¹ And after that they had mocked him, they took the robe off from him, and put his own raiment on him, and led him away to crucify him. ³² And as they came out, they found a man of Cyrene, Simon by name: him they compelled to bear his cross. ³³ And when they were come unto a place called Golgotha, that is to say, a place of a skull, ³⁴ they gave him vinegar to drink mingled with gall, and when he had tasted thereof, he would not drink. ³⁵ And they crucified him, and parted his garments, casting lots: that it might be fulfilled which was spoken by the prophet, 'They parted my garments among them, and upon my vesture did they cast lots.' ³⁶ And sitting down they watched him there; ³⁷ and set up over his head his accusation written, 'This is Jesus the King of the Jews.' ³⁸ Then were there two thieves crucified with him, one on the right hand, and another on the left.

³⁹ And they that passed by reviled him, wagging their

heads, ⁴⁰and saying, 'Thou that destroyest the temple, and buildest it in three days, save thyself. If thou be the Son of God, come down from the cross.' ⁴¹Likewise also the chief priests, mocking him, with the scribes and elders, said, ⁴²'He saved others; himself he cannot save. If he be the King of Israel, let him now come down from the cross, and we will believe him. ⁴³He trusted in God; let him deliver him now, if he will have him: for he said, "I am the Son of God."' ⁴⁴The thieves also, which were crucified with him, cast the same in his teeth. ⁴⁵Now from the sixth hour there was darkness over all the land unto the ninth hour. ⁴⁶And about the ninth hour Jesus cried with a loud voice, saying, 'Eli, Eli, lama sabach-thani?' that is to say, 'My God, my God, why hast thou for-saken me?' ⁴⁷Some of them that stood there, when they heard that, said, 'This man calleth for Elias.' ⁴⁸And straightway one of them ran, and took a spunge, and filled it with vinegar, and put it on a reed, and gave him to drink. ⁴⁹The rest said, 'Let be, let us see whether Elias will come to save him.'

⁵⁰Jesus, when he had cried again with a loud voice, yielded up the ghost. ⁵¹And, behold, the veil of the temple was rent in twain from the top to the bottom; and the earth did quake, and the rocks rent; ⁵²and the graves were opened; and many bodies of the saints which slept arose, ⁵³and came out of the graves after his resurrection, and went into the holy city, and appeared unto many. ⁵⁴Now when the centurion, and they that were with him, watching Jesus, saw the earthquake, and those things that were done, they feared greatly, saying, 'Truly this was the Son of God.' ⁵⁵And many women were there beholding afar off, which followed Jesus from Galilee,

ministering unto him, [56] among which was Mary Magdalene, and Mary the mother of James and Joses, and the mother of Zebedee's children. [57] When the even was come, there came a rich man of Arimathæa, named Joseph, who also himself was Jesus' disciple. [58] He went to Pilate, and begged the body of Jesus. Then Pilate commanded the body to be delivered. [59] And when Joseph had taken the body, he wrapped it in a clean linen cloth, [60] and laid it in his own new tomb, which he had hewn out in the rock, and he rolled a great stone to the door of the sepulchre, and departed. [61] And there was Mary Magdalene, and the other Mary, sitting over against the sepulchre.

[62] Now the next day, that followed the day of the preparation, the chief priests and Pharisees came together unto Pilate, [63] saying, 'Sir, we remember that that deceiver said, while he was yet alive, "After three days I will rise again." [64] Command therefore that the sepulchre be made sure until the third day, lest his disciples come by night, and steal him away, and say unto the people, "He is risen from the dead," so the last error shall be worse than the first.' [65] Pilate said unto them, 'Ye have a watch: go your way, make it as sure as ye can.' [66] So they went, and made the sepulchre sure, sealing the stone, and setting a watch.

28 In the end of the sabbath, as it began to dawn toward the first day of the week, came Mary Magdalene and the other Mary to see the sepulchre. [2] And, behold, there was a great earthquake: for the angel of the Lord descended from heaven, and came and rolled back the stone from the door,

and sat upon it. ³His countenance was like lightning, and his raiment white as snow, ⁴and for fear of him the keepers did shake, and became as dead men. ⁵And the angel answered and said unto the women, 'Fear not ye, for I know that ye seek Jesus, which was crucified. ⁶He is not here: for he is risen, as he said. Come, see the place where the Lord lay. ⁷And go quickly, and tell his disciples that he is risen from the dead; and, behold, he goeth before you into Galilee; there shall ye see him: lo, I have told you.' ⁸And they departed quickly from the sepulchre with fear and great joy; and did run to bring his disciples word.

⁹And as they went to tell his disciples, behold, Jesus met them, saying, 'All hail.' And they came and held him by the feet, and worshipped him. ¹⁰Then said Jesus unto them, 'Be not afraid: go tell my brethren that they go into Galilee, and there shall they see me.'

¹¹Now when they were going, behold, some of the watch came into the city, and shewed unto the chief priests all the things that were done. ¹²And when they were assembled with the elders, and had taken counsel, they gave large money unto the soldiers, ¹³saying, 'Say ye, "His disciples came by night, and stole him away while we slept." ¹⁴And if this come to the governor's ears, we will persuade him, and secure you.' ¹⁵So they took the money, and did as they were taught, and this saying is commonly reported among the Jews until this day.

¹⁶Then the eleven disciples went away into Galilee, into a mountain where Jesus had appointed them. ¹⁷And when they saw him, they worshipped him, but some doubted. ¹⁸And Jesus came and spake unto them, saying, 'All power is

given unto me in heaven and in earth.

[19] 'Go ye therefore, and teach all nations, baptizing them in the name of the Father, and of the Son, and of the Holy Ghost, [20] teaching them to observe all things whatsoever I have commanded you, and, lo, I am with you alway, even unto the end of the world. Amen.'

mark

introduction by nick cave

When I bought my first copy of the Bible, the King James version, it was to the Old Testament that I was drawn, with its maniacal, punitive God, that dealt out to His long-suffering humanity punishments that had me drop-jawed in disbelief at the very depth of their vengefulness. I had a burgeoning interest in violent literature coupled with an unnamed sense of the divinity in things and, in my early twenties, the Old Testament spoke to that part of me that railed and hissed and spat at the world. I believed in God, but I also believed that God was malign and if the Old Testament was testament to anything, it was testament to that. Evil seemed to live so close to the surface of existence within it, you could smell its mad breath, see the yellow smoke curl from its many pages, hear the blood-curdling moans of despair. It was a wonderful, terrible book and it was sacred scripture.

But you grow up. You do. You mellow out. Buds of compassion push through the cracks in the black and bitter soil. Your rage ceases to need a name. You no longer find comfort watching a whacked-out God tormenting a wretched humanity as you learn to forgive yourself and the world. That God of Old begins to transmute in your heart, base metals become silver and gold, and you warm to the world.

Then, one day, I met an Anglican vicar and he suggested

that I give the Old Testament a rest and to read *Mark* instead. I hadn't read the New Testament at that stage because the New Testament was about Jesus Christ and the Christ I remembered from my choir-boy days was that wet, all-loving, etiolated individual that the church proselytised. I spent my pre-teen years singing in the Wangarafta Cathedral Choir and even at that age I recall thinking what a wishy-washy affair the whole thing was. The Anglican Church: it was the decaf of worship and Jesus was their Lord.

'Why *Mark*?' I asked.

'Because it's short,' he replied.

Well, at that time I was willing to give anything a go so I took the vicar's advice and read it, and *The Gospel According to Mark* just swept me up.

Here, I am reminded of that picture of Christ, painted by Holman Hunt, where He appears, robed and handsome, a lantern in His hand, knocking on a door. The door to our hearts, presumably. The light is dim and buttery in the engulfing darkness. Christ came to me in this way, *lumen Christi*, with a dim light, a sad light, but light enough. Out of all the New Testament writings – from the four *Gospels*, through the *Acts*, and the complex, driven *Letters of Paul*, to the chilling, sickening *Revelation* – it is *Mark's Gospel* that has truly *held* me.

Scholars generally agree that Mark's was the first of the four *Gospels* to be written. Mark took from the mouths of teachers and prophets the jumble of events that comprised Christ's life and fixed these events into some kind of biographical form. He did this with such breathless insistence, such compulsive narrative intensity, that one is reminded of a child recounting some amazing tale, piling fact upon fact, as if the whole world depended upon it, which of course, to Mark, it did. 'Straightway' and 'immediately' link one event to another, everyone 'runs', 'shouts', is 'amazed', inflaming Christ's mission with a dazzling urgency. Mark's *Gospel* is a clatter of bones, so raw, nervy and lean on information that the narrative aches with the melancholy of absence. Scenes of deep tragedy are treated with such a matter-of-factness and raw economy they become almost palpable in their unprotected sorrowfulness. Mark's narrative begins with the Baptism and 'immediately' we are confronted with the solitary figure of Christ, who is baptised in the River Jordan and driven into the wilderness. 'And he was there in the wilderness forty days, tempted of Satan; and was with the wild beasts; and the angels ministered unto him' (1:13). This is all Mark says of the Temptation, but the verse is typically potent owing to its mysterious simplicity and spareness.

Christ's forty days and forty nights in the wilderness also say something about His aloneness, for when Christ takes on His ministry around Galilee and in Jerusalem, He enters a wilderness of the soul, where all the outpourings of His brilliant, jewel-like imagination are in turns misunderstood, rebuffed, ignored, mocked and vilified and would eventually be the death of Him. Even His disciples, who we would hope would absorb some of Christ's brilliance, seem to be in a perpetual fog of misunderstanding, following Christ from scene to scene, with little or no comprehension of what is going on around them. So much of the frustration and anger that seems at times to almost consume Christ is directed at His disciples and it is against their persistent ignorance that Christ's isolation seems at its most complete. It is Christ's divine inspiration versus the dull rationalism of those around Him that gives Mark's narrative its tension, its drive. The gulf of misunderstanding is so vast that His friends 'lay hold of Him' thinking, 'He is beside himself' (3:21). The scribes and Pharisees, with their monotonous insistence on the Law, provide the perfect springboard for Christ's luminous words. Even those Christ heals betray Him, as they run to the towns to report the doings of the miraculous healer, after Christ has insisted that they tell no one. Christ disowns His own mother for her lack of understanding. Throughout *Mark*, Christ is in deep conflict with the world. He is trying to save, and the sense of aloneness that surrounds Him is at times unbearably intense. Christ's last howl from the cross is to a God He believes has forsaken Him, 'Eloi, Eloi, lama sabachthani.'

The rite of Baptism – the dying of one's old self to be born anew – like so many of the events in Christ's life, is already flavoured metaphorically by Christ's death and it is His death on the cross that is such a powerful and haunting force, especially in *Mark*. His preoccupation with it is all the more obvious if only because of the brevity with which *Mark* deals with the events of His life. It seems that virtually everything that Christ does in Mark's narrative is in some way a preparation for His death – His frustration with His disciples and His fear that they have not comprehended the full significance of His actions, the constant taunting of the church officials, the stirring up of the crowds, His miracle-making so that witnesses will remember the extent of His divine power. Clearly *Mark* is concerned primarily with the death of Christ, to such an extent that Christ appears completely consumed by His imminent demise, thoroughly shaped by His death.

The Christ that emerges from *Mark*, tramping through the haphazard events of His life, had a ringing intensity about Him that I could not resist. Christ spoke to me through His isolation, through the burden of His death, through His rage at the mundane, through His sorrow. Christ, it seemed to me, was the victim of humanity's lack of imagination, was hammered to the cross with the nails of creative vapidity.

The Gospel According to Mark has continued to inform my life as the root source of my spirituality, my religiousness. The Christ that the Church offers us, the bloodless, placid 'Saviour' – the man smiling benignly at a group of children, or calmly, serenely hanging from the cross – denies Christ His potent, creative sorrow or His boiling anger that confronts us so forcefully in *Mark*. Thus the Church denies Christ His humanity, offering up a figure that we can perhaps 'praise', but never relate to. The essential humanness of *Mark*'s Christ provides us with a blueprint for our own lives, so that we have something that we can aspire to, rather than revere, that can lift us free of the mundanity of our existences, rather than affirming the notion that we are lowly and unworthy. Merely to praise Christ in His Perfectness, keeps us on our knees, with our heads pitifully bent. Clearly, this is not what Christ had in mind. Christ came as a liberator. Christ understood that we as humans were for ever held to the ground by the pull of gravity – our ordinariness, our mediocrity – and it was through His example that He gave our imaginations the freedom to rise and to fly. In short, to be Christ-like.

The beginning of the gospel of Jesus Christ, the Son of God; [2] as it is written in the prophets, 'Behold, I send my messenger before thy face, which shall prepare thy way before thee. [3] The voice of one crying in the wilderness, "Prepare ye the way of the Lord, make his paths straight."' [4] John did baptize in the wilderness, and preach the baptism of repentance for the remission of sins. [5] And there went out unto him all the land of Judæa, and they of Jerusalem, and were all baptized of him in the river of Jordan, confessing their sins.

[6] And John was clothed with camel's hair, and with a girdle of a skin about his loins; and he did eat locusts and wild honey; [7] and preached, saying, 'There cometh one mightier than I after me, the latchet of whose shoes I am not worthy to stoop down and unloose. [8] I indeed have baptized you with water; but he shall baptize you with the Holy Ghost.'

[9] And it came to pass in those days, that Jesus came from Nazareth of Galilee, and was baptized of John in Jordan. [10] And straightway coming up out of the water, he saw the heavens opened, and the Spirit like a dove descending upon him. [11] And there came a voice from heaven, saying, 'Thou art my beloved Son, in whom I am well pleased.'

[12] And immediately the Spirit driveth him into the wilderness. [13] And he was there in the wilderness forty days, tempted

of Satan; and was with the wild beasts; and the angels ministered unto him.

¹⁴ Now after that John was put in prison, Jesus came into Galilee, preaching the gospel of the kingdom of God, ¹⁵ and saying, 'The time is fulfilled, and the kingdom of God is at hand; repent ye, and believe the gospel.'

¹⁶ Now as he walked by the sea of Galilee, he saw Simon and Andrew his brother casting a net into the sea, for they were fishers. ¹⁷ And Jesus said unto them, 'Come ye after me, and I will make you to become fishers of men.' ¹⁸ And straightway they forsook their nets, and followed him.

¹⁹ And when he had gone a little further thence, he saw James the son of Zebedee, and John his brother, who also were in the ship mending their nets. ²⁰ And straightway he called them: and they left their father Zebedee in the ship with the hired servants, and went after him.

²¹ And they went into Capernaum; and straightway on the sabbath day he entered into the synagogue, and taught. ²² And they were astonished at his doctrine: for he taught them as one that had authority, and not as the scribes. ²³ And there was in their synagogue a man with an unclean spirit; and he cried out, ²⁴ saying, 'Let us alone; what have we to do with thee, thou Jesus of Nazareth? Art thou come to destroy us? I know thee who thou art, the Holy One of God.' ²⁵ And Jesus rebuked him, saying, 'Hold thy peace, and come out of him.' ²⁶ And when the unclean spirit had torn him, and cried with a loud voice, he came out of him. ²⁷ And they were all amazed, insomuch that they questioned among themselves, saying, 'What thing is this? What new doctrine is this? For

with authority commandeth he even the unclean spirits, and they do obey him.' ²⁸And immediately his fame spread abroad throughout all the region round about Galilee.

²⁹And forthwith, when they were come out of the synagogue, they entered into the house of Simon and Andrew, with James and John. ³⁰But Simon's wife's mother lay sick of a fever, and anon they tell him of her. ³¹And he came and took her by the hand, and lifted her up; and immediately the fever left her, and she ministered unto them.

³²And at even, when the sun did set, they brought unto him all that were diseased, and them that were possessed with devils. ³³And all the city was gathered together at the door. ³⁴And he healed many that were sick of divers diseases, and cast out many devils; and suffered not the devils to speak, because they knew him.

³⁵And in the morning, rising up a great while before day, he went out, and departed into a solitary place, and there prayed. ³⁶And Simon and they that were with him followed after him. ³⁷And when they had found him, they said unto him, 'All men seek for thee.' ³⁸And he said unto them, 'Let us go into the next towns, that I may preach there also; for therefore came I forth.' ³⁹And he preached in their synagogues throughout all Galilee, and cast out devils.

⁴⁰And there came a leper to him, beseeching him, and kneeling down to him, and saying unto him, 'If thou wilt, thou canst make me clean.' ⁴¹And Jesus, moved with compassion, put forth his hand, and touched him, and saith unto him, 'I will; be thou clean.' ⁴²And as soon as he had spoken, immediately the leprosy departed from him, and he was cleansed.

43And he straitly charged him, and forthwith sent him away; 44and saith unto him, 'See thou say nothing to any man; but go thy way, shew thyself to the priest, and offer for thy cleansing those things which Moses commanded, for a testimony unto them.' 45But he went out, and began to publish it much, and to blaze abroad the matter, insomuch that Jesus could no more openly enter into the city, but was without in desert places; and they came to him from every quarter.

2 And again he entered into Capernaum after some days; and it was noised that he was in the house. 2And straightway many were gathered together, insomuch that there was no room to receive them, no, not so much as about the door; and he preached the word unto them. 3And they come unto him, bringing one sick of the palsy, which was borne of four. 4And when they could not come nigh unto him for the press, they uncovered the roof where he was; and when they had broken it up, they let down the bed wherein the sick of the palsy lay. 5When Jesus saw their faith, he said unto the sick of the palsy, 'Son, thy sins be forgiven thee.'

6But there were certain of the scribes sitting there, and reasoning in their hearts, 7'Why doth this man thus speak blasphemies? Who can forgive sins but God only?' 8And immediately when Jesus perceived in his spirit that they so reasoned within themselves, he said unto them, 'Why reason ye these things in your hearts? 9Whether is it easier to say to the sick of the palsy, "Thy sins be forgiven thee," or to say, "Arise, and take up thy bed, and walk"? 10But that ye may know that the Son of man hath power on earth to forgive sins,' he saith to the sick of the palsy, [11]'I say unto thee, Arise, and take up thy bed, and go thy way into thine house.' [12]And immediately he arose, took up the bed, and went forth before them all; insomuch that they were all amazed, and glorified God, saying, 'We never saw it on this fashion.'

[13]And he went forth again by the sea side; and all the multitude resorted unto him, and he taught them. [14]And as he passed by, he saw Levi the son of Alphæus sitting at the receipt of custom, and said unto him, 'Follow me.' And Levi arose and followed him.

[15]And it came to pass, that, as Jesus sat at meat in his house, many publicans and sinners sat also together with Jesus and his disciples; for there were many, and they followed him. [16]And when the scribes and Pharisees saw him eat with publicans and sinners, they said unto his disciples, 'How is it that he eateth and drinketh with publicans and sinners?' [17]When Jesus heard it, he saith unto them, 'They that are whole have no need of the physician, but they that are sick; I came not to call the righteous, but sinners to repentance.'

[18]And the disciples of John and of the Pharisees used to fast; and they come and say unto him, 'Why do the disciples of John and of the Pharisees fast, but thy disciples fast not?' [19]And Jesus said unto them, 'Can the children of the bridechamber fast, while the bridegroom is with them? As long as they have the bridegroom with them, they cannot fast. [20]But the days will come, when the bridegroom shall be taken away from them, and then shall they fast in those days.

[21]'No man also seweth a piece of new cloth on an old garment; else the new piece that filled it up taketh away from

the old, and the rent is made worse. ²²And no man putteth new wine into old bottles; else the new wine doth burst the bottles, and the wine is spilled, and the bottles will be marred; but new wine must be put into new bottles.' ²³And it came to pass that he went through the corn fields on the sabbath day; and his disciples began, as they went, to pluck the ears of corn. ²⁴And the Pharisees said unto him, 'Behold, why do they on the sabbath day that which is not lawful?' ²⁵And he said unto them, 'Have ye never read what David did, when he had need, and was an hungred, he, and they that were with him? ²⁶How he went into the house of God in the days of Abiathar the high priest, and did eat the shewbread, which is not lawful to eat but for the priests, and gave also to them which were with him?'

²⁷And he said unto them, 'The sabbath was made for man, and not man for the sabbath; ²⁸therefore the Son of man is Lord also of the sabbath.'

3 And he entered again into the synagogue; and there was a man there which had a withered hand. ²And they watched him, whether he would heal him on the sabbath day; that they might accuse him.

³And he saith unto the man which had the withered hand, 'Stand forth.' ⁴And he saith unto them, 'Is it lawful to do good on the sabbath days, or to do evil? To save life, or to kill?' But they held their peace. ⁵And when he had looked round about on them with anger, being grieved for the hardness of their hearts, he saith unto the man, 'Stretch forth thine hand.' And he stretched it out; and his hand was restored

whole as the other. ⁶And the Pharisees went forth, and straightway took counsel with the Herodians against him, how they might destroy him.

⁷But Jesus withdrew himself with his disciples to the sea; and a great multitude from Galilee followed him, and from Judæa, ⁸and from Jerusalem, and from Idumæa, and from beyond Jordan; and they about Tyre and Sidon, a great multitude, when they had heard what great things he did, came unto him. ⁹And he spake to his disciples, that a small ship should wait on him because of the multitude, lest they should throng him. ¹⁰For he had healed many; insomuch that they pressed upon him for to touch him, as many as had plagues. ¹¹And unclean spirits, when they saw him, fell down before him, and cried, saying, 'Thou art the Son of God.' ¹²And he straitly charged them that they should not make him known.

¹³And he goeth up into a mountain, and calleth unto him whom he would: and they came unto him. ¹⁴And he ordained twelve, that they should be with him, and that he might send them forth to preach, ¹⁵and to have power to heal sicknesses, and to cast out devils: ¹⁶and Simon he surnamed Peter; ¹⁷and James the son of Zebedee, and John the brother of James; and he surnamed them Boanerges, which is, The sons of thunder; ¹⁸and Andrew, and Philip, and Bartholomew, and Matthew, and Thomas, and James the son of Alphæus, and Thaddæus, and Simon the Canaanite; ¹⁹and Judas Iscariot, which also betrayed him. And they went into an house. ²⁰And the multitude cometh together again, so that they could not so much as eat bread. ²¹And when his friends heard of it, they went out to lay hold on him; for they said, 'He is beside himself.'

²²And the scribes which came down from Jerusalem said, 'He hath Beelzebub, and by the prince of the devils casteth he out devils.' ²³And he called them unto him, and said unto them in parables, 'How can Satan cast out Satan? ²⁴And if a kingdom be divided against itself, that kingdom cannot stand. ²⁵And if a house be divided against itself, that house cannot stand. ²⁶And if Satan rise up against himself, and be divided, he cannot stand, but hath an end.

²⁷'No man can enter into a strong man's house, and spoil his goods, except he will first bind the strong man; and then he will spoil his house.

²⁸'Verily I say unto you, all sins shall be forgiven unto the sons of men, and blasphemies wherewith soever they shall blaspheme; ²⁹but he that shall blaspheme against the Holy Ghost hath never forgiveness, but is in danger of eternal damnation, ³⁰because they said, "He hath an unclean spirit."'

³¹There came then his brethren and his mother, and, standing without, sent unto him, calling him. ³²And the multitude sat about him, and they said unto him, 'Behold, thy mother and thy brethren without seek for thee.' ³³And he answered them, saying, 'Who is my mother, or my brethren?' ³⁴And he looked round about on them which sat about him, and said, 'Behold my mother and my brethren! ³⁵For whosoever shall do the will of God, the same is my brother, and my sister, and mother.'

4 And he began again to teach by the sea side; and there was gathered unto him a great multitude, so that he entered into a ship, and sat in the sea; and the whole multitude

was by the sea on the land. ²And he taught them many things by parables, and said unto them in his doctrine, ³'Hearken; behold, there went out a sower to sow. ⁴And it came to pass, as he sowed, some fell by the way side, and the fowls of the air came and devoured it up. ⁵And some fell on stony ground, where it had not much earth; and immediately it sprang up, because it had no depth of earth. ⁶But when the sun was up, it was scorched; and because it had no root, it withered away. ⁷And some fell among thorns, and the thorns grew up, and choked it, and it yielded no fruit. ⁸And other fell on good ground, and did yield fruit that sprang up and increased; and brought forth, some thirty, and some sixty, and some an hundred.' ⁹And he said unto them, 'He that hath ears to hear, let him hear.'

¹⁰And when he was alone, they that were about him with the twelve asked of him the parable. ¹¹And he said unto them, 'Unto you it is given to know the mystery of the kingdom of God; but unto them that are without, all these things are done in parables; ¹²that seeing they may see, and not perceive; and hearing they may hear, and not understand; lest at any time they should be converted, and their sins should be forgiven them.'

¹³And he said unto them, 'Know ye not this parable? And how then will ye know all parables?

¹⁴'The sower soweth the word. ¹⁵And these are they by the way side, where the word is sown; but when they have heard, Satan cometh immediately, and taketh away the word that was sown in their hearts. ¹⁶And these are they likewise which are sown on stony ground; who, when they have

heard the word, immediately receive it with gladness; [17]and have no root in themselves, and so endure but for a time; afterward, when affliction or persecution ariseth for the word's sake, immediately they are offended. [18]And these are they which are sown among thorns; such as hear the word, [19]and the cares of this world, and the deceitfulness of riches, and the lusts of other things entering in, choke the word, and it becometh unfruitful. [20]And these are they which are sown on good ground; such as hear the word, and receive it, and bring forth fruit, some thirtyfold, some sixty, and some an hundred.'

[21]And he said unto them, 'Is a candle brought to be put under a bushel, or under a bed? And not to be set on a candlestick? [22]For there is nothing hid, which shall not be manifested; neither was any thing kept secret, but that it should come abroad. [23]If any man have ears to hear, let him hear.' [24]And he said unto them, 'Take heed what ye hear: with what measure ye mete, it shall be measured to you; and unto you that hear shall more be given. [25]For he that hath, to him shall be given; and he that hath not, from him shall be taken even that which he hath.'

[26]And he said, 'So is the kingdom of God, as if a man should cast seed into the ground; [27]and should sleep, and rise night and day, and the seed should spring and grow up, he knoweth not how. [28]For the earth bringeth forth fruit of herself; first the blade, then the ear, after that the full corn in the ear. [29]But when the fruit is brought forth, immediately he putteth in the sickle, because the harvest is come.'

[30]And he said, 'Whereunto shall we liken the kingdom of

God? Or with what comparison shall we compare it? [31] It is like a grain of mustard seed, which, when it is sown in the earth, is less than all the seeds that be in the earth; [32] but when it is sown, it groweth up, and becometh greater than all herbs, and shooteth out great branches; so that the fowls of the air may lodge under the shadow of it.'

[33] And with many such parables spake he the word unto them, as they were able to hear it. [34] But without a parable spake he not unto them; and when they were alone, he expounded all things to his disciples.

[35] And the same day, when the even was come, he saith unto them, 'Let us pass over unto the other side.' [36] And when they had sent away the multitude, they took him even as he was in the ship. And there were also with him other little ships. [37] And there arose a great storm of wind, and the waves beat into the ship, so that it was now full. [38] And he was in the hinder part of the ship, asleep on a pillow; and they awake him, and say unto him, 'Master, carest thou not that we perish?' [39] And he arose, and rebuked the wind, and said unto the sea, 'Peace, be still.' And the wind ceased, and there was a great calm. [40] And he said unto them, 'Why are ye so fearful? How is it that ye have no faith?' [41] And they feared exceedingly, and said one to another, 'What manner of man is this, that even the wind and the sea obey him?'

5 And they came over unto the other side of the sea, into the country of the Gadarenes. [2] And when he was come out of the ship, immediately there met him out of the tombs a man with an unclean spirit, [3] who had his dwelling among

the tombs; and no man could bind him, no, not with chains; [4] because that he had been often bound with fetters and chains, and the chains had been plucked asunder by him, and the fetters broken in pieces; neither could any man tame him.

[5] And always, night and day, he was in the mountains, and in the tombs, crying, and cutting himself with stones. [6] But when he saw Jesus afar off, he ran and worshipped him, [7] and cried with a loud voice, and said, 'What have I to do with thee, Jesus, thou Son of the most high God? I adjure thee by God, that thou torment me not.' [8] For Jesus said unto him, 'Come out of the man, thou unclean spirit.' [9] And he asked him, 'What is thy name?' And the man answered, saying, 'My name is Legion: for we are many.' [10] And he besought him much that he would not send them away out of the country.

[11] Now there was there nigh unto the mountains a great herd of swine feeding. [12] And all the devils besought him, saying, 'Send us into the swine, that we may enter into them.' [13] And forthwith Jesus gave them leave. And the unclean spirits went out, and entered into the swine; and the herd ran violently down a steep place into the sea (they were about two thousand) and were choked in the sea.

[14] And they that fed the swine fled, and told it in the city, and in the country. And they went out to see what it was that was done. [15] And they come to Jesus, and see him that was possessed with the devil, and had the legion, sitting, and clothed, and in his right mind; and they were afraid. [16] And they that saw it told them how it befell to him that was possessed with the devil, and also concerning the swine. [17] And

they began to pray him to depart out of their coasts. ¹⁸And when he was come into the ship, he that had been possessed with the devil prayed him that he might be with him. ¹⁹Howbeit Jesus suffered him not, but saith unto him, 'Go home to thy friends, and tell them how great things the Lord hath done for thee, and hath had compassion on thee.' ²⁰And he departed, and began to publish in Decapolis how great things Jesus had done for him; and all men did marvel.

²¹And when Jesus was passed over again by ship unto the other side, much people gathered unto him: and he was nigh unto the sea. ²²And, behold, there cometh one of the rulers of the synagogue, Jairus by name; and when he saw him, he fell at his feet, ²³and besought him greatly, saying, 'My little daughter lieth at the point of death; I pray thee, come and lay thy hands on her, that she may be healed; and she shall live.' ²⁴And Jesus went with him; and much people followed him, and thronged him.

²⁵And a certain woman, which had an issue of blood twelve years, ²⁶and had suffered many things of many physicians, and had spent all that she had, and was nothing bettered, but rather grew worse, ²⁷when she had heard of Jesus, came in the press behind, and touched his garment. ²⁸For she said, 'If I may touch but his clothes, I shall be whole.' ²⁹And straightway the fountain of her blood was dried up; and she felt in her body that she was healed of that plague. ³⁰And Jesus, immediately knowing in himself that virtue had gone out of him, turned him about in the press, and said, 'Who touched my clothes?' ³¹And his disciples said unto him, 'Thou seest the multitude thronging thee, and sayest thou, "Who touched me?"'

³²And he looked round about to see her that had done this thing. ³³But the woman fearing and trembling, knowing what was done in her, came and fell down before him, and told him all the truth. ³⁴And he said unto her, 'Daughter, thy faith hath made thee whole; go in peace, and be whole of thy plague.'

³⁵While he yet spake, there came from the ruler of the synagogue's house certain which said, 'Thy daughter is dead; why troublest thou the Master any further?' ³⁶As soon as Jesus heard the word that was spoken, he saith unto the ruler of the synagogue, 'Be not afraid, only believe.' ³⁷And he suffered no man to follow him, save Peter, and James, and John the brother of James. ³⁸And he cometh to the house of the ruler of the synagogue, and seeth the tumult, and them that wept and wailed greatly. ³⁹And when he was come in, he saith unto them, 'Why make ye this ado, and weep? The damsel is not dead, but sleepeth.' ⁴⁰And they laughed him to scorn. But when he had put them all out, he taketh the father and the mother of the damsel, and them that were with him, and entereth in where the damsel was lying. ⁴¹And he took the damsel by the hand, and said unto her, 'Talitha cumi,' which is, being interpreted, 'Damsel, I say unto thee, arise.' ⁴²And straightway the damsel arose, and walked; for she was of the age of twelve years. And they were astonished with a great astonishment. ⁴³And he charged them straitly that no man should know it; and commanded that something should be given her to eat.

6 And he went out from thence, and came into his own country; and his disciples follow him. ²And when the

sabbath day was come, he began to teach in the synagogue; and many hearing him were astonished, saying, 'From whence hath this man these things? And what wisdom is this which is given unto him, that even such mighty works are wrought by his hands? ³Is not this the carpenter, the son of Mary, the brother of James, and Joses, and of Juda, and Simon? And are not his sisters here with us?' And they were offended at him. ⁴But Jesus said unto them, 'A prophet is not without honour, but in his own country, and among his own kin, and in his own house.' ⁵And he could there do no mighty work, save that he laid his hands upon a few sick folk, and healed them. ⁶And he marvelled because of their unbelief. And he went round about the villages, teaching.

⁷And he called unto him the twelve, and began to send them forth by two and two; and gave them power over unclean spirits; ⁸and commanded them that they should take nothing for their journey, save a staff only; no scrip, no bread, no money in their purse; ⁹but be shod with sandals; and not put on two coats. ¹⁰And he said unto them, 'In what place soever ye enter into an house, there abide till ye depart from that place. ¹¹And whosoever shall not receive you, nor hear you, when ye depart thence, shake off the dust under your feet for a testimony against them. Verily I say unto you, It shall be more tolerable for Sodom and Gomorrha in the day of judgment, than for that city.' ¹²And they went out, and preached that men should repent. ¹³And they cast out many devils, and anointed with oil many that were sick, and healed them.

¹⁴And king Herod heard of him (for his name was spread abroad) and he said, 'That John the Baptist was risen from

the dead, and therefore mighty works do shew forth themselves in him.' ¹⁵ Others said, 'That it is Elias.' And others said, 'That it is a prophet, or as one of the prophets.' ¹⁶ But when Herod heard thereof, he said, 'It is John, whom I beheaded; he is risen from the dead.'

¹⁷ For Herod himself had sent forth and laid hold upon John, and bound him in prison for Herodias' sake, his brother Philip's wife; for he had married her. ¹⁸ For John had said unto Herod, 'It is not lawful for thee to have thy brother's wife.' ¹⁹ Therefore Herodias had a quarrel against him, and would have killed him; but she could not; ²⁰ for Herod feared John, knowing that he was a just man and an holy, and observed him; and when he heard him, he did many things, and heard him gladly.

²¹ And when a convenient day was come, that Herod on his birthday made a supper to his lords, high captains, and chief estates of Galilee; ²² and when the daughter of the said Herodias came in, and danced, and pleased Herod and them that sat with him, the king said unto the damsel, 'Ask of me whatsoever thou wilt, and I will give it thee.' ²³ And he sware unto her, 'Whatsoever thou shalt ask of me, I will give it thee, unto the half of my kingdom.' ²⁴ And she went forth, and said unto her mother, 'What shall I ask?' And she said, 'The head of John the Baptist.' ²⁵ And she came in straightway with haste unto the king, and asked, saying, 'I will that thou give me by and by in a charger the head of John the Baptist.' ²⁶ And the king was exceeding sorry; yet for his oath's sake, and for their sakes which sat with him, he would not reject her. ²⁷ And immediately the king sent an executioner,

and commanded his head to be brought; and he went and beheaded him in the prison, ²⁸ and brought his head in a charger, and gave it to the damsel; and the damsel gave it to her mother.

²⁹And when his disciples heard of it, they came and took up his corpse, and laid it in a tomb.

³⁰And the apostles gathered themselves together unto Jesus, and told him all things, both what they had done, and what they had taught. ³¹And he said unto them, 'Come ye yourselves apart into a desert place, and rest a while,' for there were many coming and going, and they had no leisure so much as to eat. ³²And they departed into a desert place by ship privately. ³³And the people saw them departing, and many knew him, and ran afoot thither out of all cities, and outwent them, and came together unto him. ³⁴And Jesus, when he came out, saw much people, and was moved with compassion toward them, because they were as sheep not having a shepherd; and he began to teach them many things. ³⁵And when the day was now far spent, his disciples came unto him, and said, 'This is a desert place, and now the time is far passed; ³⁶ send them away, that they may go into the country round about, and into the villages, and buy themselves bread; for they have nothing to eat.' ³⁷ He answered and said unto them, 'Give ye them to eat.' And they say unto him, 'Shall we go and buy two hundred pennyworth of bread, and give them to eat?' ³⁸ He saith unto them, 'How many loaves have ye? Go and see.' And when they knew, they say, 'Five, and two fishes.' ³⁹And he commanded them to make all sit down by companies upon the green grass. ⁴⁰And they

sat down in ranks, by hundreds, and by fifties. ⁴¹And when he had taken the five loaves and the two fishes, he looked up to heaven, and blessed, and brake the loaves, and gave them to his disciples to set before them; and the two fishes divided he among them all. ⁴²And they did all eat, and were filled. ⁴³And they took up twelve baskets full of the fragments, and of the fishes. ⁴⁴And they that did eat of the loaves were about five thousand men.

⁴⁵And straightway he constrained his disciples to get into the ship, and to go to the other side before unto Bethsaida, while he sent away the people. ⁴⁶And when he had sent them away, he departed into a mountain to pray. ⁴⁷And when even was come, the ship was in the midst of the sea, and he alone on the land. ⁴⁸And he saw them toiling in rowing; for the wind was contrary unto them; and about the fourth watch of the night he cometh unto them, walking upon the sea, and would have passed by them. ⁴⁹But when they saw him walking upon the sea, they supposed it had been a spirit, and cried out; ⁵⁰for they all saw him, and were troubled. And immediately he talked with them, and saith unto them, 'Be of good cheer: it is I; be not afraid.' ⁵¹And he went up unto them into the ship; and the wind ceased; and they were sore amazed in themselves beyond measure, and wondered. ⁵²For they considered not the miracle of the loaves; for their heart was hardened.

⁵³And when they had passed over, they came into the land of Gennesaret, and drew to the shore. ⁵⁴And when they were come out of the ship, straightway they knew him, ⁵⁵and ran through that whole region round about, and began to

carry about in beds those that were sick, where they heard he was. [56]And whithersoever he entered, into villages, or cities, or country, they laid the sick in the streets, and besought him that they might touch if it were but the border of his garment: and as many as touched him were made whole.

7 Then came together unto him the Pharisees, and certain of the scribes, which came from Jerusalem. [2]And when they saw some of his disciples eat bread with defiled, that is to say, with unwashen, hands, they found fault. [3]For the Pharisees, and all the Jews, except they wash their hands oft, eat not, holding the tradition of the elders. [4]And when they come from the market, except they wash, they eat not. And many other things there be, which they have received to hold, as the washing of cups, and pots, brasen vessels, and of tables. [5]Then the Pharisees and scribes asked him, 'Why walk not thy disciples according to the tradition of the elders, but eat bread with unwashen hands?' [6]He answered and said unto them, 'Well hath Esaias prophesied of you hypocrites, as it is written, "This people honoureth me with their lips, but their heart is far from me. [7]Howbeit in vain do they worship me, teaching for doctrines the commandments of men." [8]For laying aside the commandment of God, ye hold the tradition of men, as the washing of pots and cups; and many other such like things ye do.'

[9]And he said unto them, 'Full well ye reject the commandment of God, that ye may keep your own tradition. [10]For Moses said, "Honour thy father and thy mother," and, "Whoso curseth father or mother, let him die the death." [11]But ye

say, "If a man shall say to his father or mother, 'It is Corban,' that is to say, a gift, by whatsoever thou mightest be profited by me; he shall be free." [12]And ye suffer him no more to do ought for his father or his mother; [13]making the word of God of none effect through your tradition, which ye have delivered: and many such like things do ye.'

[14]And when he had called all the people unto him, he said unto them, 'Hearken unto me every one of you, and understand: [15]there is nothing from without a man, that entering into him can defile him; but the things which come out of him, those are they that defile the man. [16]If any man have ears to hear, let him hear.'

[17]And when he was entered into the house from the people, his disciples asked him concerning the parable. [18]And he saith unto them, 'Are ye so without understanding also? Do ye not perceive, that whatsoever thing from without entereth into the man, it cannot defile him; [19]because it entereth not into his heart, but into the belly, and goeth out into the draught, purging all meats?' [20]And he said, 'That which cometh out of the man, that defileth the man. [21]For from within, out of the heart of men, proceed evil thoughts, adulteries, fornications, murders, [22]thefts, covetousness, wickedness, deceit, lasciviousness, an evil eye, blasphemy, pride, foolishness: [23]all these evil things come from within, and defile the man.'

[24]And from thence he arose, and went into the borders of Tyre and Sidon, and entered into an house, and would have no man know it; but he could not be hid. [25]For a certain woman, whose young daughter had an unclean spirit, heard

of him, and came and fell at his feet. ²⁶The woman was a Greek, a Syrophenician by nation; and she besought him that he would cast forth the devil out of her daughter. ²⁷But Jesus said unto her, 'Let the children first be filled: for it is not meet to take the children's bread, and to cast it unto the dogs.' ²⁸And she answered and said unto him, 'Yes, Lord: yet the dogs under the table eat of the children's crumbs.' ²⁹And he said unto her, 'For this saying go thy way; the devil is gone out of thy daughter.' ³⁰And when she was come to her house, she found the devil gone out, and her daughter laid upon the bed.

³¹And again, departing from the coasts of Tyre and Sidon, he came unto the sea of Galilee, through the midst of the coasts of Decapolis. ³²And they bring unto him one that was deaf, and had an impediment in his speech; and they beseech him to put his hand upon him. ³³And he took him aside from the multitude, and put his fingers into his ears, and he spit, and touched his tongue; ³⁴and looking up to heaven, he sighed, and saith unto him, 'Ephphatha,' that is, 'Be opened.' ³⁵And straightway his ears were opened, and the string of his tongue was loosed, and he spake plain. ³⁶And he charged them that they should tell no man; but the more he charged them, so much the more a great deal they published it; ³⁷and were beyond measure astonished, saying, 'He hath done all things well: he maketh both the deaf to hear, and the dumb to speak.'

8 In those days the multitude being very great, and having nothing to eat, Jesus called his disciples unto him,

and saith unto them, ²'I have compassion on the multitude, because they have now been with me three days, and have nothing to eat; ³and if I send them away fasting to their own houses, they will faint by the way; for divers of them came from far.' ⁴And his disciples answered him, 'From whence can a man satisfy these men with bread here in the wilderness?' ⁵And he asked them, 'How many loaves have ye?' And they said, 'Seven.' ⁶And he commanded the people to sit down on the ground: and he took the seven loaves, and gave thanks, and brake, and gave to his disciples to set before them; and they did set them before the people. ⁷And they had a few small fishes; and he blessed, and commanded to set them also before them. ⁸So they did eat, and were filled; and they took up of the broken meat that was left seven baskets. ⁹And they that had eaten were about four thousand; and he sent them away.

¹⁰And straightway he entered into a ship with his disciples, and came into the parts of Dalmanutha. ¹¹And the Pharisees came forth, and began to question with him, seeking of him a sign from heaven, tempting him. ¹²And he sighed deeply in his spirit, and saith, 'Why doth this generation seek after a sign? Verily I say unto you, There shall no sign be given unto this generation.' ¹³And he left them, and entering into the ship again departed to the other side.

¹⁴Now the disciples had forgotten to take bread, neither had they in the ship with them more than one loaf. ¹⁵And he charged them, saying, 'Take heed, beware of the leaven of the Pharisees, and of the leaven of Herod.' ¹⁶And they reasoned among themselves, saying, 'It is because we have no

bread.' ¹⁷And when Jesus knew it, he saith unto them, 'Why reason ye, because ye have no bread? Perceive ye not yet, neither understand? Have ye your heart yet hardened? ¹⁸Having eyes, see ye not? And having ears, hear ye not? And do ye not remember? ¹⁹When I brake the five loaves among five thousand, how many baskets full of fragments took ye up?' They say unto him, 'Twelve.' ²⁰'And when the seven among four thousand, how many baskets full of fragments took ye up?' And they said, 'Seven.' ²¹And he said unto them, 'How is it that ye do not understand?'

²²And he cometh to Bethsaida; and they bring a blind man unto him, and besought him to touch him. ²³And he took the blind man by the hand, and led him out of the town; and when he had spit on his eyes, and put his hands upon him, he asked him if he saw ought. ²⁴And he looked up, and said, 'I see men as trees, walking.' ²⁵After that he put his hands again upon his eyes, and made him look up: and he was restored, and saw every man clearly. ²⁶And Jesus sent him away to his house, saying, 'Neither go into the town, nor tell it to any in the town.'

²⁷And Jesus went out, and his disciples, into the towns of Cæsarea Philippi: and by the way he asked his disciples, saying unto them, 'Whom do men say that I am?' ²⁸And they answered, 'John the Baptist: but some say, Elias; and others, one of the prophets.' ²⁹And he saith unto them, 'But whom say ye that I am?' And Peter answereth and saith unto him, 'Thou art the Christ.' ³⁰And he charged them that they should tell no man of him. ³¹And he began to teach them, that the Son of man must suffer many things, and be rejected of the

elders, and of the chief priests, and scribes, and be killed, and after three days rise again. ³²And he spake that saying openly. And Peter took him, and began to rebuke him. ³³But when he had turned about and looked on his disciples, he rebuked Peter, saying, 'Get thee behind me, Satan: for thou savourest not the things that be of God, but the things that be of men.'

³⁴And when he had called the people unto him with his disciples also, he said unto them, 'Whosoever will come after me, let him deny himself, and take up his cross, and follow me. ³⁵For whosoever will save his life shall lose it; but whosoever shall lose his life for my sake and the gospel's, the same shall save it. ³⁶For what shall it profit a man, if he shall gain the whole world, and lose his own soul? ³⁷Or what shall a man give in exchange for his soul? ³⁸Whosoever therefore shall be ashamed of me and of my words in this adulterous and sinful generation; of him also shall the Son of man be ashamed, when he cometh in the glory of his Father with the holy angels.'

9 And he said unto them, 'Verily I say unto you, that there be some of them that stand here, which shall not taste of death, till they have seen the kingdom of God come with power.'

²And after six days Jesus taketh with him Peter, and James, and John, and leadeth them up into an high mountain apart by themselves; and he was transfigured before them. ³And his raiment became shining, exceeding white as snow; so as no fuller on earth can white them. ⁴And there appeared unto

them Elias with Moses; and they were talking with Jesus. [5]And Peter answered and said to Jesus, 'Master, it is good for us to be here; and let us make three tabernacles: one for thee, and one for Moses, and one for Elias.' [6]For he wist not what to say; for they were sore afraid. [7]And there was a cloud that overshadowed them; and a voice came out of the cloud, saying, 'This is my beloved Son: hear him.' [8]And suddenly, when they had looked round about, they saw no man any more, save Jesus only with themselves. [9]And as they came down from the mountain, he charged them that they should tell no man what things they had seen, till the Son of man were risen from the dead. [10]And they kept that saying with themselves, questioning one with another what the rising from the dead should mean.

[11]And they asked him, saying, 'Why say the scribes that Elias must first come?' [12]And he answered and told them, 'Elias verily cometh first, and restoreth all things; and how it is written of the Son of man, that he must suffer many things, and be set at nought. [13]But I say unto you, that Elias is indeed come, and they have done unto him whatsoever they listed, as it is written of him.'

[14]And when he came to his disciples, he saw a great multitude about them, and the scribes questioning with them. [15]And straightway all the people, when they beheld him, were greatly amazed, and running to him saluted him. [16]And he asked the scribes, 'What question ye with them?' [17]And one of the multitude answered and said, 'Master, I have brought unto thee my son, which hath a dumb spirit; [18]and wheresoever he taketh him, he teareth him: and he foameth,

and gnasheth with his teeth, and pineth away; and I spake to thy disciples that they should cast him out; and they could not.' [19] He answereth him, and saith, 'O faithless generation, how long shall I be with you? How long shall I suffer you? Bring him unto me.' [20]And they brought him unto him: and when he saw him, straightway the spirit tare him; and he fell on the ground, and wallowed foaming. [21]And he asked his father, 'How long is it ago since this came unto him?' And he said, 'Of a child. [22]And ofttimes it hath cast him into the fire, and into the waters, to destroy him; but if thou canst do any thing, have compassion on us, and help us.' [23] Jesus said unto him, 'If thou canst believe, all things are possible to him that believeth.' [24]And straightway the father of the child cried out, and said with tears, 'Lord, I believe; help thou mine unbelief.' [25] When Jesus saw that the people came running together, he rebuked the foul spirit, saying unto him, 'Thou dumb and deaf spirit, I charge thee, come out of him, and enter no more into him.' [26]And the spirit cried, and rent him sore, and came out of him: and he was as one dead; insomuch that many said, 'He is dead.' [27] But Jesus took him by the hand, and lifted him up; and he arose. [28]And when he was come into the house, his disciples asked him privately, 'Why could not we cast him out?' [29]And he said unto them, 'This kind can come forth by nothing, but by prayer and fasting.'

[30]And they departed thence, and passed through Galilee; and he would not that any man should know it. [31]For he taught his disciples, and said unto them, 'The Son of man is delivered into the hands of men, and they shall kill him; and after that he is killed, he shall rise the third day.' [32] But they

understood not that saying, and were afraid to ask him.

³³ And he came to Capernaum: and being in the house he asked them, 'What was it that ye disputed among yourselves by the way?' ³⁴ But they held their peace: for by the way they had disputed among themselves, who should be the greatest. ³⁵ And he sat down, and called the twelve, and saith unto them, 'If any man desire to be first, the same shall be last of all, and servant of all.' ³⁶ And he took a child, and set him in the midst of them; and when he had taken him in his arms, he said unto them, ³⁷ 'Whosoever shall receive one of such children in my name, receiveth me; and whosoever shall receive me, receiveth not me, but him that sent me.'

³⁸ And John answered him, saying, 'Master, we saw one casting out devils in thy name, and he followeth not us; and we forbad him, because he followeth not us.' ³⁹ But Jesus said, 'Forbid him not; for there is no man which shall do a miracle in my name, that can lightly speak evil of me. ⁴⁰ For he that is not against us is on our part. ⁴¹ For whosoever shall give you a cup of water to drink in my name, because ye belong to Christ, verily I say unto you, he shall not lose his reward.

⁴² 'And whosoever shall offend one of these little ones that believe in me, it is better for him that a millstone were hanged about his neck, and he were cast into the sea. ⁴³ And if thy hand offend thee, cut it off; it is better for thee to enter into life maimed, than having two hands to go into hell, into the fire that never shall be quenched, ⁴⁴ where their worm dieth not, and the fire is not quenched. ⁴⁵ And if thy foot offend thee, cut it off: it is better for thee to enter halt into life, than having two feet to be cast into hell, into the fire that

never shall be quenched, [46] where their worm dieth not, and the fire is not quenched. [47] And if thine eye offend thee, pluck it out; it is better for thee to enter into the kingdom of God with one eye, than having two eyes to be cast into hell fire, [48] where their worm dieth not, and the fire is not quenched. [49] For every one shall be salted with fire, and every sacrifice shall be salted with salt. [50] Salt is good; but if the salt have lost his saltness, wherewith will ye season it? Have salt in yourselves, and have peace one with another.'

10 And he arose from thence, and cometh into the coasts of Judæa by the farther side of Jordan; and the people resort unto him again; and, as he was wont, he taught them again.

[2] And the Pharisees came to him, and asked him, 'Is it lawful for a man to put away his wife?' tempting him. [3] And he answered and said unto them, 'What did Moses command you?' [4] And they said, 'Moses suffered to write a bill of divorcement, and to put her away.' [5] And Jesus answered and said unto them, 'For the hardness of your heart he wrote you this precept. [6] But from the beginning of the creation God made them male and female. [7] For this cause shall a man leave his father and mother, and cleave to his wife; [8] and they twain shall be one flesh; so then they are no more twain, but one flesh. [9] What therefore God hath joined together, let not man put asunder.' [10] And in the house his disciples asked him again of the same matter. [11] And he saith unto them, 'Whosoever shall put away his wife, and marry another, committeth adultery against her. [12] And if a woman shall put away her husband, and be married to another, she committeth adultery.'

¹³And they brought young children to him, that he should touch them; and his disciples rebuked those that brought them. ¹⁴But when Jesus saw it, he was much displeased, and said unto them, 'Suffer the little children to come unto me, and forbid them not; for of such is the kingdom of God. ¹⁵Verily I say unto you, whosoever shall not receive the kingdom of God as a little child, he shall not enter therein.' ¹⁶And he took them up in his arms, put his hands upon them, and blessed them.

¹⁷And when he was gone forth into the way, there came one running, and kneeled to him, and asked him, 'Good Master, what shall I do that I may inherit eternal life?' ¹⁸And Jesus said unto him, 'Why callest thou me good? There is none good but one, that is, God. ¹⁹Thou knowest the commandments, "Do not commit adultery, Do not kill, Do not steal, Do not bear false witness, Defraud not, Honour thy father and mother."' ²⁰And he answered and said unto him, 'Master, all these have I observed from my youth.' ²¹Then Jesus beholding him loved him, and said unto him, 'One thing thou lackest: go thy way, sell whatsoever thou hast, and give to the poor, and thou shalt have treasure in heaven; and come, take up the cross, and follow me.' ²²And he was sad at that saying, and went away grieved; for he had great possessions.

²³And Jesus looked round about, and saith unto his disciples, 'How hardly shall they that have riches enter into the kingdom of God!' ²⁴And the disciples were astonished at his words. But Jesus answereth again, and saith unto them, 'Children, how hard is it for them that trust in riches to enter into the kingdom of God! ²⁵It is easier for a camel to go

through the eye of a needle, than for a rich man to enter into the kingdom of God.' ²⁶ And they were astonished out of measure, saying among themselves, 'Who then can be saved?' ²⁷ And Jesus looking upon them saith, 'With men it is impossible, but not with God; for with God all things are possible.'

²⁸ Then Peter began to say unto him, 'Lo, we have left all, and have followed thee.' ²⁹ And Jesus answered and said, 'Verily I say unto you, there is no man that hath left house, or brethren, or sisters, or father, or mother, or wife, or children, or lands, for my sake, and the gospel's, ³⁰ but he shall receive an hundredfold now in this time, houses, and brethren, and sisters, and mothers, and children, and lands, with persecutions; and in the world to come eternal life. ³¹ But many that are first shall be last; and the last first.'

³² And they were in the way going up to Jerusalem; and Jesus went before them; and they were amazed; and as they followed, they were afraid. And he took again the twelve, and began to tell them what things should happen unto him, ³³ saying, 'Behold, we go up to Jerusalem; and the Son of man shall be delivered unto the chief priests, and unto the scribes; and they shall condemn him to death, and shall deliver him to the Gentiles; ³⁴ and they shall mock him, and shall scourge him, and shall spit upon him, and shall kill him: and the third day he shall rise again.'

³⁵ And James and John, the sons of Zebedee, come unto him, saying, 'Master, we would that thou shouldest do for us whatsoever we shall desire.' ³⁶ And he said unto them, 'What would ye that I should do for you?' ³⁷ They said unto him, 'Grant unto us that we may sit, one on thy right hand,

and the other on thy left hand, in thy glory.' ³⁸ But Jesus said unto them, 'Ye know not what ye ask: can ye drink of the cup that I drink of? And be baptized with the baptism that I am baptized with?' ³⁹And they said unto him, 'We can.' And Jesus said unto them, 'Ye shall indeed drink of the cup that I drink of; and with the baptism that I am baptized withal shall ye be baptized; ⁴⁰ but to sit on my right hand and on my left hand is not mine to give; but it shall be given to them for whom it is prepared.' ⁴¹And when the ten heard it, they began to be much displeased with James and John. ⁴²But Jesus called them to him, and saith unto them, 'Ye know that they which are accounted to rule over the Gentiles exercise lordship over them; and their great ones exercise authority upon them. ⁴³ But so shall it not be among you; but whosoever will be great among you, shall be your minister; ⁴⁴and whosoever of you will be the chiefest, shall be servant of all. ⁴⁵For even the Son of man came not to be ministered unto, but to minister, and to give his life a ransom for many.'

⁴⁶And they came to Jericho; and as he went out of Jericho with his disciples and a great number of people, blind Bartimæus, the son of Timæus, sat by the highway side begging. ⁴⁷And when he heard that it was Jesus of Nazareth, he began to cry out, and say, 'Jesus, thou Son of David, have mercy on me.' ⁴⁸And many charged him that he should hold his peace; but he cried the more a great deal, 'Thou Son of David, have mercy on me.' ⁴⁹And Jesus stood still, and commanded him to be called. And they call the blind man, saying unto him, 'Be of good comfort, rise; he calleth thee.' ⁵⁰And he, casting away his garment, rose, and came to Jesus. ⁵¹And Jesus

answered and said unto him, 'What wilt thou that I should do unto thee?' The blind man said unto him, 'Lord, that I might receive my sight.' ⁵²And Jesus said unto him, 'Go thy way; thy faith hath made thee whole.' And immediately he received his sight, and followed Jesus in the way.

11 And when they came nigh to Jerusalem, unto Bethphage and Bethany, at the mount of Olives, he sendeth forth two of his disciples, ²and saith unto them, 'Go your way into the village over against you; and as soon as ye be entered into it, ye shall find a colt tied, whereon never man sat; loose him, and bring him. ³And if any man say unto you, "Why do ye this?" say ye that the Lord hath need of him; and straightway he will send him hither.' ⁴And they went their way, and found the colt tied by the door without in a place where two ways met; and they loose him. ⁵And certain of them that stood there said unto them, 'What do ye, loosing the colt?' ⁶And they said unto them even as Jesus had commanded; and they let them go. ⁷And they brought the colt to Jesus, and cast their garments on him; and he sat upon him. ⁸And many spread their garments in the way; and others cut down branches off the trees, and strawed them in the way. ⁹And they that went before, and they that followed, cried, saying, 'Hosanna; blessed is he that cometh in the name of the Lord; ¹⁰ blessed be the kingdom of our father David, that cometh in the name of the Lord; hosanna in the highest.' ¹¹And Jesus entered into Jerusalem, and into the temple; and when he had looked round about upon all things, and now the eventide was come, he went out unto Bethany with the twelve.

¹²And on the morrow, when they were come from Bethany, he was hungry; ¹³and seeing a fig tree afar off having leaves, he came, if haply he might find any thing thereon; and when he came to it, he found nothing but leaves; for the time of figs was not yet. ¹⁴And Jesus answered and said unto it, 'No man eat fruit of thee hereafter for ever.' And his disciples heard it.

¹⁵And they come to Jerusalem; and Jesus went into the temple, and began to cast out them that sold and bought in the temple, and overthrew the tables of the moneychangers, and the seats of them that sold doves; ¹⁶and would not suffer that any man should carry any vessel through the temple. ¹⁷And he taught, saying unto them, 'Is it not written, "My house shall be called of all nations the house of prayer"? But ye have made it a den of thieves.' ¹⁸And the scribes and chief priests heard it, and sought how they might destroy him; for they feared him, because all the people was astonished at his doctrine. ¹⁹And when even was come, he went out of the city.

²⁰And in the morning, as they passed by, they saw the fig tree dried up from the roots. ²¹And Peter calling to remembrance saith unto him, 'Master, behold, the fig tree which thou cursedst is withered away.' ²²And Jesus answering saith unto them, 'Have faith in God. ²³For verily I say unto you, that whosoever shall say unto this mountain, "Be thou removed, and be thou cast into the sea"; and shall not doubt in his heart, but shall believe that those things which he saith shall come to pass; he shall have whatsoever he saith. ²⁴Therefore I say unto you, what things soever ye desire, when ye pray, believe that ye receive them, and ye shall have them. ²⁵And

when ye stand praying, forgive, if ye have ought against any: that your Father also which is in heaven may forgive you your trespasses. ²⁶ But if ye do not forgive, neither will your Father which is in heaven forgive your trespasses.'

²⁷And they come again to Jerusalem; and as he was walking in the temple, there come to him the chief priests, and the scribes, and the elders, ²⁸ and say unto him, 'By what authority doest thou these things? And who gave thee this authority to do these things?' ²⁹And Jesus answered and said unto them, 'I will also ask of you one question, and answer me, and I will tell you by what authority I do these things. ³⁰ The baptism of John, was it from heaven, or of men? Answer me.' ³¹And they reasoned with themselves, saying, 'If we shall say, "From heaven," he will say, "Why then did ye not believe him?" ³² But if we shall say, "Of men,"' they feared the people; for all men counted John, that he was a prophet indeed.' ³³And they answered and said unto Jesus, 'We cannot tell.' And Jesus answering saith unto them, 'Neither do I tell you by what authority I do these things.'

12 And he began to speak unto them by parables. 'A certain man planted a vineyard, and set an hedge about it, and digged a place for the winefat, and built a tower, and let it out to husbandmen, and went into a far country. ²And at the season he sent to the husbandmen a servant, that he might receive from the husbandmen of the fruit of the vineyard. ³And they caught him, and beat him, and sent him away empty. ⁴And again he sent unto them another servant; and at him they cast stones, and wounded him in the head,

and sent him away shamefully handled. ⁵And again he sent another; and him they killed, and many others; beating some, and killing some. ⁶Having yet therefore one son, his wellbeloved, he sent him also last unto them, saying, "They will reverence my son." ⁷But those husbandmen said among themselves, "This is the heir; come, let us kill him, and the inheritance shall be ours." ⁸And they took him, and killed him, and cast him out of the vineyard. ⁹What shall therefore the lord of the vineyard do? He will come and destroy the husbandmen, and will give the vineyard unto others. ¹⁰And have ye not read this scripture: "The stone which the builders rejected is become the head of the corner. ¹¹This was the Lord's doing, and it is marvellous in our eyes"?' ¹²And they sought to lay hold on him, but feared the people; for they knew that he had spoken the parable against them: and they left him, and went their way.

¹³And they send unto him certain of the Pharisees and of the Herodians, to catch him in his words. ¹⁴And when they were come, they say unto him, 'Master, we know that thou art true, and carest for no man; for thou regardest not the person of men, but teachest the way of God in truth. Is it lawful to give tribute to Caesar, or not? ¹⁵Shall we give, or shall we not give?' But he, knowing their hypocrisy, said unto them, 'Why tempt ye me? Bring me a penny, that I may see it.' ¹⁶And they brought it. And he saith unto them, 'Whose is this image and superscription?' And they said unto him, 'Caesar's.' ¹⁷And Jesus answering said unto them, 'Render to Caesar the things that are Caesar's, and to God the things that are God's.' And they marvelled at him.

¹⁸ Then come unto him the Sadducees, which say there is no resurrection; and they asked him, saying, ¹⁹ 'Master, Moses wrote unto us, "If a man's brother die, and leave his wife behind him, and leave no children, that his brother should take his wife, and raise up seed unto his brother." ²⁰ Now there were seven brethren; and the first took a wife, and dying left no seed. ²¹And the second took her, and died, neither left he any seed; and the third likewise. ²²And the seven had her, and left no seed; last of all the woman died also. ²³ In the resurrection therefore, when they shall rise, whose wife shall she be of them? For the seven had her to wife.' ²⁴And Jesus answering said unto them, 'Do ye not therefore err, because ye know not the scriptures, neither the power of God? ²⁵ For when they shall rise from the dead, they neither marry, nor are given in marriage; but are as the angels which are in heaven. ²⁶And as touching the dead, that they rise; have ye not read in the book of Moses, how in the bush God spake unto him, saying, "I am the God of Abraham, and the God of Isaac, and the God of Jacob?" ²⁷ He is not the God of the dead, but the God of the living; ye therefore do greatly err.'

²⁸And one of the scribes came, and having heard them reasoning together, and perceiving that he had answered them well, asked him, 'Which is the first commandment of all?' ²⁹And Jesus answered him, 'The first of all the commandments is, "Hear, O Israel; the Lord our God is one Lord: ³⁰and thou shalt love the Lord thy God with all thy heart, and with all thy soul, and with all thy mind, and with all thy strength": this is the first commandment. ³¹And the second is like, namely this, "Thou shalt love thy neighbour as thyself." There

is none other commandment greater than these.' ³²And the scribe said unto him, 'Well, Master, thou hast said the truth: for there is one God; and there is none other but he; ³³and to love him with all the heart, and with all the understanding, and with all the soul, and with all the strength, and to love his neighbour as himself, is more than all whole burnt offerings and sacrifices.' ³⁴And when Jesus saw that he answered discreetly, he said unto him, 'Thou art not far from the kingdom of God.' And no man after that durst ask him any question.

³⁵And Jesus answered and said, while he taught in the temple, 'How say the scribes that Christ is the Son of David? ³⁶For David himself said by the Holy Ghost, "The Lord said to my Lord, 'Sit thou on my right hand, till I make thine enemies thy footstool.'" ³⁷David therefore himself calleth him "Lord"; and whence is he then his son?' And the common people heard him gladly.

³⁸And he said unto them in his doctrine, 'Beware of the scribes, which love to go in long clothing, and love salutations in the marketplaces, ³⁹and the chief seats in the synagogues, and the uppermost rooms at feasts, ⁴⁰which devour widows' houses, and for a pretence make long prayers: these shall receive greater damnation.'

⁴¹And Jesus sat over against the treasury, and beheld how the people cast money into the treasury; and many that were rich cast in much. ⁴²And there came a certain poor widow, and she threw in two mites, which make a farthing. ⁴³And he called unto him his disciples, and saith unto them, 'Verily I say unto you, that this poor widow hath cast more in, than all they which have cast into the treasury: ⁴⁴for all they did

cast in of their abundance; but she of her want did cast in all that she had, even all her living.'

13 And as he went out of the temple, one of his disciples saith unto him, 'Master, see what manner of stones and what buildings are here!' ²And Jesus answering said unto him, 'Seest thou these great buildings? There shall not be left one stone upon another, that shall not be thrown down.' ³And as he sat upon the mount of Olives over against the temple, Peter and James and John and Andrew asked him privately, ⁴'Tell us, when shall these things be? And what shall be the sign when all these things shall be fulfilled?' ⁵And Jesus answering them began to say, 'Take heed lest any man deceive you; ⁶for many shall come in my name, saying, "I am Christ," and shall deceive many. ⁷And when ye shall hear of wars and rumours of wars, be ye not troubled; for such things must needs be; but the end shall not be yet. ⁸For nation shall rise against nation, and kingdom against kingdom; and there shall be earthquakes in divers places, and there shall be famines and troubles: these are the beginnings of sorrows.

⁹'But take heed to yourselves: for they shall deliver you up to councils; and in the synagogues ye shall be beaten; and ye shall be brought before rulers and kings for my sake, for a testimony against them. ¹⁰And the gospel must first be published among all nations. ¹¹But when they shall lead you, and deliver you up, take no thought beforehand what ye shall speak, neither do ye premeditate; but whatsoever shall be given you in that hour, that speak ye: for it is not ye that

speak, but the Holy Ghost. ¹²Now the brother shall betray the brother to death, and the father the son; and children shall rise up against their parents, and shall cause them to be put to death. ¹³And ye shall be hated of all men for my name's sake: but he that shall endure unto the end, the same shall be saved.

¹⁴'But when ye shall see the abomination of desolation, spoken of by Daniel the prophet, standing where it ought not (let him that readeth understand) then let them that be in Judæa flee to the mountains; ¹⁵and let him that is on the house-top not go down into the house, neither enter therein, to take any thing out of his house; ¹⁶and let him that is in the field not turn back again for to take up his garment. ¹⁷But woe to them that are with child, and to them that give suck in those days! ¹⁸And pray ye that your flight be not in the winter. ¹⁹For in those days shall be affliction, such as was not from the beginning of the creation which God created unto this time, neither shall be. ²⁰And except that the Lord had shortened those days, no flesh should be saved; but for the elect's sake, whom he hath chosen, he hath shortened the days. ²¹And then if any man shall say to you, "Lo, here is Christ," or, "lo, he is there," believe him not; ²²for false Christs and false prophets shall rise, and shall shew signs and wonders, to seduce, if it were possible, even the elect. ²³But take ye heed: behold, I have foretold you all things.

²⁴'But in those days, after that tribulation, the sun shall be darkened, and the moon shall not give her light, ²⁵and the stars of heaven shall fall, and the powers that are in heaven shall be shaken. ²⁶And then shall they see the Son of man coming in the clouds with great power and glory. ²⁷And then

shall he send his angels, and shall gather together his elect from the four winds, from the uttermost part of the earth to the uttermost part of heaven. ²⁸ Now learn a parable of the fig tree: when her branch is yet tender, and putteth forth leaves, ye know that summer is near; ²⁹ so ye in like manner, when ye shall see these things come to pass, know that it is nigh, even at the doors. ³⁰ Verily I say unto you, that this generation shall not pass, till all these things be done. ³¹ Heaven and earth shall pass away: but my words shall not pass away.

³² 'But of that day and that hour knoweth no man, no, not the angels which are in heaven, neither the Son, but the Father. ³³ Take ye heed, watch and pray: for ye know not when the time is. ³⁴ For the Son of man is as a man taking a far journey, who left his house, and gave authority to his servants, and to every man his work, and commanded the porter to watch. ³⁵ Watch ye therefore: for ye know not when the master of the house cometh, at even, or at midnight, or at the cockcrowing, or in the morning, ³⁶ lest coming suddenly he find you sleeping. ³⁷ And what I say unto you I say unto all, Watch.'

14 After two days was the feast of the passover, and of unleavened bread; and the chief priests and the scribes sought how they might take him by craft, and put him to death. ² But they said, 'Not on the feast day, lest there be an uproar of the people.'

³ And being in Bethany in the house of Simon the leper, as he sat at meat, there came a woman having an alabaster box of ointment of spikenard very precious; and she brake the box, and poured it on his head. ⁴ And there were some

that had indignation within themselves, and said, 'Why was this waste of the ointment made?' ⁵For it might have been sold for more than three hundred pence, and have been given to the poor.' And they murmured against her. ⁶And Jesus said, 'Let her alone; why trouble ye her? She hath wrought a good work on me. ⁷For ye have the poor with you always, and whensoever ye will ye may do them good; but me ye have not always. ⁸She hath done what she could: she is come aforehand to anoint my body to the burying. ⁹Verily I say unto you, wheresoever this gospel shall be preached throughout the whole world, this also that she hath done shall be spoken of for a memorial of her.'

¹⁰And Judas Iscariot, one of the twelve, went unto the chief priests, to betray him unto them. ¹¹And when they heard it, they were glad, and promised to give him money. And he sought how he might conveniently betray him.

¹²And the first day of unleavened bread, when they killed the passover, his disciples said unto him, 'Where wilt thou that we go and prepare that thou mayest eat the passover?' ¹³And he sendeth forth two of his disciples, and saith unto them, 'Go ye into the city, and there shall meet you a man bearing a pitcher of water; follow him. ¹⁴And wheresoever he shall go in, say ye to the goodman of the house, "The Master saith, 'Where is the guestchamber, where I shall eat the passover with my disciples?'" ¹⁵And he will shew you a large upper room furnished and prepared; there make ready for us.' ¹⁶And his disciples went forth, and came into the city, and found as he had said unto them; and they made ready the passover. ¹⁷And in the evening he cometh with the twelve.

[18]And as they sat and did eat, Jesus said, 'Verily I say unto you, one of you which eateth with me shall betray me.' [19]And they began to be sorrowful, and to say unto him one by one, 'Is it I?' and another said, 'Is it I?' [20]And he answered and said unto them, 'It is one of the twelve, that dippeth with me in the dish. [21]The Son of man indeed goeth, as it is written of him; but woe to that man by whom the Son of man is betrayed! Good were it for that man if he had never been born.'

[22]And as they did eat, Jesus took bread, and blessed, and brake it, and gave to them, and said, 'Take, eat: this is my body.' [23]And he took the cup, and when he had given thanks, he gave it to them; and they all drank of it. [24]And he said unto them, 'This is my blood of the new testament, which is shed for many. [25]Verily I say unto you, I will drink no more of the fruit of the vine, until that day that I drink it new in the kingdom of God.'

[26]And when they had sung an hymn, they went out into the mount of Olives. [27]And Jesus saith unto them, 'All ye shall be offended because of me this night; for it is written, I will smite the shepherd, and the sheep shall be scattered. [28]But after that I am risen, I will go before you into Galilee.' [29]But Peter said unto him, 'Although all shall be offended, yet will not I.' [30]And Jesus saith unto him, 'Verily I say unto thee, that this day, even in this night, before the cock crow twice, thou shalt deny me thrice.' [31]But he spake the more vehemently, 'If I should die with thee, I will not deny thee in any wise.' Likewise also said they all. [32]And they came to a place which was named Gethsemane; and he saith to his disciples, 'Sit ye here, while I shall pray.' [33]And he taketh with

him Peter and James and John, and began to be sore amazed, and to be very heavy; ³⁴ and saith unto them, 'My soul is exceeding sorrowful unto death; tarry ye here, and watch.' ³⁵ And he went forward a little, and fell on the ground, and prayed that, if it were possible, the hour might pass from him. ³⁶ And he said, 'Abba, Father, all things are possible unto thee; take away this cup from me; nevertheless not what I will, but what thou wilt.' ³⁷ And he cometh, and findeth them sleeping, and saith unto Peter, 'Simon, sleepest thou? Couldest not thou watch one hour? ³⁸ Watch ye and pray, lest ye enter into temptation. The spirit truly is ready, but the flesh is weak.' ³⁹ And again he went away, and prayed, and spake the same words. ⁴⁰ And when he returned, he found them asleep again (for their eyes were heavy), neither wist they what to answer him. ⁴¹ And he cometh the third time, and saith unto them, 'Sleep on now, and take your rest: it is enough, the hour is come; behold, the Son of man is betrayed into the hands of sinners. ⁴² Rise up, let us go; lo, he that betrayeth me is at hand.'

⁴³ And immediately, while he yet spake, cometh Judas, one of the twelve, and with him a great multitude with swords and staves, from the chief priests and the scribes and the elders. ⁴⁴ And he that betrayed him had given them a token, saying, 'Whomsoever I shall kiss, that same is he; take him, and lead him away safely.' ⁴⁵ And as soon as he was come, he goeth straightway to him, and saith, 'Master, master,' and kissed him.

⁴⁶ And they laid their hands on him, and took him. ⁴⁷ And one of them that stood by drew a sword, and smote a servant

of the high priest, and cut off his ear. ⁴⁸And Jesus answered and said unto them, 'Are ye come out, as against a thief, with swords and with staves to take me? ⁴⁹I was daily with you in the temple teaching, and ye took me not: but the scriptures must be fulfilled.' ⁵⁰And they all forsook him, and fled. ⁵¹And there followed him a certain young man, having a linen cloth cast about his naked body; and the young men laid hold on him; ⁵²and he left the linen cloth, and fled from them naked.

⁵³And they led Jesus away to the high priest; and with him were assembled all the chief priests and the elders and the scribes. ⁵⁴And Peter followed him afar off, even into the palace of the high priest: and he sat with the servants, and warmed himself at the fire. ⁵⁵And the chief priests and all the council sought for witness against Jesus to put him to death; and found none. ⁵⁶For many bare false witness against him, but their witness agreed not together. ⁵⁷And there arose certain, and bare false witness against him, saying, ⁵⁸'We heard him say, "I will destroy this temple that is made with hands, and within three days I will build another made without hands."' ⁵⁹But neither so did their witness agree together. ⁶⁰And the high priest stood up in the midst, and asked Jesus, saying, 'Answerest thou nothing? What is it which these witness against thee?' ⁶¹But he held his peace, and answered nothing. Again the high priest asked him, and said unto him, 'Art thou the Christ, the Son of the Blessed?' ⁶²And Jesus said, 'I am; and ye shall see the Son of man sitting on the right hand of power, and coming in the clouds of heaven.' ⁶³Then the high priest rent his clothes, and saith, 'What need we any further witnesses? ⁶⁴Ye have heard the blasphemy: what think

ye?' And they all condemned him to be guilty of death. ⁶⁵And some began to spit on him, and to cover his face, and to buffet him, and to say unto him, 'Prophesy,' and the servants did strike him with the palms of their hands.

⁶⁶And as Peter was beneath in the palace, there cometh one of the maids of the high priest; ⁶⁷and when she saw Peter warming himself, she looked upon him, and said, 'And thou also wast with Jesus of Nazareth.' ⁶⁸But he denied, saying, 'I know not, neither understand I what thou sayest.' And he went out into the porch; and the cock crew. ⁶⁹And a maid saw him again, and began to say to them that stood by, 'This is one of them.' ⁷⁰And he denied it again. And a little after, they that stood by said again to Peter, 'Surely thou art one of them; for thou art a Galilæan, and thy speech agreeth thereto.' ⁷¹But he began to curse and to swear, saying, 'I know not this man of whom ye speak.' ⁷²And the second time the cock crew. And Peter called to mind the word that Jesus said unto him, 'Before the cock crow twice, thou shalt deny me thrice.' And when he thought thereon, he wept.

15 And straightway in the morning the chief priests held a consultation with the elders and scribes and the whole council, and bound Jesus, and carried him away, and delivered him to Pilate. ²And Pilate asked him, 'Art thou the King of the Jews?' And he answering said unto him, 'Thou sayest it.' ³And the chief priests accused him of many things: but he answered nothing. ⁴And Pilate asked him again, saying, 'Answerest thou nothing? Behold how many things they witness against thee.' ⁵But Jesus yet answered nothing; so that

Pilate marvelled. ⁶Now at that feast he released unto them one prisoner, whomsoever they desired. ⁷And there was one named Barabbas, which lay bound with them that had made insurrection with him, who had committed murder in the insurrection. ⁸And the multitude crying aloud began to desire him to do as he had ever done unto them. ⁹But Pilate answered them, saying, 'Will ye that I release unto you the King of the Jews?' ¹⁰For he knew that the chief priests had delivered him for envy. ¹¹But the chief priests moved the people, that he should rather release Barabbas unto them. ¹²And Pilate answered and said again unto them, 'What will ye then that I shall do unto him whom ye call the King of the Jews?' ¹³And they cried out again, 'Crucify him.' ¹⁴Then Pilate said unto them, 'Why, what evil hath he done?' And they cried out the more exceedingly, 'Crucify him.'

¹⁵And so Pilate, willing to content the people, released Barabbas unto them, and delivered Jesus, when he had scourged him, to be crucified. ¹⁶And the soldiers led him away into the hall, called Prætorium; and they call together the whole band. ¹⁷And they clothed him with purple, and platted a crown of thorns, and put it about his head, ¹⁸and began to salute him, 'Hail, King of the Jews!' ¹⁹And they smote him on the head with a reed, and did spit upon him, and bowing their knees worshipped him. ²⁰And when they had mocked him, they took off the purple from him, and put his own clothes on him, and led him out to crucify him. ²¹And they compel one Simon a Cyrenian, who passed by, coming out of the country, the father of Alexander and Rufus, to bear his cross. ²²And they bring him unto the place Golgotha,

which is, being interpreted, 'The place of a skull.' ²³And they gave him to drink wine mingled with myrrh: but he received it not. ²⁴And when they had crucified him, they parted his garments, casting lots upon them, what every man should take. ²⁵And it was the third hour, and they crucified him. ²⁶And the superscription of his accusation was written over, 'The king of the Jews'. ²⁷And with him they crucify two thieves; the one on his right hand, and the other on his left. ²⁸And the scripture was fulfilled, which saith, 'And he was numbered with the transgressors.' ²⁹And they that passed by railed on him, wagging their heads, and saying, 'Ah, thou that destroyest the temple, and buildest it in three days, ³⁰save thyself, and come down from the cross.' ³¹Likewise also the chief priests mocking said among themselves with the scribes, 'He saved others; himself he cannot save. ³²Let Christ the King of Israel descend now from the cross, that we may see and believe.' And they that were crucified with him reviled him. ³³And when the sixth hour was come, there was darkness over the whole land until the ninth hour. ³⁴And at the ninth hour Jesus cried with a loud voice, saying, 'Eloi, Eloi, lama sabachthani?' which is, being interpreted, 'My God, my God, why hast thou forsaken me?' ³⁵And some of them that stood by, when they heard it, said, 'Behold, he calleth Elias.' ³⁶And one ran and filled a spunge full of vinegar, and put it on a reed, and gave him to drink, saying, 'Let alone; let us see whether Elias will come to take him down.' ³⁷And Jesus cried with a loud voice, and gave up the ghost. ³⁸And the veil of the temple was rent in twain from the top to the bottom.

³⁹And when the centurion, which stood over against him,

saw that he so cried out, and gave up the ghost, he said, 'Truly this man was the Son of God.' ⁴⁰There were also women looking on afar off; among whom was Mary Magdalene, and Mary the mother of James the less and of Joses, and Salome ⁴¹(who also, when he was in Galilee, followed him, and ministered unto him), and many other women which came up with him unto Jerusalem.

⁴²And now when the even was come, because it was the preparation, that is, the day before the sabbath, ⁴³Joseph of Arimathæa, an honourable counsellor, which also waited for the kingdom of God, came, and went in boldly unto Pilate, and craved the body of Jesus. ⁴⁴And Pilate marvelled if he were already dead; and calling unto him the centurion, he asked him whether he had been any while dead. ⁴⁵And when he knew it of the centurion, he gave the body to Joseph. ⁴⁶And he bought fine linen, and took him down, and wrapped him in the linen, and laid him in a sepulchre which was hewn out of a rock, and rolled a stone unto the door of the sepulchre. ⁴⁷And Mary Magdalene and Mary the mother of Joses beheld where he was laid.

16 And when the sabbath was past, Mary Magdalene, and Mary the mother of James, and Salome, had bought sweet spices, that they might come and anoint him. ²And very early in the morning the first day of the week, they came unto the sepulchre at the rising of the sun. ³And they said among themselves, 'Who shall roll us away the stone from the door of the sepulchre?' ⁴And when they looked, they saw that the stone was rolled away; for it was very great.

⁵And entering into the sepulchre, they saw a young man sitting on the right side, clothed in a long white garment; and they were affrighted. ⁶And he saith unto them, 'Be not affrighted: ye seek Jesus of Nazareth, which was crucified. He is risen; he is not here; behold the place where they laid him. ⁷But go your way, tell his disciples and Peter that he goeth before you into Galilee: there shall ye see him, as he said unto you.' ⁸And they went out quickly, and fled from the sepulchre; for they trembled and were amazed; neither said they any thing to any man; for they were afraid.

* ⁹Now when Jesus was risen early the first day of the week, he appeared first to Mary Magdalene, out of whom he had cast seven devils. ¹⁰And she went and told them that had been with him, as they mourned and wept. ¹¹And they, when they had heard that he was alive, and had been seen of her, believed not.

¹²After that he appeared in another form unto two of them, as they walked, and went into the country. ¹³And they went and told it unto the residue; neither believed they them.

¹⁴Afterward he appeared unto the eleven as they sat at meat, and upbraided them with their unbelief and hardness of heart, because they believed not them which had seen him after he was risen. ¹⁵And he said unto them, 'Go ye into all the world, and preach the gospel to every creature. ¹⁶He that believeth and is baptised shall be saved; but he that believeth not shall be damned. ¹⁷And these signs shall follow them that believe: in my name shall they cast out devils; they shall speak with new tongues; ¹⁸they shall take up serpents; and if they drink any deadly thing, it shall not hurt

them; they shall lay hands on the sick, and they shall recover.'

[19] So then after the Lord had spoken unto them, he was received up into heaven, and sat on the right hand of God. [20] And they went forth, and preached every where, the Lord working with them, and confirming the word with signs following. Amen.

* In the most reliable manuscripts Mark's gospel ends at ch. 16:8.

luke

introduction by richard holloway

There is a lot to be said for attaching a health warning to religion. It can be a hazardous business, because it is often based on a seductive deceit. In its most dangerous form it claims to have found words that exactly express one of the great mysteries that obsess the imagination, the possibility of God. So words *about* God are treated as though they were equivalent to God, and religious authorities demand our assent to them. Our fidelity or infidelity is tested by our relationship to the official vocabulary that is supposed to express the divine mystery. Since there is no final way of either verifying or falsifying such claims, the opportunity religious language offers us for violence and discord is endless. This is why many of the sanest minds in history have been wary of religion and its explosive, but unsustainable claims.

Apart from the danger religion may pose to our physical health, it can also endanger us spiritually, because it can trap us in language *about* mysteries rather than open us to the mysteries themselves. One of our problems as humans is that our greatest gift, language, is also our greatest danger. We destroy ourselves by our words. The difficulty is that things are not what we say they are. The word 'water' is not itself drinkable. Words point to things, but they can never be the things they point to. This may seem too obvious to waste time on, but it is a truth that is often ignored in religious circles. All theology is a doomed but necessary attempt to express the inexpressible. God is the elusive mystery we try to capture and convey in language, but how can that ever be done? If the word 'water' is not itself drinkable, how can the words we use to express the mystery of God be themselves absolute? They are metaphors, analogies, figures of speech, yet religious people have slaughtered and condemned each other over these experimental uncertainties. Our glory and agony is that we long to find words that will no longer be words, mere signifiers, but the very experience they are trying to signify; and our tragedy is that we can never succeed. This is the anguish that lies at the heart of all religion, because, though our words can describe our thirst for the absolute, they can never satisfy it.

But there is something that comes close. There is a human experience that sometimes captures the mystery that haunts us. Music is usually held to be the experience that does this best. In music there is an almost perfect equivalence of form and content. Music evidences itself, is itself the experience we experience, and is not just a sign or symbol for something else. All great art does this. It breaks through the frustration of language and unites us with that which words only usually signify. I say, 'only usually', because there is a language that, like music and art, is also capable of this same perfect tautology, this mysterious equivalence between the longing and the thing longed for. I am, of course, talking about poetry. Art, particularly music and poetry, unites us with the thing beyond, places us in its midst, rather than talks unceasingly and ineffectively about it, which is what religion usually does.

One test of great art is the shiver factor, the prickle at the back of the neck, the involuntary twitch of muscle that shows that a connection has been made between us and the matter to which we are paying attention. By this standard, Luke's gospel is a work of great art. In place after place it achieves that mysterious equivalence between the word spoken and the word felt, the situation described and the situation experienced. This is why it has influenced other artists who have translated Luke's words into painting of equivalent power. One of these paintings hangs in the Royal Scottish Gallery in Edinburgh. It was painted by Giovanni Francesco Barbieri for Cardinal Rocci in 1639 and it is called *Peter the Penitent*. It shows Peter crying bitterly, tormented by anguish and guilt, just after his third denial of Jesus. All the gospels recount the prediction of Jesus that Peter would deny him, and they all go on to describe Peter's betrayal. Only in *Luke*, however, do we get the detail that makes dramatic sense of Peter's desolation. After the third denial the cock crows, and Luke tells us: 'And the Lord turned, and looked upon Peter. And Peter remembered the word of the Lord, how he had said unto him, "Before the cock crow, thou shalt deny me thrice." And Peter went out, and wept bitterly' (22:61–2). The words are few and simple, yet they have carried that look of grieving love through history. And they connect us to our own denials. Peter's tragedy is not that he was a bad or cynical man, but that he was an ordinary man who could not live up to his own ideals. Luke does not use abstract language about human remorse and the nature of guilt, yet in a few brush-strokes he

introduction

brings us right into the experience and we confront ourselves. Unlike much conventional religious teaching that alienates us by its hectoring abstractions, Luke connects with us again and again by the immediacy of his art.

But that way of putting it is misleading, because it suggests the self-conscious presence of a writer working away to put a perfect polish on the text. We do not know who Luke was, and it does not matter, because it is the very anonymity of this text that confirms its power. All great art is essentially anonymous in its impact. We do not need to know anything about its provenance for it to affect us. We do not really know who wrote *Genesis* or many of the other ancient writings and we need not care, because these great texts communicate truth to us at a level that goes beyond the artistry of any particular individual. They create archetypes that express the general condition of humanity, and its sorrow and loss, heroism and betrayal. This is also why the gospels go on touching us long after we have abandoned the orthodoxies that have been built on them. We do not know who wrote them or when, but they still have power to connect with our lives today, so that, reading them, we sometimes have to put them down and look into the distance as their words strike ancient chords within us.

If we fed the four gospels into a computer programmed to do literary detective work, we would make some interesting discoveries. The first thing we would notice is that *John*, the fourth gospel, is unlike the other three in voice and perspective. There are differences among the first three gospels as well, of course, but not only do they have a similar feel, they actually share a lot of material. For instance, it is quite obvious that *Matthew* and *Luke* simply repeat large chunks of *Mark*; they each quote another another source, not found in *Mark*; and there is a certain amount of material peculiar to each of them. And all these layers of text had their own history. The gospels were not written down the way a biographer would work today. The process would be more like that of a musical historian who goes round the highlands and islands of Scotland to record folk tales, poetry and songs that are in the memories of people, but have never been written down in hard form. Most of our ancient literature comes from a long-standing oral tradition before it was committed to ink on parchment. The gospel writers would have been engaged in a similar exercise. They would collect stories about Jesus, remembrances that were handed down and sermons or meditations that were the result of long contemplation on the meaning of his story. In time, these would be woven into a whole garment, but only whole in the sense that a patchwork quilt is whole, stitched together out of many pieces.

Some of the most attractive and colourful of the patches are found only in *Luke*. It is Luke who tells us that at his birth Jesus was laid in a manger, 'because there was no room for them in the inn'. Luke brings more women, and more details about them, into his narrative than any of the other gospel writers. We have already noted the little thread of narrative that frames Peter's grief at his denials of Jesus; even more vivid are the parables that have gone into the memory and vocabulary of the western world, such as the Good Samaritan and the Prodigal Son. The message of Jesus, the good news, or gospel, as it was called, was expressed most memorably in the immediacy of stories rather than in religious abstractions. This is why the parables in *Luke* continue to connect with us today. They are about our experience of guilt, and our need for forgiveness; they are about the dangers of tribe and religion, and the way they insulate us against the needs of our neighbours. This is the point of the parable of the Good Samaritan in chapter 10. It is not about religious hypocrisy, and the way religion often says one thing and does another. The reason why the priest and the Levite passed by on the other side, leaving the man lying by the roadside, is that their code would not allow them to come to the aid of a stranger who might be a source of religious pollution to them. Interestingly, the Samaritan also followed a code that was just as defensive towards strangers, but it was simply blown away by the force of the pity he felt for the man who had fallen among thieves. Jesus is warning us that the codes that define our religious and national identities can shut our hearts against one another. Compassion should overrule code.

The story of the Prodigal Son in chapter 15 is even more profound. It is about the ways we hurt one another, and withhold the forgiveness that alone can heal the wounds we have inflicted. The most difficult of the predicaments that face us is what to do about the evil we do to one another. Our pain at being injured, as well as our sense of justice, require confession and repentance from the offender. Being the offender is even more imprisoning. The complexity of guilty self-knowledge often leads to a blustering defensiveness, rather like Peter's denials of Jesus, that prevents us from asking for the forgiveness we desperately want. In this way a dynamic of mutual recrimination is created that traps us in anger and despair. In the parable of the Prodigal the father rushes to forgive the son before he can say a word: 'When he was yet a great way off, his father saw him, and had compassion, and ran, and fell on his neck, and kissed him'. And it is this act of compassionate forgiveness that frees the son from the burden of his own guilt and gives him the strength to confess it: 'Father, I have sinned against heaven, and in thy sight, and am no more worthy to be called thy son'. Jesus is not discussing the ethics of forgiveness, how we can earn it and under what circumstances we can offer it. He simply shows us that without it we are all in prison, so we should try to get our forgiveness in first. If we refuse to forgive, we tear down the very bridge we ourselves will one day have to cross.

The Gospel of Luke is an old book and there is much in it that will seem strange to someone picking it up for the first time today. Nevertheless, it is impossible to read it without being challenged by the mysterious presence of Jesus. As well as a sense of enormous compassion for the human condition, we find in him a burning anger against all systems, religious or political, that come between God and the poor of the earth. In the furious pity of Jesus we catch a glimpse of God's dream for a transformed humanity. But the long narrative of the crucifixion at the end of the gospel reminds us that dreamers are usually disposed of with cruel efficiency by the people who have put themselves in charge of the world. Yet Jesus keeps breaking out of the tombs into which we have consigned him, so the dream lives on.

introduction

the gospel according to st luke

Forasmuch as many have taken in hand to set forth in order a declaration of those things which are most surely believed among us, ²even as they delivered them unto us, which from the beginning were eye-witnesses, and ministers of the word; ³it seemed good to me also, having had perfect understanding of all things from the very first, to write unto thee in order, most excellent Theophilus, ⁴that thou mightest know the certainty of those things, wherein thou hast been instructed.

⁵There was in the days of Herod, the king of Judæa, a certain priest named Zacharias, of the course of Abia; and his wife was of the daughters of Aaron, and her name was Elisabeth. ⁶And they were both righteous before God, walking in all the commandments and ordinances of the Lord blameless. ⁷And they had no child, because that Elisabeth was barren, and they both were now well stricken in years.

⁸And it came to pass, that while he executed the priest's office before God in the order of his course, ⁹according to the custom of the priest's office, his lot was to burn incense when he went into the temple of the Lord. ¹⁰And the whole multitude of the people were praying without at the time of incense. ¹¹And there appeared unto him an angel of the Lord standing on the right side of the altar of incense. ¹²And when Zacharias saw him, he was troubled, and fear fell upon him. ¹³But the angel said unto him, 'Fear not, Zacharias, for thy

prayer is heard; and thy wife Elisabeth shall bear thee a son, and thou shalt call his name John. ¹⁴And thou shalt have joy and gladness; and many shall rejoice at his birth. ¹⁵For he shall be great in the sight of the Lord, and shall drink neither wine nor strong drink; and he shall be filled with the Holy Ghost, even from his mother's womb. ¹⁶And many of the children of Israel shall he turn to the Lord their God. ¹⁷And he shall go before him in the spirit and power of Elias, to turn the hearts of the fathers to the children, and the disobedient to the wisdom of the just; to make ready a people prepared for the Lord.' ¹⁸And Zacharias said unto the angel, 'Whereby shall I know this? For I am an old man, and my wife well stricken in years.' ¹⁹And the angel answering said unto him, 'I am Gabriel, that stand in the presence of God; and am sent to speak unto thee, and to shew thee these glad tidings. ²⁰And, behold, thou shalt be dumb, and not able to speak, until the day that these things shall be performed, because thou believest not my words, which shall be fulfilled in their season.'

²¹And the people waited for Zacharias, and marvelled that he tarried so long in the temple. ²²And when he came out, he could not speak unto them; and they perceived that he had seen a vision in the temple, for he beckoned unto them, and remained speechless. ²³And it came to pass, that, as soon as the days of his ministration were accomplished, he departed to his own house.

²⁴And after those days his wife Elisabeth conceived, and hid herself five months, saying, ²⁵'Thus hath the Lord dealt with me in the days wherein he looked on me, to take away my reproach among men.'

²⁶And in the sixth month the angel Gabriel was sent from God unto a city of Galilee, named Nazareth, ²⁷to a virgin espoused to a man whose name was Joseph, of the house of David; and the virgin's name was Mary. ²⁸And the angel came in unto her, and said, 'Hail, thou that art highly favoured, the Lord is with thee: blessed art thou among women.' ²⁹And when she saw him, she was troubled at his saying, and cast in her mind what manner of salutation this should be. ³⁰And the angel said unto her, 'Fear not, Mary, for thou hast found favour with God. ³¹And, behold, thou shalt conceive in thy womb, and bring forth a son, and shalt call his name JESUS. ³²He shall be great, and shall be called the Son of the Highest; and the Lord God shall give unto him the throne of his father David. ³³And he shall reign over the house of Jacob for ever; and of his kingdom there shall be no end.' ³⁴Then said Mary unto the angel, 'How shall this be, seeing I know not a man?' ³⁵And the angel answered and said unto her, 'The Holy Ghost shall come upon thee, and the power of the Highest shall overshadow thee; therefore also that holy thing which shall be born of thee shall be called the Son of God. ³⁶And, behold, thy cousin Elisabeth, she hath also conceived a son in her old age; and this is the sixth month with her, who was called barren. ³⁷For with God nothing shall be impossible.' ³⁸And Mary said, 'Behold the handmaid of the Lord; be it unto me according to thy word.' And the angel departed from her.

³⁹And Mary arose in those days, and went into the hill country with haste, into a city of Juda; ⁴⁰and entered into the house of Zacharias, and saluted Elisabeth. ⁴¹And it came to pass, that, when Elisabeth heard the salutation of Mary, the babe leaped in her womb; and Elisabeth was filled with the

Holy Ghost. 42 And she spake out with a loud voice, and said,
'Blessed art thou among women, and blessed is the fruit of
thy womb. 43 And whence is this to me, that the mother of my
Lord should come to me? 44 For, lo, as soon as the voice of
thy salutation sounded in mine ears, the babe leaped in my
womb for joy. 45 And blessed is she that believed: for there
shall be a performance of those things which were told her
from the Lord.' 46 And Mary said,

'My soul doth magnify the Lord,
47 and my spirit hath rejoiced in God my Saviour.
48 For he hath regarded the low estate
of his handmaiden;
for, behold, from henceforth
all generations shall call me blessed.
49 For he that is mighty hath done to me great things;
and holy is his name.
50 And his mercy is on them that fear him
from generation to generation.
51 He hath shewed strength with his arm;
he hath scattered the proud
in the imagination of their hearts.
52 He hath put down the mighty from their seats,
and exalted them of low degree.
53 He hath filled the hungry with good things;
and the rich he hath sent empty away.
54 He hath holpen his servant Israel,
in remembrance of his mercy;
55 as he spake to our fathers, to Abraham,
and to his seed for ever.'

⁵⁶And Mary abode with her about three months, and returned to her own house.

⁵⁷ Now Elisabeth's full time came that she should be delivered; and she brought forth a son. ⁵⁸And her neighbours and her cousins heard how the Lord had shewed great mercy upon her; and they rejoiced with her.

⁵⁹And it came to pass, that on the eighth day they came to circumcise the child; and they called him Zacharias, after the name of his father. ⁶⁰And his mother answered and said, 'Not so; but he shall be called John.' ⁶¹And they said unto her, 'There is none of thy kindred that is called by this name.' ⁶²And they made signs to his father, how he would have him called. ⁶³And he asked for a writing table, and wrote, saying, 'His name is John.' And they marvelled all. ⁶⁴And his mouth was opened immediately, and his tongue loosed, and he spake, and praised God. ⁶⁵And fear came on all that dwelt round about them: and all these sayings were noised abroad throughout all the hill country of Judæa. ⁶⁶And all they that heard them laid them up in their hearts, saying, 'What manner of child shall this be!' And the hand of the Lord was with him.

⁶⁷And his father Zacharias was filled with the Holy Ghost, and prophesied, saying, ⁶⁸'Blessed be the Lord God of Israel; for he hath visited and redeemed his people, ⁶⁹and hath raised up an horn of salvation for us in the house of his servant David, ⁷⁰as he spake by the mouth of his holy prophets, which have been since the world began, ⁷¹that we should be saved from our enemies, and from the hand of all that hate us, ⁷² to perform the mercy promised to our fathers, and to remember his holy covenant, ⁷³ the oath which he sware to our father Abraham, ⁷⁴that he would grant unto us, that we

being delivered out of the hand of our enemies might serve him without fear, ⁷⁵ in holiness and righteousness before him, all the days of our life. ⁷⁶And thou, child, shalt be called the prophet of the Highest; for thou shalt go before the face of the Lord to prepare his ways, ⁷⁷to give knowledge of salvation unto his people by the remission of their sins, ⁷⁸through the tender mercy of our God; whereby the dayspring from on high hath visited us, ⁷⁹to give light to them that sit in darkness and in the shadow of death, to guide our feet into the way of peace.' ⁸⁰And the child grew, and waxed strong in spirit, and was in the deserts till the day of his shewing unto Israel.

2 And it came to pass in those days, that there went out a decree from Caesar Augustus, that all the world should be taxed. ²(And this taxing was first made when Cyrenius was governor of Syria.) ³And all went to be taxed, every one into his own city. ⁴And Joseph also went up from Galilee, out of the city of Nazareth, into Judæa, unto the city of David, which is called Bethlehem (because he was of the house and lineage of David), ⁵to be taxed with Mary his espoused wife, being great with child. ⁶And so it was, that, while they were there, the days were accomplished that she should be delivered. ⁷And she brought forth her firstborn son, and wrapped him in swaddling clothes, and laid him in a manger; because there was no room for them in the inn. ⁸And there were in the same country shepherds abiding in the field, keeping watch over their flock by night. ⁹And, lo, the angel of the Lord came upon them, and the glory of the Lord shone round about them; and they were sore afraid. ¹⁰And the angel said unto them, 'Fear not: for, behold, I bring you good tidings of

great joy, which shall be to all people. [11]For unto you is born this day in the city of David a Saviour, which is Christ the Lord. [12]And this shall be a sign unto you: ye shall find the babe wrapped in swaddling clothes, lying in a manger.' [13]And suddenly there was with the angel a multitude of the heavenly host praising God, and saying, [14]'Glory to God in the highest, and on earth peace, good will toward men.'

[15]And it came to pass, as the angels were gone away from them into heaven, the shepherds said one to another, 'Let us now go even unto Bethlehem, and see this thing which is come to pass, which the Lord hath made known unto us.' [16]And they came with haste, and found Mary, and Joseph, and the babe lying in a manger. [17]And when they had seen it, they made known abroad the saying which was told them concerning this child. [18]And all they that heard it wondered at those things which were told them by the shepherds. [19]But Mary kept all these things, and pondered them in her heart. [20]And the shepherds returned, glorifying and praising God for all the things that they had heard and seen, as it was told unto them.

[21]And when eight days were accomplished for the circumcising of the child, his name was called JESUS, which was so named of the angel before he was conceived in the womb.

[22]And when the days of her purification according to the law of Moses were accomplished, they brought him to Jerusalem, to present him to the Lord [23](as it is written in the law of the Lord, 'Every male that openeth the womb shall be called holy to the Lord'), [24]and to offer a sacrifice according to that which is said in the law of the Lord, 'a pair of turtledoves, or two young pigeons.' [25]And, behold, there was a man

in Jerusalem, whose name was Simeon; and the same man was just and devout, waiting for the consolation of Israel, and the Holy Ghost was upon him. ²⁶And it was revealed unto him by the Holy Ghost that he should not see death before he had seen the Lord's Christ. ²⁷And he came by the Spirit into the temple; and when the parents brought in the child Jesus, to do for him after the custom of the law, ²⁸then took he him up in his arms, and blessed God, and said, ²⁹'Lord, now lettest thou thy servant depart in peace, according to thy word: ³⁰'For mine eyes have seen thy salvation, ³¹which thou hast prepared before the face of all people, ³²a light to lighten the Gentiles, and the glory of thy people Israel.'

³³And Joseph and his mother marvelled at those things which were spoken of him. ³⁴And Simeon blessed them, and said unto Mary his mother, 'Behold, this child is set for the fall and rising again of many in Israel; and for a sign which shall be spoken against ³⁵(yea, a sword shall pierce through thy own soul also), that the thoughts of many hearts may be revealed.'

³⁶And there was one Anna, a prophetess, the daughter of Phanuel, of the tribe of Aser. She was of a great age, and had lived with an husband seven years from her virginity; ³⁷and she was a widow of about fourscore and four years, which departed not from the temple, but served God with fastings and prayers night and day. ³⁸And she coming in that instant gave thanks likewise unto the Lord, and spake of him to all them that looked for redemption in Jerusalem.

³⁹And when they had performed all things according to the law of the Lord, they returned into Galilee, to their own city Nazareth. ⁴⁰And the child grew, and waxed strong in spirit,

filled with wisdom; and the grace of God was upon him.

⁴¹Now his parents went to Jerusalem every year at the feast of the passover. ⁴²And when he was twelve years old, they went up to Jerusalem after the custom of the feast. ⁴³And when they had fulfilled the days, as they returned, the child Jesus tarried behind in Jerusalem; and Joseph and his mother knew not of it. ⁴⁴But they, supposing him to have been in the company, went a day's journey; and they sought him among their kinsfolk and acquaintance. ⁴⁵And when they found him not, they turned back again to Jerusalem, seeking him. ⁴⁶And it came to pass, that after three days they found him in the temple, sitting in the midst of the doctors, both hearing them, and asking them questions. ⁴⁷And all that heard him were astonished at his understanding and answers. ⁴⁸And when they saw him, they were amazed; and his mother said unto him, 'Son, why hast thou thus dealt with us? Behold, thy father and I have sought thee sorrowing.'

⁴⁹And he said unto them, 'How is it that ye sought me? Wist ye not that I must be about my Father's business?' ⁵⁰And they understood not the saying which he spake unto them. ⁵¹And he went down with them, and came to Nazareth, and was subject unto them; but his mother kept all these sayings in her heart.

⁵²And Jesus increased in wisdom and stature, and in favour with God and man.

3 Now in the fifteenth year of the reign of Tiberius Cæsar, Pontius Pilate being governor of Judæa, and Herod being tetrarch of Galilee, and his brother Philip tetrarch of Ituræa and of the region of Trachonitis, and Lysanias the tetrarch of

Abilene, ²Annas and Caiaphas being the high priests, the word of God came unto John the son of Zacharias in the wilderness. ³And he came into all the country about Jordan, preaching the baptism of repentance for the remission of sins; ⁴as it is written in the book of the words of Esaias the prophet, saying, 'The voice of one crying in the wilderness, "Prepare ye the way of the Lord, make his paths straight. ⁵Every valley shall be filled, and every mountain and hill shall be brought low; and the crooked shall be made straight, and the rough ways shall be made smooth; ⁶and all flesh shall see the salvation of God."' ⁷Then said he to the multitude that came forth to be baptized of him, 'O generation of vipers, who hath warned you to flee from the wrath to come? ⁸Bring forth therefore fruits worthy of repentance, and begin not to say within yourselves, "We have Abraham to our father," for I say unto you that God is able of these stones to raise up children unto Abraham. ⁹And now also the axe is laid unto the root of the trees; every tree therefore which bringeth not forth good fruit is hewn down, and cast into the fire.'

¹⁰And the people asked him, saying, 'What shall we do then?' ¹¹He answereth and saith unto them, 'He that hath two coats, let him impart to him that hath none; and he that hath meat, let him do likewise.' ¹²Then came also publicans to be baptized, and said unto him, 'Master, what shall we do?' ¹³And he said unto them, 'Exact no more than that which is appointed you.' ¹⁴And the soldiers likewise demanded of him, saying, 'And what shall we do?' And he said unto them, 'Do violence to no man, neither accuse any falsely; and be content with your wages.'

¹⁵And as the people were in expectation, and all men

mused in their hearts of John, whether he were the Christ, or not, ¹⁶ John answered, saying unto them all, 'I indeed baptize you with water; but one mightier than I cometh, the latchet of whose shoes I am not worthy to unloose; he shall baptize you with the Holy Ghost and with fire, ¹⁷ whose fan is in his hand, and he will throughly purge his floor, and will gather the wheat into his garner; but the chaff he will burn with fire unquenchable.'

¹⁸ And many other things in his exhortation preached he unto the people. ¹⁹ But Herod the tetrarch, being reproved by him for Herodias his brother Philip's wife, and for all the evils which Herod had done, ²⁰ added yet this above all, that he shut up John in prison.

²¹ Now when all the people were baptized, it came to pass, that Jesus also being baptized, and praying, the heaven was opened, ²² and the Holy Ghost descended in a bodily shape like a dove upon him, and a voice came from heaven, which said, 'Thou art my beloved Son; in thee I am well pleased.'

²³ And Jesus himself began to be about thirty years of age, being (as was supposed) the son of Joseph, which was the son of Heli, ²⁴ which was the son of Matthat, which was the son of Levi, which was the son of Melchi, which was the son of Janna, which was the son of Joseph, ²⁵ which was the son of Mattathias, which was the son of Amos, which was the son of Naum, which was the son of Esli, which was the son of Nagge, ²⁶ which was the son of Maath, which was the son of Mattathias, which was the son of Semei, which was the son of Joseph, which was the son of Juda, ²⁷ which was the son of Joanna, which was the son of Rhesa, which was the son of Zorobabel, which was the son of Salathiel, which was the son of Neri,

²⁸ which was the son of Melchi, which was the son of Addi, which was the son of Cosam, which was the son of Elmodam, which was the son of Er, ²⁹ which was the son of Jose, which was the son of Eliezer, which was the son of Jorim, which was the son of Matthat, which was the son of Levi, ³⁰ which was the son of Simeon, which was the son of Juda, which was the son of Joseph, which was the son of Jonan, which was the son of Eliakim, ³¹ which was the son of Melea, which was the son of Menan, which was the son of Mattatha, which was the son of Nathan, which was the son of David, ³² which was the son of Jesse, which was the son of Obed, which was the son of Booz, which was the son of Salmon, which was the son of Naasson, ³³ which was the son of Aminadab, which was the son of Aram, which was the son of Esrom, which was the son of Phares, which was the son of Juda, ³⁴ which was the son of Jacob, which was the son of Isaac, which was the son of Abraham, which was the son of Thara, which was the son of Nachor, ³⁵ which was the son of Saruch, which was the son of Ragau, which was the son of Phalec, which was the son of Heber, which was the son of Sala, ³⁶ which was the son of Cainan, which was the son of Arphaxad, which was the son of Sem, which was the son of Noe, which was the son of Lamech, ³⁷ which was the son of Mathusala, which was the son of Enoch, which was the son of Jared, which was the son of Maleleel, which was the son of Cainan, ³⁸ which was the son of Enos, which was the son of Seth, which was the son of Adam, which was the son of God.

4 And Jesus being full of the Holy Ghost returned from Jordan, and was led by the Spirit into the wilderness,

² being forty days tempted of the devil. And in those days he did eat nothing: and when they were ended, he afterward hungered. ³And the devil said unto him, 'If thou be the Son of God, command this stone that it be made bread.' ⁴And Jesus answered him, saying, 'It is written, "That man shall not live by bread alone, but by every word of God."'

⁵And the devil, taking him up into an high mountain, shewed unto him all the kingdoms of the world in a moment of time. ⁶And the devil said unto him, 'All this power will I give thee, and the glory of them; for that is delivered unto me, and to whomsoever I will I give it. ⁷If thou therefore wilt worship me, all shall be thine.' ⁸And Jesus answered and said unto him, 'Get thee behind me, Satan; for it is written, "Thou shalt worship the Lord thy God, and him only shalt thou serve."'

⁹And he brought him to Jerusalem, and set him on a pinnacle of the temple, and said unto him, 'If thou be the Son of God, cast thyself down from hence. ¹⁰For it is written, "He shall give his angels charge over thee, to keep thee: ¹¹and in their hands they shall bear thee up, lest at any time thou dash thy foot against a stone."' ¹²And Jesus answering said unto him, 'It is said, "Thou shalt not tempt the Lord thy God."' ¹³And when the devil had ended all the temptation, he departed from him for a season.

¹⁴And Jesus returned in the power of the Spirit into Galilee: and there went out a fame of him through all the region round about. ¹⁵And he taught in their synagogues, being glorified of all.

¹⁶And he came to Nazareth, where he had been brought up: and, as his custom was, he went into the synagogue on

the sabbath day, and stood up for to read. ¹⁷And there was delivered unto him the book of the prophet Esaias. And when he had opened the book, he found the place where it was written, ¹⁸ 'The Spirit of the Lord is upon me, because he hath anointed me to preach the gospel to the poor; he hath sent me to heal the brokenhearted, to preach deliverance to the captives, and recovering of sight to the blind, to set at liberty them that are bruised, ¹⁹to preach the acceptable year of the Lord.' ²⁰And he closed the book, and he gave it again to the minister, and sat down. And the eyes of all them that were in the synagogue were fastened on him. ²¹And he began to say unto them, 'This day is this scripture fulfilled in your ears.' ²²And all bare him witness, and wondered at the gracious words which proceeded out of his mouth. And they said, 'Is not this Joseph's son?' ²³And he said unto them, 'Ye will surely say unto me this proverb, "Physician, heal thyself: whatsoever we have heard done in Capernaum, do also here in thy country."' ²⁴And he said, 'Verily I say unto you, no prophet is accepted in his own country. ²⁵But I tell you of a truth, many widows were in Israel in the days of Elias, when the heaven was shut up three years and six months, when great famine was throughout all the land; ²⁶but unto none of them was Elias sent, save unto Sarepta, a city of Sidon, unto a woman that was a widow. ²⁷And many lepers were in Israel in the time of Eliseus the prophet; and none of them was cleansed, saving Naaman the Syrian.' ²⁸And all they in the synagogue, when they heard these things, were filled with wrath, ²⁹and rose up, and thrust him out of the city, and led him unto the brow of the hill whereon their city was built, that they might cast him down headlong. ³⁰But he passing through the midst of them went his way, ³¹ and came down to Capernaum, a city of Galilee, and taught them on the sabbath days. ³²And they were astonished at his doctrine: for his word was with power.

³³And in the synagogue there was a man, which had a spirit of an unclean devil, and cried out with a loud voice, ³⁴saying, 'Let us alone; what have we to do with thee, thou Jesus of Nazareth? Art thou come to destroy us? I know thee who thou art; the Holy One of God.' ³⁵And Jesus rebuked him, saying, 'Hold thy peace, and come out of him.' And when the devil had thrown him in the midst, he came out of him, and hurt him not. ³⁶And they were all amazed, and spake among themselves, saying, 'What a word is this! For with authority and power he commandeth the unclean spirits, and they come out.' ³⁷And the fame of him went out into every place of the country round about.

³⁸And he arose out of the synagogue, and entered into Simon's house. And Simon's wife's mother was taken with a great fever; and they besought him for her. ³⁹And he stood over her, and rebuked the fever, and it left her; and immediately she arose and ministered unto them.

⁴⁰Now when the sun was setting, all they that had any sick with divers diseases brought them unto him; and he laid his hands on every one of them, and healed them. ⁴¹And devils also came out of many, crying out, and saying, 'Thou art Christ the Son of God.' And he rebuking them suffered them not to speak; for they knew that he was Christ. ⁴²And when it was day, he departed and went into a desert place; and the people sought him, and came unto him, and stayed him, that he should not depart from them. ⁴³And he said

unto them, 'I must preach the kingdom of God to other cities also: for therefore am I sent.' ⁴⁴And he preached in the synagogues of Galilee.

5 And it came to pass, that, as the people pressed upon him to hear the word of God, he stood by the lake of Gennesaret, ²and saw two ships standing by the lake; but the fishermen were gone out of them, and were washing their nets. ³And he entered into one of the ships, which was Simon's, and prayed him that he would thrust out a little from the land. And he sat down, and taught the people out of the ship. ⁴Now when he had left speaking, he said unto Simon, 'Launch out into the deep, and let down your nets for a draught.' ⁵And Simon answering said unto him, 'Master, we have toiled all the night, and have taken nothing; nevertheless at thy word I will let down the net.' ⁶And when they had this done, they inclosed a great multitude of fishes; and their net brake. ⁷And they beckoned unto their partners, which were in the other ship, that they should come and help them. And they came, and filled both the ships, so that they began to sink. ⁸When Simon Peter saw it, he fell down at Jesus' knees, saying, 'Depart from me; for I am a sinful man, O Lord.' ⁹For he was astonished, and all that were with him, at the draught of the fishes which they had taken. ¹⁰And so was also James, and John, the sons of Zebedee, which were partners with Simon. And Jesus said unto Simon, 'Fear not; from henceforth thou shalt catch men.' ¹¹And when they had brought their ships to land, they forsook all, and followed him.

¹²And it came to pass, when he was in a certain city, behold a man full of leprosy, who seeing Jesus fell on his face, and

besought him, saying, 'Lord, if thou wilt, thou canst make me clean.' ¹³And he put forth his hand, and touched him, saying, 'I will: be thou clean.' And immediately the leprosy departed from him. ¹⁴And he charged him to tell no man, 'But go, and shew thyself to the priest, and offer for thy cleansing, according as Moses commanded, for a testimony unto them.' ¹⁵But so much the more went there a fame abroad of him; and great multitudes came together to hear, and to be healed by him of their infirmities.

¹⁶And he withdrew himself into the wilderness, and prayed. ¹⁷And it came to pass on a certain day, as he was teaching, that there were Pharisees and doctors of the law sitting by, which were come out of every town of Galilee, and Judæa, and Jerusalem; and the power of the Lord was present to heal them.

¹⁸And, behold, men brought in a bed a man which was taken with a palsy: and they sought means to bring him in, and to lay him before him. ¹⁹And when they could not find by what way they might bring him in because of the multitude, they went upon the housetop, and let him down through the tiling with his couch into the midst before Jesus. ²⁰And when he saw their faith, he said unto him, 'Man, thy sins are forgiven thee.' ²¹And the scribes and the Pharisees began to reason, saying, 'Who is this which speaketh blasphemies? Who can forgive sins, but God alone?' ²²But when Jesus perceived their thoughts, he answering said unto them, 'What reason ye in your hearts? ²³Whether is easier, to say, "Thy sins be forgiven thee," or to say, "Rise up and walk"? ²⁴But that ye may know that the Son of man hath power upon earth to forgive sins (he said unto the sick of the palsy), I say

unto thee, "Arise, and take up thy couch, and go into thine house."' ²⁵And immediately he rose up before them, and took up that whereon he lay, and departed to his own house, glorifying God. ²⁶And they were all amazed, and they glorified God, and were filled with fear, saying, 'We have seen strange things today.'

²⁷And after these things he went forth, and saw a publican, named Levi, sitting at the receipt of custom; and he said unto him, 'Follow me.' ²⁸And he left all, rose up, and followed him. ²⁹And Levi made him a great feast in his own house; and there was a great company of publicans and of others that sat down with them. ³⁰But their scribes and Pharisees murmured against his disciples, saying, 'Why do ye eat and drink with publicans and sinners?' ³¹And Jesus answering said unto them, 'They that are whole need not a physician; but they that are sick. ³²I came not to call the righteous, but sinners to repentance.'

³³And they said unto him, 'Why do the disciples of John fast often, and make prayers, and likewise the disciples of the Pharisees; but thine eat and drink?' ³⁴And he said unto them, 'Can ye make the children of the bridechamber fast, while the bridegroom is with them? ³⁵But the days will come, when the bridegroom shall be taken away from them, and then shall they fast in those days.'

³⁶And he spake also a parable unto them: 'No man putteth a piece of a new garment upon an old; if otherwise, then both the new maketh a rent, and the piece that was taken out of the new agreeth not with the old. ³⁷And no man putteth new wine into old bottles; else the new wine will burst the bottles, and be spilled, and the bottles shall perish. ³⁸But new

wine must be put into new bottles; and both are preserved. ³⁹ No man also having drunk old wine straightway desireth new: for he saith, "The old is better."'

6 And it came to pass on the second sabbath after the first, that he went through the corn fields; and his disciples plucked the ears of corn, and did eat, rubbing them in their hands. ²And certain of the Pharisees said unto them, 'Why do ye that which is not lawful to do on the sabbath days?' ³And Jesus answering them said, 'Have ye not read so much as this, what David did, when himself was an hungred, and they which were with him; ⁴how he went into the house of God, and did take and eat the shewbread, and gave also to them that were with him; which it is not lawful to eat but for the priests alone?' ⁵And he said unto them that 'The Son of man is Lord also of the sabbath.'

⁶And it came to pass also on another sabbath, that he entered into the synagogue and taught; and there was a man whose right hand was withered. ⁷And the scribes and Pharisees watched him, whether he would heal on the sabbath day; that they might find an accusation against him. ⁸But he knew their thoughts, and said to the man which had the withered hand, 'Rise up, and stand forth in the midst.' And he arose and stood forth. ⁹Then said Jesus unto them, 'I will ask you one thing: Is it lawful on the sabbath days to do good, or to do evil? To save life, or to destroy it?' ¹⁰And looking round about upon them all, he said unto the man, 'Stretch forth thy hand.' And he did so; and his hand was restored whole as the other. ¹¹And they were filled with madness; and communed one with another what they might do to Jesus.

¹²And it came to pass in those days, that he went out into a mountain to pray, and continued all night in prayer to God. ¹³And when it was day, he called unto him his disciples: and of them he chose twelve, whom also he named apostles: ¹⁴Simon (whom he also named Peter) and Andrew his brother, James and John, Philip and Bartholomew, ¹⁵Matthew and Thomas, James the son of Alphæus, and Simon called Zelotes, ¹⁶and Judas the brother of James, and Judas Iscariot, which also was the traitor.

¹⁷And he came down with them, and stood in the plain, and the company of his disciples, and a great multitude of people out of all Judæa and Jerusalem, and from the sea coast of Tyre and Sidon, which came to hear him, and to be healed of their diseases; ¹⁸and they that were vexed with unclean spirits. And they were healed. ¹⁹And the whole multitude sought to touch him; for there went virtue out of him, and healed them all.

²⁰And he lifted up his eyes on his disciples, and said, 'Blessed be ye poor; for yours is the kingdom of God. ²¹Blessed are ye that hunger now; for ye shall be filled. Blessed are ye that weep now; for ye shall laugh. ²²Blessed are ye, when men shall hate you, and when they shall separate you from their company, and shall reproach you, and cast out your name as evil, for the Son of man's sake. ²³Rejoice ye in that day, and leap for joy; for, behold, your reward is great in heaven, for in the like manner did their fathers unto the prophets. ²⁴But woe unto you that are rich! For ye have received your consolation. ²⁵Woe unto you that are full! For ye shall hunger. Woe unto you that laugh now! For ye shall mourn and weep. ²⁶Woe unto you, when all men shall speak

well of you! For so did their fathers to the false prophets.

²⁷'But I say unto you which hear, Love your enemies, do good to them which hate you, ²⁸ bless them that curse you, and pray for them which despitefully use you. ²⁹And unto him that smiteth thee on the one cheek offer also the other; and him that taketh away thy cloke forbid not to take thy coat also. ³⁰ Give to every man that asketh of thee; and of him that taketh away thy goods ask them not again. ³¹And as ye would that men should do to you, do ye also to them likewise. ³² For if ye love them which love you, what thank have ye? For sinners also love those that love them. ³³And if ye do good to them which do good to you, what thank have ye? For sinners also do even the same. ³⁴And if ye lend to them of whom ye hope to receive, what thank have ye? For sinners also lend to sinners, to receive as much again. ³⁵But love ye your enemies, and do good, and lend, hoping for nothing again; and your reward shall be great, and ye shall be the children of the Highest: for he is kind unto the unthankful and to the evil. ³⁶ Be ye therefore merciful, as your Father also is merciful. ³⁷ Judge not, and ye shall not be judged; condemn not, and ye shall not be condemned; forgive, and ye shall be forgiven; ³⁸ give, and it shall be given unto you; good measure, pressed down, and shaken together, and running over, shall men give into your bosom. For with the same measure that ye mete withal it shall be measured to you again.'

³⁹And he spake a parable unto them, 'Can the blind lead the blind? Shall they not both fall into the ditch? ⁴⁰The disciple is not above his master: but every one that is perfect shall be as his master. ⁴¹And why beholdest thou the mote that is in thy brother's eye, but perceivest not the beam that is in

thine own eye? ⁴²Either how canst thou say to thy brother, "Brother, let me pull out the mote that is in thine eye," when thou thyself beholdest not the beam that is in thine own eye? Thou hypocrite, cast out first the beam out of thine own eye, and then shalt thou see clearly to pull out the mote that is in thy brother's eye. ⁴³For a good tree bringeth not forth corrupt fruit; neither doth a corrupt tree bring forth good fruit. ⁴⁴For every tree is known by his own fruit. For of thorns men do not gather figs, nor of a bramble bush gather they grapes. ⁴⁵A good man out of the good treasure of his heart bringeth forth that which is good; and an evil man out of the evil treasure of his heart bringeth forth that which is evil: for of the abundance of the heart his mouth speaketh.

⁴⁶'And why call ye me, "Lord, Lord," and do not the things which I say? ⁴⁷Whosoever cometh to me, and heareth my sayings, and doeth them, I will shew you to whom he is like. ⁴⁸He is like a man which built an house, and digged deep, and laid the foundation on a rock: and when the flood arose, the stream beat vehemently upon that house, and could not shake it: for it was founded upon a rock. ⁴⁹But he that heareth, and doeth not, is like a man that without a foundation built an house upon the earth; against which the stream did beat vehemently, and immediately it fell; and the ruin of that house was great.'

7 Now when he had ended all his sayings in the audience of the people, he entered into Capernaum. ²And a certain centurion's servant, who was dear unto him, was sick, and ready to die. ³And when he heard of Jesus, he sent unto him the elders of the Jews, beseeching him that he would

come and heal his servant. ⁴And when they came to Jesus, they besought him instantly, saying, that 'He was worthy for whom he should do this, ⁵for he loveth our nation, and he hath built us a synagogue.' ⁶Then Jesus went with them. And when he was now not far from the house, the centurion sent friends to him, saying unto him, 'Lord, trouble not thyself; for I am not worthy that thou shouldest enter under my roof. ⁷Wherefore neither thought I myself worthy to come unto thee; but say in a word, and my servant shall be healed. ⁸For I also am a man set under authority, having under me soldiers, and I say unto one, "Go," and he goeth; and to another, "Come," and he cometh; and to my servant, "Do this," and he doeth it.' ⁹When Jesus heard these things, he marvelled at him, and turned him about, and said unto the people that followed him, 'I say unto you, I have not found so great faith, no, not in Israel.' ¹⁰And they that were sent, returning to the house, found the servant whole that had been sick.

¹¹And it came to pass the day after, that he went into a city called Nain; and many of his disciples went with him, and much people. ¹²Now when he came nigh to the gate of the city, behold, there was a dead man carried out, the only son of his mother, and she was a widow; and much people of the city was with her. ¹³And when the Lord saw her, he had compassion on her, and said unto her, 'Weep not.' ¹⁴And he came and touched the bier: and they that bare him stood still. And he said, 'Young man, I say unto thee, Arise.' ¹⁵And he that was dead sat up, and began to speak. And he delivered him to his mother. ¹⁶And there came a fear on all: and they glorified God, saying, that 'a great prophet is risen up

among us'; and, that 'God hath visited his people.' ¹⁷And this rumour of him went forth throughout all Judæa, and throughout all the region round about. ¹⁸And the disciples of John shewed him of all these things.

¹⁹And John calling unto him two of his disciples sent them to Jesus, saying, 'Art thou he that should come? Or look we for another?' ²⁰When the men were come unto him, they said, 'John Baptist hath sent us unto thee, saying, "Art thou he that should come? Or look we for another?"' ²¹And in that same hour he cured many of their infirmities and plagues, and of evil spirits; and unto many that were blind he gave sight. ²²Then Jesus answering said unto them, 'Go your way, and tell John what things ye have seen and heard; how that the blind see, the lame walk, the lepers are cleansed, the deaf hear, the dead are raised, to the poor the gospel is preached. ²³And blessed is he, whosoever shall not be offended in me.'

²⁴And when the messengers of John were departed, he began to speak unto the people concerning John, 'What went ye out into the wilderness for to see? A reed shaken with the wind? ²⁵But what went ye out for to see? A man clothed in soft raiment? Behold, they which are gorgeously apparelled, and live delicately, are in kings' courts. ²⁶But what went ye out for to see? A prophet? Yea, I say unto you, and much more than a prophet. ²⁷This is he, of whom it is written, "Behold, I send my messenger before thy face, which shall prepare thy way before thee." ²⁸For I say unto you, Among those that are born of women there is not a greater prophet than John the Baptist: but he that is least in the kingdom of God is greater than he.' ²⁹And all the people that heard him, and the publicans, justified God, being baptized with the baptism of John.

³⁰ But the Pharisees and lawyers rejected the counsel of God against themselves, being not baptized of him.

³¹And the Lord said, 'Whereunto then shall I liken the men of this generation? And to what are they like? ³²They are like unto children sitting in the marketplace, and calling one to another, and saying, "We have piped unto you, and ye have not danced; we have mourned to you, and ye have not wept." ³³For John the Baptist came neither eating bread nor drinking wine; and ye say, "He hath a devil." ³⁴The Son of man is come eating and drinking; and ye say, "Behold a gluttonous man, and a winebibber, a friend of publicans and sinners!" ³⁵But wisdom is justified of all her children.'

³⁶And one of the Pharisees desired him that he would eat with him. And he went into the Pharisee's house, and sat down to meat. ³⁷And, behold, a woman in the city, which was a sinner, when she knew that Jesus sat at meat in the Pharisee's house, brought an alabaster box of ointment, ³⁸and stood at his feet behind him weeping, and began to wash his feet with tears, and did wipe them with the hairs of her head, and kissed his feet, and anointed them with the ointment. ³⁹Now when the Pharisee which had bidden him saw it, he spake within himself, saying, 'This man, if he were a prophet, would have known who and what manner of woman this is that toucheth him: for she is a sinner.' ⁴⁰And Jesus answering said unto him, 'Simon, I have somewhat to say unto thee.' And he saith, 'Master, say on.' ⁴¹'There was a certain creditor which had two debtors: the one owed five hundred pence, and the other fifty. ⁴²And when they had nothing to pay, he frankly forgave them both. Tell me therefore, which of them will love him most?' ⁴³Simon answered

and said, 'I suppose that he, to whom he forgave most.' And he said unto him, 'Thou hast rightly judged.' ⁴⁴And he turned to the woman, and said unto Simon, 'Seest thou this woman? I entered into thine house, thou gavest me no water for my feet: but she hath washed my feet with tears, and wiped them with the hairs of her head. ⁴⁵Thou gavest me no kiss: but this woman since the time I came in hath not ceased to kiss my feet. ⁴⁶My head with oil thou didst not anoint: but this woman hath anointed my feet with ointment. ⁴⁷Wherefore I say unto thee, her sins, which are many, are forgiven; for she loved much; but to whom little is forgiven, the same loveth little.' ⁴⁸And he said unto her, 'Thy sins are forgiven.' ⁴⁹And they that sat at meat with him began to say within themselves, 'Who is this that forgiveth sins also?' ⁵⁰And he said to the woman, 'Thy faith hath saved thee; go in peace.'

8 And it came to pass afterward, that he went throughout every city and village, preaching and shewing the glad tidings of the kingdom of God; and the twelve were with him, ²and certain women, which had been healed of evil spirits and infirmities: Mary called Magdalene, out of whom went seven devils, ³and Joanna the wife of Chuza Herod's steward, and Susanna, and many others, which ministered unto him of their substance.

⁴And when much people were gathered together, and were come to him out of every city, he spake by a parable: ⁵'A sower went out to sow his seed; and as he sowed, some fell by the way side; and it was trodden down, and the fowls of the air devoured it. ⁶And some fell upon a rock; and as soon as it was sprung up, it withered away, because it lacked

moisture. [7]And some fell among thorns; and the thorns sprang up with it, and choked it. [8]And other fell on good ground, and sprang up, and bare fruit an hundred-fold.' And when he had said these things, he cried, 'He that hath ears to hear, let him hear.'

[9]And his disciples asked him, saying, 'What might this parable be?' [10]And he said, 'Unto you it is given to know the mysteries of the kingdom of God; but to others in parables, that seeing they might not see, and hearing they might not understand. [11]Now the parable is this: The seed is the word of God. [12]Those by the way side are they that hear; then cometh the devil, and taketh away the word out of their hearts, lest they should believe and be saved. [13]They on the rock are they, which, when they hear, receive the word with joy; and these have no root, which for a while believe, and in time of temptation fall away. [14]And that which fell among thorns are they, which, when they have heard, go forth, and are choked with cares and riches and pleasures of this life, and bring no fruit to perfection. [15]But that on the good ground are they, which in an honest and good heart, having heard the word, keep it, and bring forth fruit with patience.

[16]'No man, when he hath lighted a candle, covereth it with a vessel, or putteth it under a bed; but setteth it on a candlestick, that they which enter in may see the light. [17]For nothing is secret, that shall not be made manifest; neither any thing hid, that shall not be known and come abroad. [18]Take heed therefore how ye hear; for whosoever hath, to him shall be given; and whosoever hath not, from him shall be taken even that which he seemeth to have.'

[19]Then came to him his mother and his brethren, and

could not come at him for the press. ²⁰And it was told him by certain which said, 'Thy mother and thy brethren stand without, desiring to see thee.' ²¹And he answered and said unto them, 'My mother and my brethren are these which hear the word of God, and do it.'

²² Now it came to pass on a certain day, that he went into a ship with his disciples; and he said unto them, 'Let us go over unto the other side of the lake.' And they launched forth. ²³ But as they sailed he fell asleep; and there came down a storm of wind on the lake; and they were filled with water, and were in jeopardy. ²⁴And they came to him, and awoke him, saying, 'Master, master, we perish.' Then he arose, and rebuked the wind and the raging of the water; and they ceased, and there was a calm. ²⁵And he said unto them, 'Where is your faith?' And they being afraid wondered, saying one to another, 'What manner of man is this! For he commandeth even the winds and water, and they obey him.'

²⁶And they arrived at the country of the Gadarenes, which is over against Galilee. ²⁷And when he went forth to land, there met him out of the city a certain man, which had devils long time, and ware no clothes, neither abode in any house, but in the tombs. ²⁸ When he saw Jesus, he cried out, and fell down before him, and with a loud voice said, 'What have I to do with thee, Jesus, thou Son of God most high? I beseech thee, torment me not.' ²⁹(For he had commanded the unclean spirit to come out of the man. For often-times it had caught him; and he was kept bound with chains and in fetters; and he brake the bands, and was driven of the devil into the wilderness.) ³⁰And Jesus asked him, saying, 'What is thy name?' And he said, 'Legion', because many devils were

entered into him. ³¹And they besought him that he would not command them to go out into the deep.

³²And there was there an herd of many swine feeding on the mountain; and they besought him that he would suffer them to enter into them. And he suffered them. ³³Then went the devils out of the man, and entered into the swine; and the herd ran violently down a steep place into the lake, and were choked. ³⁴When they that fed them saw what was done, they fled, and went and told it in the city and in the country. ³⁵Then they went out to see what was done; and came to Jesus, and found the man, out of whom the devils were departed, sitting at the feet of Jesus, clothed, and in his right mind; and they were afraid. ³⁶They also which saw it told them by what means he that was possessed of the devils was healed.

³⁷Then the whole multitude of the country of the Gadarenes round about besought him to depart from them; for they were taken with great fear: and he went up into the ship, and returned back again. ³⁸Now the man out of whom the devils were departed besought him that he might be with him; but Jesus sent him away, saying, ³⁹'Return to thine own house, and shew how great things God hath done unto thee.' And he went his way, and published throughout the whole city how great things Jesus had done unto him. ⁴⁰And it came to pass, that, when Jesus was returned, the people gladly received him; for they were all waiting for him.

⁴¹And, behold, there came a man named Jairus, and he was a ruler of the synagogue; and he fell down at Jesus' feet, and besought him that he would come into his house. ⁴²For he had one only daughter, about twelve years of age, and

she lay a dying. But as he went the people thronged him.

⁴³And a woman having an issue of blood twelve years, which had spent all her living upon physicians, neither could be healed of any, ⁴⁴came behind him, and touched the border of his garment: and immediately her issue of blood stanched. ⁴⁵And Jesus said, 'Who touched me?' When all denied, Peter and they that were with him said, 'Master, the multitude throng thee and press thee, and sayest thou, "Who touched me?"' ⁴⁶And Jesus said, 'Somebody hath touched me; for I perceive that virtue is gone out of me.' ⁴⁷And when the woman saw that she was not hid, she came trembling, and falling down before him, she declared unto him before all the people for what cause she had touched him, and how she was healed immediately. ⁴⁸And he said unto her, 'Daughter, be of good comfort: thy faith hath made thee whole; go in peace.'

⁴⁹While he yet spake, there cometh one from the ruler of the synagogue's house, saying to him, 'Thy daughter is dead; trouble not the Master.' ⁵⁰But when Jesus heard it, he answered him, saying, 'Fear not: believe only, and she shall be made whole.' ⁵¹And when he came into the house, he suffered no man to go in, save Peter, and James, and John, and the father and the mother of the maiden. ⁵²And all wept, and bewailed her; but he said, 'Weep not; she is not dead, but sleepeth.' ⁵³And they laughed him to scorn, knowing that she was dead. ⁵⁴And he put them all out, and took her by the hand, and called, saying, 'Maid, arise.' ⁵⁵And her spirit came again, and she arose straightway: and he commanded to give her meat. ⁵⁶And her parents were astonished: but he charged them that they should tell no man what was done.

9 Then he called his twelve disciples together, and gave them power and authority over all devils, and to cure diseases. ²And he sent them to preach the kingdom of God, and to heal the sick. ³And he said unto them, 'Take nothing for your journey, neither staves, nor scrip, neither bread, neither money; neither have two coats apiece. ⁴And whatsoever house ye enter into, there abide, and thence depart. ⁵And whosoever will not receive you, when ye go out of that city, shake off the very dust from your feet for a testimony against them.' ⁶And they departed, and went through the towns, preaching the gospel, and healing every where.

⁷Now Herod the tetrarch heard of all that was done by him: and he was perplexed, because that it was said of some, that John was risen from the dead; ⁸and of some, that Elias had appeared; and of others, that one of the old prophets was risen again. ⁹And Herod said, 'John have I beheaded: but who is this, of whom I hear such things?' And he desired to see him.

¹⁰And the apostles, when they were returned, told him all that they had done. And he took them, and went aside privately into a desert place belonging to the city called Bethsaida. ¹¹And the people, when they knew it, followed him: and he received them, and spake unto them of the kingdom of God, and healed them that had need of healing. ¹²And when the day began to wear away, then came the twelve, and said unto him, 'Send the multitude away, that they may go into the towns and country round about, and lodge, and get victuals: for we are here in a desert place.' ¹³But he said unto them, 'Give ye them to eat.' And they said, 'We have no more but five loaves and two fishes; except we should go

and buy meat for all this people.' ¹⁴For they were about five thousand men. And he said to his disciples, 'Make them sit down by fifties in a company.' ¹⁵And they did so, and made them all sit down. ¹⁶Then he took the five loaves and the two fishes, and looking up to heaven, he blessed them, and brake, and gave to the disciples to set before the multitude. ¹⁷And they did eat, and were all filled: and there was taken up of fragments that remained to them twelve baskets.

¹⁸And it came to pass, as he was alone praying, his disciples were with him: and he asked them, saying, 'Whom say the people that I am?' ¹⁹They answering said, 'John the Baptist; but some say, Elias; and others say, that one of the old prophets is risen again.' ²⁰He said unto them, 'But whom say ye that I am?' Peter answering said, 'The Christ of God.' ²¹And he straitly charged them, and commanded them to tell no man that thing, ²²saying, 'The Son of man must suffer many things, and be rejected of the elders and chief priests and scribes, and be slain, and be raised the third day.'

²³And he said to them all, 'If any man will come after me, let him deny himself, and take up his cross daily, and follow me. ²⁴For whosoever will save his life shall lose it; but whosoever will lose his life for my sake, the same shall save it. ²⁵For what is a man advantaged, if he gain the whole world, and lose himself, or be cast away? ²⁶For whosoever shall be ashamed of me and of my words, of him shall the Son of man be ashamed, when he shall come in his own glory, and in his Father's, and of the holy angels. ²⁷But I tell you of a truth, there be some standing here, which shall not taste of death, till they see the kingdom of God.'

²⁸And it came to pass about an eight days after these

sayings, he took Peter and John and James, and went up into a mountain to pray. ²⁹And as he prayed, the fashion of his countenance was altered, and his raiment was white and glistering. ³⁰And, behold, there talked with him two men, which were Moses and Elias, ³¹who appeared in glory, and spake of his decease which he should accomplish at Jerusalem. ³²But Peter and they that were with him were heavy with sleep; and when they were awake, they saw his glory, and the two men that stood with him. ³³And it came to pass, as they departed from him, Peter said unto Jesus, 'Master, it is good for us to be here: and let us make three tabernacles: one for thee, and one for Moses, and one for Elias,' not knowing what he said. ³⁴While he thus spake, there came a cloud, and overshadowed them; and they feared as they entered into the cloud. ³⁵And there came a voice out of the cloud, saying, 'This is my beloved Son: hear him.' ³⁶And when the voice was past, Jesus was found alone. And they kept it close, and told no man in those days any of those things which they had seen.

³⁷And it came to pass that on the next day, when they were come down from the hill, much people met him. ³⁸And, behold, a man of the company cried out, saying, 'Master, I beseech thee, look upon my son; for he is mine only child. ³⁹And, lo, a spirit taketh him, and he suddenly crieth out; and it teareth him that he foameth again, and bruising him hardly departeth from him. ⁴⁰And I besought thy disciples to cast him out; and they could not.' ⁴¹And Jesus answering said, 'O faithless and perverse generation, how long shall I be with you, and suffer you? Bring thy son hither.' ⁴²And as he was yet a coming, the devil threw him down, and tare him. And

Jesus rebuked the unclean spirit, and healed the child, and delivered him again to his father.

⁴³And they were all amazed at the mighty power of God. But while they wondered every one at all things which Jesus did, he said unto his disciples, ⁴⁴'Let these sayings sink down into your ears: for the Son of man shall be delivered into the hands of men.' ⁴⁵But they understood not this saying, and it was hid from them, that they perceived it not: and they feared to ask him of that saying.

⁴⁶Then there arose a reasoning among them, which of them should be greatest. ⁴⁷And Jesus, perceiving the thought of their heart, took a child, and set him by him, ⁴⁸and said unto them, 'Whosoever shall receive this child in my name receiveth me: and whosoever shall receive me receiveth him that sent me; for he that is least among you all, the same shall be great.'

⁴⁹And John answered and said, 'Master, we saw one casting out devils in thy name; and we forbad him, because he followeth not with us.' ⁵⁰And Jesus said unto him, 'Forbid him not: for he that is not against us is for us.'

⁵¹And it came to pass, when the time was come that he should be received up, he stedfastly set his face to go to Jerusalem, ⁵²and sent messengers before his face: and they went, and entered into a village of the Samaritans, to make ready for him. ⁵³And they did not receive him, because his face was as though he would go to Jerusalem. ⁵⁴And when his disciples James and John saw this, they said, 'Lord, wilt thou that we command fire to come down from heaven, and consume them, even as Elias did?' ⁵⁵But he turned, and rebuked them, and said, 'Ye know not what manner of spirit ye are of. ⁵⁶For

the Son of man is not come to destroy men's lives, but to save them.' And they went to another village.

⁵⁷And it came to pass, that, as they went in the way, a certain man said unto him, 'Lord, I will follow thee whithersoever thou goest.' ⁵⁸And Jesus said unto him, 'Foxes have holes, and birds of the air have nests; but the Son of man hath not where to lay his head.' ⁵⁹And he said unto another, 'Follow me.' But he said, 'Lord, suffer me first to go and bury my father.' ⁶⁰Jesus said unto him, 'Let the dead bury their dead; but go thou and preach the kingdom of God.' ⁶¹And another also said, 'Lord, I will follow thee; but let me first go bid them farewell, which are at home at my house.' ⁶²And Jesus said unto him, 'No man, having put his hand to the plough, and looking back, is fit for the kingdom of God.'

10 After these things the Lord appointed other seventy also, and sent them two and two before his face into every city and place, whither he himself would come. ²Therefore said he unto them, 'The harvest truly is great, but the labourers are few; pray ye therefore the Lord of the harvest, that he would send forth labourers into his harvest. ³Go your ways: behold, I send you forth as lambs among wolves. ⁴Carry neither purse, nor scrip, nor shoes: and salute no man by the way. ⁵And into whatsoever house ye enter, first say, "Peace be to this house." ⁶And if the son of peace be there, your peace shall rest upon it: if not, it shall turn to you again. ⁷And in the same house remain, eating and drinking such things as they give: for the labourer is worthy of his hire. Go not from house to house. ⁸And into whatsoever city ye enter, and they receive you, eat such things as are set

before you. ⁹And heal the sick that are therein, and say unto them, "The kingdom of God is come nigh unto you." ¹⁰But into whatsoever city ye enter, and they receive you not, go your ways out into the streets of the same, and say, ¹¹"Even the very dust of your city, which cleaveth on us, we do wipe off against you; notwithstanding be ye sure of this, that the kingdom of God is come nigh unto you." ¹²But I say unto you, that it shall be more tolerable in that day for Sodom, than for that city. ¹³Woe unto thee, Chorazin! Woe unto thee, Bethsaida! For if the mighty works had been done in Tyre and Sidon, which have been done in you, they had a great while ago repented, sitting in sackcloth and ashes. ¹⁴But it shall be more tolerable for Tyre and Sidon at the judgment, than for you. ¹⁵And thou, Capernaum, which art exalted to heaven, shalt be thrust down to hell. ¹⁶He that heareth you heareth me; and he that despiseth you despiseth me; and he that despiseth me despiseth him that sent me.'

¹⁷And the seventy returned again with joy, saying, 'Lord, even the devils are subject unto us through thy name.' ¹⁸And he said unto them, 'I beheld Satan as lightning fall from heaven. ¹⁹Behold, I give unto you power to tread on serpents and scorpions, and over all the power of the enemy; and nothing shall by any means hurt you. ²⁰Notwithstanding in this rejoice not, that the spirits are subject unto you; but rather rejoice, because your names are written in heaven.'

²¹In that hour Jesus rejoiced in spirit, and said, 'I thank thee, O Father, Lord of heaven and earth, that thou hast hid these things from the wise and prudent, and hast revealed them unto babes: even so, Father; for so it seemed good in thy sight. ²²All things are delivered to me of my Father; and

no man knoweth who the Son is, but the Father; and who the Father is, but the Son, and he to whom the Son will reveal him.'

²³And he turned him unto his disciples, and said privately, 'Blessed are the eyes which see the things that ye see. ²⁴For I tell you that many prophets and kings have desired to see those things which ye see, and have not seen them; and to hear those things which ye hear, and have not heard them.'

²⁵And, behold, a certain lawyer stood up, and tempted him, saying, 'Master, what shall I do to inherit eternal life?' ²⁶He said unto him, 'What is written in the law? How readest thou?' ²⁷And he answering said, 'Thou shalt love the Lord thy God with all thy heart, and with all thy soul, and with all thy strength, and with all thy mind; and thy neighbour as thyself.' ²⁸And he said unto him, 'Thou hast answered right: this do, and thou shalt live.' ²⁹But he, willing to justify himself, said unto Jesus, 'And who is my neighbour?' ³⁰And Jesus answering said, 'A certain man went down from Jerusalem to Jericho, and fell among thieves, which stripped him of his raiment, and wounded him, and departed, leaving him half dead. ³¹And by chance there came down a certain priest that way: and when he saw him, he passed by on the other side. ³²And likewise a Levite, when he was at the place, came and looked on him, and passed by on the other side. ³³But a certain Samaritan, as he journeyed, came where he was; and when he saw him, he had compassion on him, ³⁴and went to him, and bound up his wounds, pouring in oil and wine, and set him on his own beast, and brought him to an inn, and took care of him. ³⁵And on the morrow when he departed, he took out two pence, and gave them to the host, and said

unto him, "Take care of him; and whatsoever thou spendest more, when I come again, I will repay thee." ³⁶ Which now of these three, thinkest thou, was neighbour unto him that fell among the thieves?' ³⁷ And he said, 'He that shewed mercy on him.' Then said Jesus unto him, 'Go, and do thou likewise.'

³⁸ Now it came to pass, as they went, that he entered into a certain village: and a certain woman named Martha received him into her house. ³⁹ And she had a sister called Mary, which also sat at Jesus' feet, and heard his word. ⁴⁰ But Martha was cumbered about much serving, and came to him, and said, 'Lord, dost thou not care that my sister hath left me to serve alone? Bid her therefore that she help me.' ⁴¹ And Jesus answered and said unto her, 'Martha, Martha, thou art careful and troubled about many things, ⁴² but one thing is needful; and Mary hath chosen that good part, which shall not be taken away from her.'

11 And it came to pass, that, as he was praying in a certain place, when he ceased, one of his disciples said unto him, 'Lord, teach us to pray, as John also taught his disciples.' ² And he said unto them, 'When ye pray, say,

> Our Father which art in heaven,
>> Hallowed be thy name.
>>> Thy kingdom come.
>>> Thy will be done, as in heaven, so in earth.
> ³ Give us day by day our daily bread.
> ⁴ And forgive us our sins;
>> for we also forgive every one
>>> that is indebted to us.

And lead us not into temptation;
but deliver us from evil.'

5And he said unto them, 'Which of you shall have a friend, and shall go unto him at midnight, and say unto him, "Friend, lend me three loaves; 6for a friend of mine in his journey is come to me, and I have nothing to set before him?" 7And he from within shall answer and say, "Trouble me not: the door is now shut, and my children are with me in bed; I cannot rise and give thee." 8I say unto you, though he will not rise and give him, because he is his friend, yet because of his importunity he will rise and give him as many as he needeth.

9'And I say unto you, ask, and it shall be given you; seek, and ye shall find; knock, and it shall be opened unto you. 10For every one that asketh receiveth; and he that seeketh findeth; and to him that knocketh it shall be opened. 11If a son shall ask bread of any of you that is a father, will he give him a stone? Or if he ask a fish, will he for a fish give him a serpent? 12Or if he shall ask an egg, will he offer him a scorpion? 13If ye then, being evil, know how to give good gifts unto your children, how much more shall your heavenly Father give the Holy Spirit to them that ask him?'

14And he was casting out a devil, and it was dumb. And it came to pass, when the devil was gone out, the dumb spake; and the people wondered. 15But some of them said, 'He casteth out devils through Beelzebub the chief of the devils.' 16And others, tempting him, sought of him a sign from heaven. 17But he, knowing their thoughts, said unto them, 'Every kingdom divided against itself is brought to desolation; and a house divided against a house falleth. 18If Satan also be divided against himself, how shall his kingdom stand? Because ye say that I cast out devils through Beelzebub. ¹⁹And if I by Beelzebub cast out devils, by whom do your sons cast them out? Therefore shall they be your judges. ²⁰But if I with the finger of God cast out devils, no doubt the kingdom of God is come upon you. ²¹When a strong man armed keepeth his palace, his goods are in peace. ²²But when a stronger man than he shall come upon him, and overcome him, he taketh from him all his armour wherein he trusted, and divideth his spoils. ²³He that is not with me is against me; and he that gathereth not with me scattereth. ²⁴When the unclean spirit is gone out of a man, he walketh through dry places, seeking rest; and finding none, he saith, "I will return unto my house whence I came out." ²⁵And when he cometh, he findeth it swept and garnished. ²⁶Then goeth he, and taketh to him seven other spirits more wicked than himself; and they enter in, and dwell there; and the last state of that man is worse than the first.'

²⁷And it came to pass, as he spake these things, a certain woman of the company lifted up her voice, and said unto him, 'Blessed is the womb that bare thee, and the paps which thou hast sucked.' ²⁸But he said, 'Yea rather, blessed are they that hear the word of God, and keep it.'

²⁹And when the people were gathered thick together, he began to say, 'This is an evil generation: they seek a sign; and there shall no sign be given it, but the sign of Jonas the prophet. ³⁰For as Jonas was a sign unto the Ninevites, so shall also the Son of man be to this generation. ³¹The queen of the south shall rise up in the judgment with the men of this generation, and condemn them; for she came from the

utmost parts of the earth to hear the wisdom of Solomon; and, behold, a greater than Solomon is here. ³²The men of Nineveh shall rise up in the judgment with this generation, and shall condemn it; for they repented at the preaching of Jonas; and, behold, a greater than Jonas is here. ³³No man, when he hath lighted a candle, putteth it in a secret place, neither under a bushel, but on a candlestick, that they which come in may see the light. ³⁴The light of the body is the eye: therefore when thine eye is single, thy whole body also is full of light; but when thine eye is evil, thy body also is full of darkness. ³⁵Take heed therefore that the light which is in thee be not darkness. ³⁶If thy whole body therefore be full of light, having no part dark, the whole shall be full of light, as when the bright shining of a candle doth give thee light.'

³⁷And as he spake, a certain Pharisee besought him to dine with him; and he went in, and sat down to meat. ³⁸And when the Pharisee saw it, he marvelled that he had not first washed before dinner. ³⁹And the Lord said unto him, 'Now do ye Pharisees make clean the outside of the cup and the platter; but your inward part is full of ravening and wickedness. ⁴⁰Ye fools, did not he that made that which is without make that which is within also? ⁴¹But rather give alms of such things as ye have; and, behold, all things are clean unto you. ⁴²But woe unto you, Pharisees! For ye tithe mint and rue and all manner of herbs, and pass over judgment and the love of God; these ought ye to have done, and not to leave the other undone. ⁴³Woe unto you, Pharisees! For ye love the uppermost seats in the synagogues, and greetings in the markets. ⁴⁴Woe unto you, scribes and Pharisees, hypocrites! For ye are as graves which appear not, and the men

that walk over them are not aware of them.'

⁴⁵ Then answered one of the lawyers, and said unto him, 'Master, thus saying thou reproachest us also.' ⁴⁶And he said, 'Woe unto you also, ye lawyers! For ye lade men with burdens grievous to be borne, and ye yourselves touch not the burdens with one of your fingers. ⁴⁷Woe unto you! For ye build the sepulchres of the prophets, and your fathers killed them. ⁴⁸Truly ye bear witness that ye allow the deeds of your fathers; for they indeed killed them, and ye build their sepulchres. ⁴⁹Therefore also said the wisdom of God, "I will send them prophets and apostles, and some of them they shall slay and persecute," ⁵⁰that the blood of all the prophets, which was shed from the foundation of the world, may be required of this generation; ⁵¹from the blood of Abel unto the blood of Zacharias, which perished between the altar and the temple: verily I say unto you, it shall be required of this generation. ⁵²Woe unto you, lawyers! For ye have taken away the key of knowledge; ye entered not in yourselves, and them that were entering in ye hindered.'

⁵³And as he said these things unto them, the scribes and the Pharisees began to urge him vehemently, and to provoke him to speak of many things: ⁵⁴laying wait for him, and seeking to catch something out of his mouth, that they might accuse him.

12 In the mean time, when there were gathered together an innumerable multitude of people, insomuch that they trode one upon another, he began to say unto his disciples first of all, 'Beware ye of the leaven of the Pharisees, which is hypocrisy. ²For there is nothing covered, that shall not be revealed; neither hid, that shall not be known. ³Therefore

whatsoever ye have spoken in darkness shall be heard in the light; and that which ye have spoken in the ear in closets shall be proclaimed upon the housetops. ⁴And I say unto you my friends, be not afraid of them that kill the body, and after that have no more that they can do. ⁵But I will forewarn you whom ye shall fear: fear him, which after he hath killed hath power to cast into hell; yea, I say unto you, Fear him. ⁶Are not five sparrows sold for two farthings, and not one of them is forgotten before God? ⁷But even the very hairs of your head are all numbered. Fear not therefore: ye are of more value than many sparrows. ⁸Also I say unto you, whosoever shall confess me before men, him shall the Son of man also confess before the angels of God; ⁹but he that denieth me before men shall be denied before the angels of God. ¹⁰And whosoever shall speak a word against the Son of man, it shall be forgiven him; but unto him that blasphemeth against the Holy Ghost it shall not be forgiven. ¹¹And when they bring you unto the synagogues, and unto magistrates, and powers, take ye no thought how or what thing ye shall answer, or what ye shall say. ¹²For the Holy Ghost shall teach you in the same hour what ye ought to say.'

¹³And one of the company said unto him, 'Master, speak to my brother, that he divide the inheritance with me.' ¹⁴And he said unto him, 'Man, who made me a judge or a divider over you?' ¹⁵And he said unto them, 'Take heed, and beware of covetousness; for a man's life consisteth not in the abundance of the things which he possesseth.' ¹⁶And he spake a parable unto them, saying, 'The ground of a certain rich man brought forth plentifully, ¹⁷and he thought within himself, saying, "What shall I do, because I have no room where to bestow

my fruits?" ¹⁸And he said, "This will I do: I will pull down my barns, and build greater; and there will I bestow all my fruits and my goods. ¹⁹And I will say to my soul, Soul, thou hast much goods laid up for many years; take thine ease, eat, drink, and be merry." ²⁰But God said unto him, "Thou fool, this night thy soul shall be required of thee; then whose shall those things be, which thou hast provided?" ²¹So is he that layeth up treasure for himself, and is not rich toward God.'

²²And he said unto his disciples, 'Therefore I say unto you, take no thought for your life, what ye shall eat; neither for the body, what ye shall put on. ²³The life is more than meat, and the body is more than raiment. ²⁴Consider the ravens, for they neither sow nor reap; which neither have store-house nor barn; and God feedeth them: how much more are ye better than the fowls? ²⁵And which of you with taking thought can add to his stature one cubit? ²⁶If ye then be not able to do that thing which is least, why take ye thought for the rest? ²⁷Consider the lilies how they grow: they toil not, they spin not; and yet I say unto you, that Solomon in all his glory was not arrayed like one of these. ²⁸If then God so clothe the grass, which is today in the field, and tomorrow is cast into the oven, how much more will he clothe you, O ye of little faith? ²⁹And seek not ye what ye shall eat, or what ye shall drink, neither be ye of doubtful mind. ³⁰For all these things do the nations of the world seek after: and your Father knoweth that ye have need of these things.

³¹'But rather seek ye the kingdom of God; and all these things shall be added unto you. ³²Fear not, little flock; for it is your Father's good pleasure to give you the kingdom. ³³Sell that ye have, and give alms; provide yourselves bags

which wax not old, a treasure in the heavens that faileth not, where no thief approacheth, neither moth corrupteth. [34] For where your treasure is, there will your heart be also. [35] Let your loins be girded about, and your lights burning; [36] and ye yourselves like unto men that wait for their lord, when he will return from the wedding; that when he cometh and knocketh, they may open unto him immediately. [37] Blessed are those servants whom the lord when he cometh shall find watching: verily I say unto you that he shall gird himself, and make them to sit down to meat, and will come forth and serve them. [38] And if he shall come in the second watch, or come in the third watch, and find them so, blessed are those servants. [39] And this know, that if the goodman of the house had known what hour the thief would come, he would have watched, and not have suffered his house to be broken through. [40] Be ye therefore ready also: for the Son of man cometh at an hour when ye think not.'

[41] Then Peter said unto him, 'Lord, speakest thou this parable unto us, or even to all?' [42] And the Lord said, 'Who then is that faithful and wise steward, whom his lord shall make ruler over his household, to give them their portion of meat in due season? [43] Blessed is that servant, whom his lord when he cometh shall find so doing. [44] Of a truth I say unto you that he will make him ruler over all that he hath. [45] But and if that servant say in his heart, "My lord delayeth his coming," and shall begin to beat the menservants and maidens, and to eat and drink, and to be drunken, [46] the lord of that servant will come in a day when he looketh not for him, and at an hour when he is not aware, and will cut him in sunder, and will appoint him his portion with the unbelievers. [47] And that servant, which

knew his lord's will, and prepared not himself, neither did according to his will, shall be beaten with many stripes. ⁴⁸ But he that knew not, and did commit things worthy of stripes, shall be beaten with few stripes. For unto whomsoever much is given, of him shall be much required: and to whom men have committed much, of him they will ask the more.

⁴⁹ 'I am come to send fire on the earth; and what will I, if it be already kindled? ⁵⁰ But I have a baptism to be baptized with; and how am I straitened till it be accomplished! ⁵¹ Suppose ye that I am come to give peace on earth? I tell you, nay; but rather division. ⁵² For from henceforth there shall be five in one house divided, three against two, and two against three. ⁵³ The father shall be divided against the son, and the son against the father; the mother against the daughter, and the daughter against the mother; the mother in law against her daughter in law, and the daughter in law against her mother in law.'

⁵⁴ And he said also to the people, 'When ye see a cloud rise out of the west, straightway ye say, "There cometh a shower," and so it is. ⁵⁵ And when ye see the south wind blow, ye say, "There will be heat," and it cometh to pass. ⁵⁶ Ye hypocrites, ye can discern the face of the sky and of the earth; but how is it that ye do not discern this time? ⁵⁷ Yea, and why even of yourselves judge ye not what is right?

⁵⁸ 'When thou goest with thine adversary to the magistrate, as thou art in the way, give diligence that thou mayest be delivered from him; lest he hale thee to the judge, and the judge deliver thee to the officer, and the officer cast thee into prison. ⁵⁹ I tell thee, thou shalt not depart thence, till thou hast paid the very last mite.'

13 There were present at that season some that told him of the Galilæans, whose blood Pilate had mingled with their sacrifices. ²And Jesus answering said unto them, 'Suppose ye that these Galilæans were sinners above all the Galilæans, because they suffered such things? ³I tell you, nay: but, except ye repent, ye shall all likewise perish. ⁴Or those eighteen, upon whom the tower in Siloam fell, and slew them, think ye that they were sinners above all men that dwelt in Jerusalem? ⁵I tell you, nay: but, except ye repent, ye shall all likewise perish.'

⁶He spake also this parable: 'A certain man had a fig tree planted in his vineyard; and he came and sought fruit thereon, and found none. ⁷Then said he unto the dresser of his vineyard, "Behold, these three years I come seeking fruit on this fig tree, and find none; cut it down; why cumbereth it the ground?" ⁸And he answering said unto him, "Lord, let it alone this year also, till I shall dig about it, and dung it; ⁹and if it bear fruit, well; and if not, then after that thou shalt cut it down."'

¹⁰And he was teaching in one of the synagogues on the sabbath. ¹¹And, behold, there was a woman which had a spirit of infirmity eighteen years, and was bowed together, and could in no wise lift up herself. ¹²And when Jesus saw her, he called her to him, and said unto her, 'Woman, thou art loosed from thine infirmity.' ¹³And he laid his hands on her: and immediately she was made straight, and glorified God. ¹⁴And the ruler of the synagogue answered with indignation, because that Jesus had healed on the sabbath day, and said unto the people, 'There are six days in which men ought to work; in them therefore come and be healed, and

not on the sabbath day.' ¹⁵ The Lord then answered him, and said, 'Thou hypocrite, doth not each one of you on the sabbath loose his ox or his ass from the stall, and lead him away to watering? ¹⁶ And ought not this woman, being a daughter of Abraham, whom Satan hath bound, lo, these eighteen years, be loosed from this bond on the sabbath day?' ¹⁷ And when he had said these things, all his adversaries were ashamed: and all the people rejoiced for all the glorious things that were done by him.

¹⁸ Then said he, 'Unto what is the kingdom of God like? And whereunto shall I resemble it? ¹⁹ It is like a grain of mustard seed, which a man took, and cast into his garden; and it grew, and waxed a great tree; and the fowls of the air lodged in the branches of it.' ²⁰ And again he said, 'Whereunto shall I liken the kingdom of God?' ²¹ It is like leaven, which a woman took and hid in three measures of meal, till the whole was leavened.'

²² And he went through the cities and villages, teaching, and journeying toward Jerusalem. ²³ Then said one unto him, 'Lord, are there few that be saved?' And he said unto them, ²⁴ 'Strive to enter in at the strait gate; for many, I say unto you, will seek to enter in, and shall not be able. ²⁵ When once the master of the house is risen up, and hath shut to the door, and ye begin to stand without, and to knock at the door, saying, "Lord, Lord, open unto us"; and he shall answer and say unto you, "I know you not whence ye are," ²⁶ then shall ye begin to say, "We have eaten and drunk in thy presence, and thou hast taught in our streets." ²⁷ But he shall say, "I tell you, I know you not whence ye are; depart from me, all ye workers of iniquity." ²⁸ There shall be weeping and

gnashing of teeth, when ye shall see Abraham, and Isaac, and Jacob, and all the prophets, in the kingdom of God, and you yourselves thrust out. [29]And they shall come from the east, and from the west, and from the north, and from the south, and shall sit down in the kingdom of God. [30]And, behold, there are last which shall be first, and there are first which shall be last.'

[31]The same day there came certain of the Pharisees, saying unto him, 'Get thee out, and depart hence; for Herod will kill thee.' [32]And he said unto them, 'Go ye, and tell that fox, "Behold, I cast out devils, and I do cures today and tomorrow, and the third day I shall be perfected. [33]Nevertheless I must walk today, and tomorrow, and the day following; for it cannot be that a prophet perish out of Jerusalem." [34]O Jerusalem, Jerusalem, which killest the prophets, and stonest them that are sent unto thee; how often would I have gathered thy children together, as a hen doth gather her brood under her wings, and ye would not! [35]Behold, your house is left unto you desolate: and verily I say unto you, ye shall not see me, until the time come when ye shall say, "Blessed is he that cometh in the name of the Lord."'

14 And it came to pass, as he went into the house of one of the chief Pharisees to eat bread on the sabbath day, that they watched him. [2]And, behold, there was a certain man before him which had the dropsy. [3]And Jesus answering spake unto the lawyers and Pharisees, saying, 'Is it lawful to heal on the sabbath day?' [4]And they held their peace. And he took him, and healed him, and let him go; [5]and answered them, saying, 'Which of you shall have an ass or

an ox fallen into a pit, and will not straightway pull him out on the sabbath day?' ⁶And they could not answer him again to these things.

⁷And he put forth a parable to those which were bidden, when he marked how they chose out the chief rooms; saying unto them, ⁸'When thou art bidden of any man to a wedding, sit not down in the highest room, lest a more honourable man than thou be bidden of him; ⁹and he that bade thee and him come and say to thee, "Give this man place"; and thou begin with shame to take the lowest room. ¹⁰But when thou art bidden, go and sit down in the lowest room; that when he that bade thee cometh, he may say unto thee, "Friend, go up higher," then shalt thou have worship in the presence of them that sit at meat with thee. ¹¹For whosoever exalteth himself shall be abased; and he that humbleth himself shall be exalted.'

¹²Then said he also to him that bade him, 'When thou makest a dinner or a supper, call not thy friends, nor thy brethren, neither thy kinsmen, nor thy rich neighbours, lest they also bid thee again, and a recompence be made thee. ¹³But when thou makest a feast, call the poor, the maimed, the lame, the blind; ¹⁴and thou shalt be blessed; for they cannot recompense thee; for thou shalt be recompensed at the resurrection of the just.'

¹⁵And when one of them that sat at meat with him heard these things, he said unto him, 'Blessed is he that shall eat bread in the kingdom of God.' ¹⁶Then said he unto him, 'A certain man made a great supper, and bade many, ¹⁷and sent his servant at supper time to say to them that were bidden, "Come; for all things are now ready." ¹⁸And they all with

one consent began to make excuse. The first said unto him, "I have bought a piece of ground, and I must needs go and see it: I pray thee have me excused." ¹⁹And another said, "I have bought five yoke of oxen, and I go to prove them: I pray thee have me excused." ²⁰And another said, "I have married a wife, and therefore I cannot come." ²¹So that servant came, and shewed his lord these things. Then the master of the house being angry said to his servant, "Go out quickly into the streets and lanes of the city, and bring in hither the poor, and the maimed, and the halt, and the blind." ²²And the servant said, "Lord, it is done as thou hast commanded, and yet there is room." ²³And the lord said unto the servant, "Go out into the highways and hedges, and compel them to come in, that my house may be filled. ²⁴For I say unto you that none of those men which were bidden shall taste of my supper.'"

²⁵And there went great multitudes with him; and he turned, and said unto them, ²⁶'If any man come to me, and hate not his father, and mother, and wife, and children, and brethren, and sisters, yea, and his own life also, he cannot be my disciple. ²⁷And whosoever doth not bear his cross, and come after me, cannot be my disciple. ²⁸For which of you, intending to build a tower, sitteth not down first, and counteth the cost, whether he have sufficient to finish it? ²⁹Lest haply, after he hath laid the foundation, and is not able to finish it, all that behold it begin to mock him, ³⁰saying, "This man began to build, and was not able to finish." ³¹Or what king, going to make war against another king, sitteth not down first, and consulteth whether he be able with ten thousand to meet him that cometh against him with twenty thousand?

³² Or else, while the other is yet a great way off, he sendeth an ambassage, and desireth conditions of peace. ³³ So likewise, whosoever he be of you that forsaketh not all that he hath, he cannot be my disciple.

³⁴ 'Salt is good: but if the salt have lost his savour, wherewith shall it be seasoned? ³⁵ It is neither fit for the land, nor yet for the dunghill; but men cast it out. He that hath ears to hear, let him hear.'

15 Then drew near unto him all the publicans and sinners for to hear him. ²And the Pharisees and scribes murmured, saying, 'This man receiveth sinners, and eateth with them.'

³And he spake this parable unto them, saying, ⁴'What man of you, having an hundred sheep, if he lose one of them, doth not leave the ninety and nine in the wilderness, and go after that which is lost, until he find it? ⁵And when he hath found it, he layeth it on his shoulders, rejoicing. ⁶And when he cometh home, he calleth together his friends and neighbours, saying unto them, "Rejoice with me; for I have found my sheep which was lost." ⁷I say unto you, that likewise joy shall be in heaven over one sinner that repenteth, more than over ninety and nine just persons, which need no repentance.

⁸'Either what woman having ten pieces of silver, if she lose one piece, doth not light a candle, and sweep the house, and seek diligently till she find it? ⁹And when she hath found it, she calleth her friends and her neighbours together, saying, "Rejoice with me; for I have found the piece which I had lost." ¹⁰Likewise, I say unto you, there is joy in the presence of the angels of God over one sinner that repenteth.'

¹¹And he said, 'A certain man had two sons: ¹²and the younger of them said to his father, "Father, give me the portion of goods that falleth to me." And he divided unto them his living. ¹³And not many days after the younger son gathered all together, and took his journey into a far country, and there wasted his substance with riotous living. ¹⁴And when he had spent all, there arose a mighty famine in that land; and he began to be in want. ¹⁵And he went and joined himself to a citizen of that country; and he sent him into his fields to feed swine. ¹⁶And he would fain have filled his belly with the husks that the swine did eat; and no man gave unto him. ¹⁷And when he came to himself, he said, "How many hired servants of my father's have bread enough and to spare, and I perish with hunger! ¹⁸I will arise and go to my father, and will say unto him, Father, I have sinned against heaven, and before thee, ¹⁹and am no more worthy to be called thy son; make me as one of thy hired servants." ²⁰And he arose, and came to his father. But when he was yet a great way off, his father saw him, and had compassion, and ran, and fell on his neck, and kissed him. ²¹And the son said unto him, "Father, I have sinned against heaven, and in thy sight, and am no more worthy to be called thy son." ²²But the father said to his servants, "Bring forth the best robe, and put it on him; and put a ring on his hand, and shoes on his feet: ²³and bring hither the fatted calf, and kill it; and let us eat, and be merry. ²⁴For this my son was dead, and is alive again; he was lost, and is found." And they began to be merry. ²⁵Now his elder son was in the field; and as he came and drew nigh to the house, he heard musick and dancing. ²⁶And he called one of the servants, and asked what these things meant. ²⁷And he

said unto him, "Thy brother is come; and thy father hath killed the fatted calf, because he hath received him safe and sound." ²⁸And he was angry, and would not go in; therefore came his father out, and intreated him. ²⁹And he answering said to his father, "Lo, these many years do I serve thee, neither transgressed I at any time thy commandment: and yet thou never gavest me a kid, that I might make merry with my friends. ³⁰But as soon as this thy son was come, which hath devoured thy living with harlots, thou hast killed for him the fatted calf." ³¹And he said unto him, "Son, thou art ever with me, and all that I have is thine. ³²It was meet that we should make merry, and be glad; for this thy brother was dead, and is alive again; and was lost, and is found."'

16 And he said also unto his disciples, 'There was a certain rich man, which had a steward; and the same was accused unto him that he had wasted his goods. ²And he called him, and said unto him, "How is it that I hear this of thee? Give an account of thy stewardship; for thou mayest be no longer steward." ³Then the steward said within himself, "What shall I do? For my lord taketh away from me the stewardship. I cannot dig; to beg I am ashamed. ⁴I am resolved what to do, that, when I am put out of the stewardship, they may receive me into their houses." ⁵So he called every one of his lord's debtors unto him, and said unto the first, "How much owest thou unto my lord?" ⁶And he said, "An hundred measures of oil." And he said unto him, "Take thy bill, and sit down quickly, and write fifty." ⁷Then said he to another, "And how much owest thou?" And he said, "An hundred measures of wheat." And he said unto him, "Take

thy bill, and write fourscore." ⁸And the lord commended the unjust steward, because he had done wisely: for the children of this world are in their generation wiser than the children of light. ⁹And I say unto you, make to yourselves friends of the mammon of unrighteousness; that, when ye fail, they may receive you into everlasting habitations.

¹⁰'He that is faithful in that which is least is faithful also in much: and he that is unjust in the least is unjust also in much. ¹¹If therefore ye have not been faithful in the unrighteous mammon, who will commit to your trust the true riches? ¹²And if ye have not been faithful in that which is another man's, who shall give you that which is your own?

¹³'No servant can serve two masters: for either he will hate the one, and love the other; or else he will hold to the one, and despise the other. Ye cannot serve God and mammon.'

¹⁴And the Pharisees also, who were covetous, heard all these things: and they derided him. ¹⁵And he said unto them, 'Ye are they which justify yourselves before men, but God knoweth your hearts, for that which is highly esteemed among men is abomination in the sight of God. ¹⁶The law and the prophets were until John; since that time the kingdom of God is preached, and every man presseth into it. ¹⁷And it is easier for heaven and earth to pass, than one tittle of the law to fail. ¹⁸Whosoever putteth away his wife, and marrieth another, committeth adultery; and whosoever marrieth her that is put away from her husband committeth adultery.

¹⁹'There was a certain rich man, which was clothed in purple and fine linen, and fared sumptuously every day; ²⁰and there was a certain beggar named Lazarus, which was laid at his gate, full of sores, ²¹and desiring to be fed with the

crumbs which fell from the rich man's table; moreover the dogs came and licked his sores. ²²And it came to pass that the beggar died, and was carried by the angels into Abraham's bosom; the rich man also died, and was buried; ²³and in hell he lift up his eyes, being in torments, and seeth Abraham afar off, and Lazarus in his bosom. ²⁴And he cried and said, "Father Abraham, have mercy on me, and send Lazarus that he may dip the tip of his finger in water, and cool my tongue; for I am tormented in this flame." ²⁵But Abraham said, "Son, remember that thou in thy lifetime receivedst thy good things, and likewise Lazarus evil things; but now he is comforted, and thou art tormented. ²⁶And beside all this, between us and you there is a great gulf fixed: so that they which would pass from hence to you cannot; neither can they pass to us, that would come from thence." ²⁷Then he said, "I pray thee therefore, father, that thou wouldest send him to my father's house, ²⁸for I have five brethren; that he may testify unto them, lest they also come into this place of torment." ²⁹Abraham saith unto him, "They have Moses and the prophets; let them hear them." ³⁰And he said, "Nay, father Abraham: but if one went unto them from the dead, they will repent." ³¹And he said unto him, "If they hear not Moses and the prophets, neither will they be persuaded, though one rose from the dead."'

17 Then said he unto the disciples, 'It is impossible but that offences will come: but woe unto him, through whom they come! ²It were better for him that a millstone were hanged about his neck, and he cast into the sea, than that he should offend one of these little ones.

³ 'Take heed to yourselves: if thy brother trespass against thee, rebuke him; and if he repent, forgive him. ⁴And if he trespass against thee seven times in a day, and seven times in a day turn again to thee, saying, "I repent," thou shalt forgive him.'

⁵And the apostles said unto the Lord, 'Increase our faith.' ⁶And the Lord said, 'If ye had faith as a grain of mustard seed, ye might say unto this sycamine tree, "Be thou plucked up by the root, and be thou planted in the sea"; and it should obey you. ⁷But which of you, having a servant plowing or feeding cattle, will say unto him by and by, when he is come from the field, "Go and sit down to meat"? ⁸And will not rather say unto him, "Make ready wherewith I may sup, and gird thyself, and serve me, till I have eaten and drunken; and afterward thou shalt eat and drink"? ⁹Doth he thank that servant because he did the things that were commanded him? I trow not. ¹⁰So likewise ye, when ye shall have done all those things which are commanded you, say, "We are unprofitable servants: we have done that which was our duty to do."'

¹¹And it came to pass, as he went to Jerusalem, that he passed through the midst of Samaria and Galilee. ¹²And as he entered into a certain village, there met him ten men that were lepers, which stood afar off. ¹³And they lifted up their voices, and said, 'Jesus, Master, have mercy on us.' ¹⁴And when he saw them, he said unto them, 'Go shew yourselves unto the priests.' And it came to pass, that, as they went, they were cleansed. ¹⁵And one of them, when he saw that he was healed, turned back, and with a loud voice glorified God, ¹⁶and fell down on his face at his feet, giving him thanks; and he was a Samaritan. ¹⁷And Jesus answering said,

'Were there not ten cleansed? But where are the nine? ¹⁸There are not found that returned to give glory to God, save this stranger.' ¹⁹And he said unto him, 'Arise, go thy way; thy faith hath made thee whole.'

²⁰And when he was demanded of the Pharisees, when the kingdom of God should come, he answered them and said, 'The kingdom of God cometh not with observation. ²¹Neither shall they say, "Lo here!" or, "Lo there!" For, behold, the kingdom of God is within you.' ²²And he said unto the disciples, 'The days will come, when ye shall desire to see one of the days of the Son of man, and ye shall not see it. ²³And they shall say to you, "See here," or, "See there": go not after them, nor follow them. ²⁴For as the lightning, that lighteneth out of the one part under heaven, shineth unto the other part under heaven; so shall also the Son of man be in his day. ²⁵But first must he suffer many things, and be rejected of this generation. ²⁶And as it was in the days of Noe, so shall it be also in the days of the Son of man. ²⁷They did eat, they drank, they married wives, they were given in marriage, until the day that Noe entered into the ark, and the flood came, and destroyed them all. ²⁸Likewise also as it was in the days of Lot; they did eat, they drank, they bought, they sold, they planted, they builded; ²⁹but the same day that Lot went out of Sodom it rained fire and brimstone from heaven, and destroyed them all. ³⁰Even thus shall it be in the day when the Son of man is revealed. ³¹In that day, he which shall be upon the housetop, and his stuff in the house, let him not come down to take it away; and he that is in the field, let him likewise not return back. ³²Remember Lot's wife. ³³Whosoever shall seek to save his life shall lose it; and

whosoever shall lose his life shall preserve it. ³⁴I tell you, in that night there shall be two men in one bed; the one shall be taken, and the other shall be left. ³⁵Two women shall be grinding together; the one shall be taken, and the other left. ³⁶Two men shall be in the field; the one shall be taken, and the other left.' ³⁷And they answered and said unto him, 'Where, Lord?' And he said unto them, 'Wheresoever the body is, thither will the eagles be gathered together.'

18 And he spake a parable unto them to this end, that men ought always to pray, and not to faint; ²saying, 'There was in a city a judge, which feared not God, neither regarded man; ³and there was a widow in that city; and she came unto him, saying, "Avenge me of mine adversary." ⁴And he would not for a while; but afterward he said within himself, "Though I fear not God, nor regard man; ⁵yet because this widow troubleth me, I will avenge her, lest by her continual coming she weary me."' ⁶And the Lord said, 'Hear what the unjust judge saith. ⁷And shall not God avenge his own elect, which cry day and night unto him, though he bear long with them? ⁸I tell you that he will avenge them speedily. Nevertheless when the Son of man cometh, shall he find faith on the earth?'

⁹And he spake this parable unto certain which trusted in themselves that they were righteous, and despised others. ¹⁰'Two men went up into the temple to pray: the one a Pharisee, and the other a publican. ¹¹The Pharisee stood and prayed thus with himself, "God, I thank thee, that I am not as other men are, extortioners, unjust, adulterers, or even as this publican. ¹²I fast twice in the week, I give tithes of all that I possess."

¹³And the publican, standing afar off, would not lift up so much as his eyes unto heaven, but smote upon his breast, saying, "God be merciful to me a sinner." ¹⁴I tell you, this man went down to his house justified rather than the other: for every one that exalteth himself shall be abased; and he that humbleth himself shall be exalted.'

¹⁵And they brought unto him also infants, that he would touch them; but when his disciples saw it, they rebuked them. ¹⁶But Jesus called them unto him, and said, 'Suffer little children to come unto me, and forbid them not; for of such is the kingdom of God. ¹⁷Verily I say unto you, whosoever shall not receive the kingdom of God as a little child shall in no wise enter therein.'

¹⁸And a certain ruler asked him, saying, 'Good Master, what shall I do to inherit eternal life?' ¹⁹And Jesus said unto him, 'Why callest thou me good? None is good, save one, that is, God. ²⁰Thou knowest the commandments: Do not commit adultery, Do not kill, Do not steal, Do not bear false witness, Honour thy father and thy mother.' ²¹And he said, 'All these have I kept from my youth up.' ²²Now when Jesus heard these things, he said unto him, 'Yet lackest thou one thing: sell all that thou hast, and distribute unto the poor, and thou shalt have treasure in heaven; and come, follow me.' ²³And when he heard this, he was very sorrowful; for he was very rich. ²⁴And when Jesus saw that he was very sorrowful, he said, 'How hardly shall they that have riches enter into the kingdom of God! ²⁵For it is easier for a camel to go through a needle's eye, than for a rich man to enter into the kingdom of God.' ²⁶And they that heard it said, 'Who then can be saved?' ²⁷And he said, 'The things which are impossible with men

are possible with God.' ²⁸Then Peter said, 'Lo, we have left all, and followed thee.' ²⁹And he said unto them, 'Verily I say unto you, there is no man that hath left house, or parents, or brethren, or wife, or children, for the kingdom of God's sake, ³⁰who shall not receive manifold more in this present time, and in the world to come life everlasting.'

³¹Then he took unto him the twelve, and said unto them, 'Behold, we go up to Jerusalem, and all things that are written by the prophets concerning the Son of man shall be accomplished. ³²For he shall be delivered unto the Gentiles, and shall be mocked, and spitefully entreated, and spitted on. ³³And they shall scourge him, and put him to death; and the third day he shall rise again.' ³⁴And they understood none of these things; and this saying was hid from them, neither knew they the things which were spoken.

³⁵And it came to pass that, as he was come nigh unto Jericho, a certain blind man sat by the way side begging, ³⁶and hearing the multitude pass by, he asked what it meant. ³⁷And they told him that Jesus of Nazareth passeth by. ³⁸And he cried, saying, 'Jesus, thou Son of David, have mercy on me.' ³⁹And they which went before rebuked him, that he should hold his peace: but he cried so much the more, 'Thou Son of David, have mercy on me.' ⁴⁰And Jesus stood, and commanded him to be brought unto him; and when he was come near, he asked him, ⁴¹saying, 'What wilt thou that I shall do unto thee?' And he said, 'Lord, that I may receive my sight.' ⁴²And Jesus said unto him, 'Receive thy sight; thy faith hath saved thee.' ⁴³And immediately he received his sight, and followed him, glorifying God: and all the people, when they saw it, gave praise unto God.

19

And Jesus entered and passed through Jericho. ²And, behold, there was a man named Zacchæus, which was the chief among the publicans, and he was rich. ³And he sought to see Jesus who he was; and could not for the press, because he was little of stature. ⁴And he ran before, and climbed up into a sycomore tree to see him; for he was to pass that way. ⁵And when Jesus came to the place, he looked up, and saw him, and said unto him, 'Zacchæus, make haste, and come down; for today I must abide at thy house.' ⁶And he made haste, and came down, and received him joyfully. ⁷And when they saw it, they all murmured, saying that he was gone to be guest with a man that is a sinner. ⁸And Zacchæus stood, and said unto the Lord, 'Behold, Lord, the half of my goods I give to the poor; and if I have taken any thing from any man by false accusation, I restore him fourfold.' ⁹And Jesus said unto him, 'This day is salvation come to this house, forsomuch as he also is a son of Abraham. ¹⁰For the Son of man is come to seek and to save that which was lost.'

¹¹And as they heard these things, he added and spake a parable, because he was nigh to Jerusalem, and because they thought that the kingdom of God should immediately appear. ¹²He said therefore, 'A certain nobleman went into a far country to receive for himself a kingdom, and to return. ¹³And he called his ten servants, and delivered them ten pounds, and said unto them, "Occupy till I come." ¹⁴But his citizens hated him, and sent a message after him, saying, "We will not have this man to reign over us." ¹⁵And it came to pass that, when he was returned, having received the kingdom, then he commanded these servants to be called unto him, to whom he had given the money, that he might know

how much every man had gained by trading. ¹⁶Then came the first, saying, "Lord, thy pound hath gained ten pounds." ¹⁷And he said unto him, "Well, thou good servant, because thou hast been faithful in a very little, have thou authority over ten cities." ¹⁸And the second came, saying, "Lord, thy pound hath gained five pounds." ¹⁹And he said likewise to him, "Be thou also over five cities." ²⁰And another came, saying, "Lord, behold, here is thy pound, which I have kept laid up in a napkin; ²¹for I feared thee, because thou art an austere man: thou takest up that thou layedst not down, and reapest that thou didst not sow." ²²And he saith unto him, "Out of thine own mouth will I judge thee, thou wicked servant. Thou knewest that I was an austere man, taking up that I laid not down, and reaping that I did not sow. ²³Wherefore then gavest not thou my money into the bank, that at my coming I might have required mine own with usury?" ²⁴And he said unto them that stood by, "Take from him the pound, and give it to him that hath ten pounds." ²⁵(And they said unto him, "Lord, he hath ten pounds.") ²⁶For I say unto you that unto every one which hath shall be given; and from him that hath not, even that he hath shall be taken away from him. ²⁷But those mine enemies, which would not that I should reign over them, bring hither, and slay them before me.'

²⁸And when he had thus spoken, he went before, ascending up to Jerusalem. ²⁹And it came to pass, when he was come nigh to Bethphage and Bethany, at the mount called the mount of Olives, he sent two of his disciples, ³⁰saying, 'Go ye into the village over against you, in the which at your entering ye shall find a colt tied, whereon yet never man sat: loose him, and bring him hither. ³¹And if any man ask you,

"Why do ye loose him?" Thus shall ye say unto him, "Because the Lord hath need of him."' ³²And they that were sent went their way, and found even as he had said unto them. ³³And as they were loosing the colt, the owners thereof said unto them, 'Why loose ye the colt?' ³⁴And they said, 'The Lord hath need of him.' ³⁵And they brought him to Jesus: and they cast their garments upon the colt, and they set Jesus thereon. ³⁶And as he went, they spread their clothes in the way. ³⁷And when he was come nigh, even now at the descent of the mount of Olives, the whole multitude of the disciples began to rejoice and praise God with a loud voice for all the mighty works that they had seen, ³⁸saying, 'Blessed be the King that cometh in the name of the Lord; peace in heaven, and glory in the highest.' ³⁹And some of the Pharisees from among the multitude said unto him, 'Master, rebuke thy disciples.' ⁴⁰And he answered and said unto them, 'I tell you that, if these should hold their peace, the stones would immediately cry out.'

⁴¹And when he was come near, he beheld the city, and wept over it, ⁴²saying, 'If thou hadst known, even thou, at least in this thy day, the things which belong unto thy peace! But now they are hid from thine eyes. ⁴³For the days shall come upon thee, that thine enemies shall cast a trench about thee, and compass thee round, and keep thee in on every side, ⁴⁴and shall lay thee even with the ground, and thy children within thee; and they shall not leave in thee one stone upon another; because thou knewest not the time of thy visitation.' ⁴⁵And he went into the temple, and began to cast out them that sold therein, and them that bought, ⁴⁶saying unto them, 'It is written, "My house is the house of prayer," but ye have

made it a den of thieves.' ⁴⁷And he taught daily in the temple. But the chief priests and the scribes and the chief of the people sought to destroy him, ⁴⁸and could not find what they might do; for all the people were very attentive to hear him.

20 And it came to pass that on one of those days, as he taught the people in the temple, and preached the gospel, the chief priests and the scribes came upon him with the elders, ²and spake unto him, saying, 'Tell us, by what authority doest thou these things? Or who is he that gave thee this authority?' ³And he answered and said unto them, 'I will also ask you one thing; and answer me: ⁴the baptism of John, was it from heaven, or of men?' ⁵And they reasoned with themselves, saying, 'If we shall say, "From heaven," he will say, "Why then believed ye him not?"; ⁶but and if we say, "Of men; all the people will stone us; for they be persuaded that John was a prophet.' ⁷And they answered that they could not tell whence it was. ⁸And Jesus said unto them, 'Neither tell I you by what authority I do these things.'

⁹Then began he to speak to the people this parable: 'A certain man planted a vineyard, and let it forth to husbandmen, and went into a far country for a long time. ¹⁰And at the season he sent a servant to the husbandmen, that they should give him of the fruit of the vineyard; but the husbandmen beat him, and sent him away empty. ¹¹And again he sent another servant: and they beat him also, and entreated him shamefully, and sent him away empty. ¹²And again he sent a third; and they wounded him also, and cast him out. ¹³Then said the lord of the vineyard, "What shall I do? I will send my beloved son; it may be they will reverence him when

they see him." ¹⁴ But when the husbandmen saw him, they reasoned among themselves, saying, "This is the heir: come, let us kill him, that the inheritance may be ours." ¹⁵ So they cast him out of the vineyard, and killed him. What therefore shall the lord of the vineyard do unto them? ¹⁶ He shall come and destroy these husbandmen, and shall give the vineyard to others.' And when they heard it, they said, 'God forbid.' ¹⁷ And he beheld them, and said, 'What is this then that is written, "The stone which the builders rejected, the same is become the head of the corner"? ¹⁸ Whosoever shall fall upon that stone shall be broken; but on whomsoever it shall fall, it will grind him to powder.'

¹⁹ And the chief priests and the scribes the same hour sought to lay hands on him; and they feared the people; for they perceived that he had spoken this parable against them. ²⁰ And they watched him, and sent forth spies, which should feign themselves just men, that they might take hold of his words, that so they might deliver him unto the power and authority of the governor. ²¹ And they asked him, saying, 'Master, we know that thou sayest and teachest rightly, neither acceptest thou the person of any, but teachest the way of God truly. ²² Is it lawful for us to give tribute unto Cæsar, or no?' ²³ But he perceived their craftiness, and said unto them, 'Why tempt ye me? ²⁴ Shew me a penny. Whose image and superscription hath it?' They answered and said, 'Cæsar's.' ²⁵ And he said unto them, 'Render therefore unto Cæsar the things which be Cæsar's, and unto God the things which be God's.' ²⁶ And they could not take hold of his words before the people: and they marvelled at his answer, and held their peace.

²⁷ Then came to him certain of the Sadducees, which deny

that there is any resurrection; and they asked him, [28] saying, 'Master, Moses wrote unto us, if any man's brother die, having a wife, and he die without children, that his brother should take his wife, and raise up seed unto his brother. [29] There were therefore seven brethren; and the first took a wife, and died without children. [30] And the second took her to wife, and he died childless. [31] And the third took her; and in like manner the seven also: and they left no children, and died. [32] Last of all the woman died also. [33] Therefore in the resurrection whose wife of them is she? For seven had her to wife.' [34] And Jesus answering said unto them, 'The children of this world marry, and are given in marriage, [35] but they which shall be accounted worthy to obtain that world, and the resurrection from the dead, neither marry, nor are given in marriage; [36] neither can they die any more: for they are equal unto the angels; and are the children of God, being the children of the resurrection. [37] Now that the dead are raised, even Moses shewed at the bush, when he calleth the Lord the God of Abraham, and the God of Isaac, and the God of Jacob. [38] For he is not a God of the dead, but of the living: for all live unto him.'

[39] Then certain of the scribes answering said, 'Master, thou hast well said.' [40] And after that they durst not ask him any question at all. [41] And he said unto them, 'How say they that Christ is David's son? [42] And David himself saith in the book of Psalms, "The Lord said unto my Lord, 'Sit thou on my right hand, [43] till I make thine enemies thy footstool." [44] David therefore calleth him Lord, how is he then his son?'

[45] Then in the audience of all the people he said unto his disciples, [46] 'Beware of the scribes, which desire to walk in long robes, and love greetings in the markets, and the

highest seats in the synagogues, and the chief rooms at feasts; ⁴⁷which devour widows' houses, and for a shew make long prayers: the same shall receive greater damnation.'

21 And he looked up, and saw the rich men casting their gifts into the treasury. ²And he saw also a certain poor widow casting in thither two mites. ³And he said, 'Of a truth I say unto you that this poor widow hath cast in more than they all. ⁴For all these have of their abundance cast in unto the offerings of God, but she of her penury hath cast in all the living that she had.'

⁵And as some spake of the temple, how it was adorned with goodly stones and gifts, he said, ⁶'As for these things which ye behold, the days will come, in the which there shall not be left one stone upon another, that shall not be thrown down.' ⁷And they asked him, saying, 'Master, but when shall these things be? And what sign will there be when these things shall come to pass?' ⁸And he said, 'Take heed that ye be not deceived; for many shall come in my name, saying, "I am Christ," and the time draweth near: go ye not therefore after them.

⁹'But when ye shall hear of wars and commotions, be not terrified; for these things must first come to pass, but the end is not by and by.' ¹⁰Then said he unto them, 'Nation shall rise against nation, and kingdom against kingdom. ¹¹And great earthquakes shall be in divers places, and famines, and pestilences; and fearful sights and great signs shall there be from heaven.

¹²'But before all these, they shall lay their hands on you, and persecute you, delivering you up to the synagogues, and

into prisons, being brought before kings and rulers for my name's sake. ¹³And it shall turn to you for a testimony. ¹⁴Settle it therefore in your hearts, not to meditate before what ye shall answer, ¹⁵for I will give you a mouth and wisdom, which all your adversaries shall not be able to gainsay nor resist. ¹⁶And ye shall be betrayed both by parents, and brethren, and kinsfolks, and friends; and some of you shall they cause to be put to death. ¹⁷And ye shall be hated of all men for my name's sake. ¹⁸But there shall not an hair of your head perish. ¹⁹In your patience possess ye your souls. ²⁰And when ye shall see Jerusalem compassed with armies, then know that the desolation thereof is nigh. ²¹Then let them which are in Judæa flee to the mountains; and let them which are in the midst of it depart out; and let not them that are in the countries enter thereinto. ²²For these be the days of vengeance, that all things which are written may be fulfilled. ²³But woe unto them that are with child, and to them that give suck, in those days! For there shall be great distress in the land, and wrath upon this people. ²⁴And they shall fall by the edge of the sword, and shall be led away captive into all nations: and Jerusalem shall be trodden down of the Gentiles, until the times of the Gentiles be fulfilled.

²⁵'And there shall be signs in the sun, and in the moon, and in the stars; and upon the earth distress of nations, with perplexity; the sea and the waves roaring; ²⁶men's hearts failing them for fear, and for looking after those things which are coming on the earth: for the powers of heaven shall be shaken. ²⁷And then shall they see the Son of man coming in a cloud with power and great glory. ²⁸And when these things begin to come to pass, then look up, and lift up your heads;

for your redemption draweth nigh.' ²⁹And he spake to them a parable: 'Behold the fig tree, and all the trees; ³⁰when they now shoot forth, ye see and know of your own selves that summer is now nigh at hand. ³¹So likewise ye, when ye see these things come to pass, know ye that the kingdom of God is nigh at hand. ³²Verily I say unto you, this generation shall not pass away, till all be fulfilled. ³³Heaven and earth shall pass away, but my words shall not pass away.

³⁴And take heed to yourselves, lest at any time your hearts be overcharged with surfeiting, and drunkenness, and cares of this life, and so that day come upon you unawares. ³⁵For as a snare shall it come on all them that dwell on the face of the whole earth. ³⁶Watch ye therefore, and pray always, that ye may be accounted worthy to escape all these things that shall come to pass, and to stand before the Son of man.' ³⁷And in the day time he was teaching in the temple; and at night he went out, and abode in the mount that is called the mount of Olives. ³⁸And all the people came early in the morning to him in the temple, for to hear him.

22 Now the feast of unleavened bread drew nigh, which is called the Passover. ²And the chief priests and scribes sought how they might kill him; for they feared the people.

³Then entered Satan into Judas surnamed Iscariot, being of the number of the twelve. ⁴And he went his way, and communed with the chief priests and captains, how he might betray him unto them. ⁵And they were glad, and covenanted to give him money. ⁶And he promised, and sought opportunity to betray him unto them in the absence of the multitude.

⁷Then came the day of unleavened bread, when the passover must be killed. ⁸And he sent Peter and John, saying, 'Go and prepare us the passover, that we may eat.' ⁹And they said unto him, 'Where wilt thou that we prepare?' ¹⁰And he said unto them, 'Behold, when ye are entered into the city, there shall a man meet you, bearing a pitcher of water; follow him into the house where he entereth in. ¹¹And ye shall say unto the goodman of the house, "The Master saith unto thee, 'Where is the guestchamber, where I shall eat the passover with my disciples?' " ¹²And he shall shew you a large upper room furnished; there make ready.' ¹³And they went, and found as he had said unto them: and they made ready the passover.

¹⁴And when the hour was come, he sat down, and the twelve apostles with him. ¹⁵And he said unto them, 'With desire I have desired to eat this passover with you before I suffer. ¹⁶For I say unto you, I will not any more eat thereof, until it be fulfilled in the kingdom of God.' ¹⁷And he took the cup, and gave thanks, and said, 'Take this, and divide it among yourselves. ¹⁸For I say unto you, I will not drink of the fruit of the vine, until the kingdom of God shall come.'

¹⁹And he took bread, and gave thanks, and brake it, and gave unto them, saying, 'This is my body which is given for you: this do in remembrance of me.' ²⁰Likewise also the cup after supper, saying, 'This cup is the new testament in my blood, which is shed for you. ²¹But, behold, the hand of him that betrayeth me is with me on the table. ²²And truly the Son of man goeth, as it was determined: but woe unto that man by whom he is betrayed!' ²³And they began to enquire among themselves, which of them it was that should do this thing.

²⁴And there was also a strife among them, which of them should be accounted the greatest. ²⁵And he said unto them, 'The kings of the Gentiles exercise lordship over them; and they that exercise authority upon them are called benefactors. ²⁶But ye shall not be so: but he that is greatest among you, let him be as the younger; and he that is chief, as he that doth serve. ²⁷For whether is greater, he that sitteth at meat, or he that serveth? Is not he that sitteth at meat? But I am among you as he that serveth. ²⁸Ye are they which have continued with me in my temptations. ²⁹And I appoint unto you a kingdom, as my Father hath appointed unto me; ³⁰that ye may eat and drink at my table in my kingdom, and sit on thrones judging the twelve tribes of Israel.'

³¹And the Lord said, 'Simon, Simon, behold, Satan hath desired to have you, that he may sift you as wheat; ³²but I have prayed for thee, that thy faith fail not; and when thou art converted, strengthen thy brethren.' ³³And he said unto him, 'Lord, I am ready to go with thee, both into prison, and to death.' ³⁴And he said, 'I tell thee, Peter, the cock shall not crow this day, before that thou shalt thrice deny that thou knowest me.' ³⁵And he said unto them, 'When I sent you without purse, and scrip, and shoes, lacked ye any thing?' And they said, 'Nothing.' ³⁶Then said he unto them, 'But now, he that hath a purse, let him take it, and likewise his scrip: and he that hath no sword, let him sell his garment, and buy one. ³⁷For I say unto you that this that is written must yet be accomplished in me, and he was reckoned among the transgressors: for the things concerning me have an end.' ³⁸And they said, 'Lord, behold, here are two swords.' And he said unto them, 'It is enough.'

³⁹And he came out, and went, as he was wont, to the mount of Olives; and his disciples also followed him. ⁴⁰And when he was at the place, he said unto them, 'Pray that ye enter not into temptation.' ⁴¹And he was withdrawn from them about a stone's cast, and kneeled down, and prayed, ⁴²saying, 'Father, if thou be willing, remove this cup from me; nevertheless not my will, but thine, be done.' ⁴³And there appeared an angel unto him from heaven, strengthening him. ⁴⁴And being in an agony he prayed more earnestly; and his sweat was as it were great drops of blood falling down to the ground. ⁴⁵And when he rose up from prayer, and was come to his disciples, he found them sleeping for sorrow, ⁴⁶and said unto them, 'Why sleep ye? Rise and pray, lest ye enter into temptation.'

⁴⁷And while he yet spake, behold a multitude, and he that was called Judas, one of the twelve, went before them, and drew near unto Jesus to kiss him. ⁴⁸But Jesus said unto him, 'Judas, betrayest thou the Son of man with a kiss?' ⁴⁹When they which were about him saw what would follow, they said unto him, 'Lord, shall we smite with the sword?'

⁵⁰And one of them smote the servant of the high priest, and cut off his right ear. ⁵¹And Jesus answered and said, 'Suffer ye thus far.' And he touched his ear, and healed him. ⁵²Then Jesus said unto the chief priests, and captains of the temple, and the elders, which were come to him, 'Be ye come out, as against a thief, with swords and staves? ⁵³When I was daily with you in the temple, ye stretched forth no hands against me: but this is your hour, and the power of darkness.'

⁵⁴Then took they him, and led him, and brought him into the high priest's house. And Peter followed afar off. ⁵⁵And

when they had kindled a fire in the midst of the hall, and were set down together, Peter sat down among them. ⁵⁶But a certain maid beheld him as he sat by the fire, and earnestly looked upon him, and said, 'This man was also with him.' ⁵⁷And he denied him, saying, 'Woman, I know him not.' ⁵⁸And after a little while another saw him, and said, 'Thou art also of them.' And Peter said, 'Man, I am not.' ⁵⁹And about the space of one hour after another confidently affirmed, saying, 'Of a truth this fellow also was with him; for he is a Galilæan.' ⁶⁰And Peter said, 'Man, I know not what thou sayest.' And immediately, while he yet spake, the cock crew. ⁶¹And the Lord turned, and looked upon Peter. And Peter remembered the word of the Lord, how he had said unto him, 'Before the cock crow, thou shalt deny me thrice.' ⁶²And Peter went out, and wept bitterly.

⁶³And the men that held Jesus mocked him, and smote him. ⁶⁴And when they had blindfolded him, they struck him on the face, and asked him, saying, 'Prophesy, who is it that smote thee?' ⁶⁵And many other things blasphemously spake they against him.

⁶⁶And as soon as it was day, the elders of the people and the chief priests and the scribes came together, and led him into their council, saying, ⁶⁷'Art thou the Christ? Tell us.' And he said unto them, 'If I tell you, ye will not believe. ⁶⁸And if I also ask you, ye will not answer me, nor let me go. ⁶⁹Hereafter shall the Son of man sit on the right hand of the power of God.' ⁷⁰Then said they all, 'Art thou then the Son of God?' And he said unto them, 'Ye say that I am.' ⁷¹And they said, 'What need we any further witness? For we ourselves have heard of his own mouth.'

23

And the whole multitude of them arose, and led him unto Pilate. ²And they began to accuse him, saying, 'We found this fellow perverting the nation, and forbidding to give tribute to Cæsar, saying that he himself is Christ a King.' ³And Pilate asked him, saying, 'Art thou the King of the Jews?' And he answered him and said, 'Thou sayest it.' ⁴Then said Pilate to the chief priests and to the people, 'I find no fault in this man.' ⁵And they were the more fierce, saying, 'He stirreth up the people, teaching throughout all Jewry, beginning from Galilee to this place.' ⁶When Pilate heard of Galilee, he asked whether the man were a Galilæan. ⁷And as soon as he knew that he belonged unto Herod's jurisdiction, he sent him to Herod, who himself also was at Jerusalem at that time.

⁸And when Herod saw Jesus, he was exceeding glad, for he was desirous to see him of a long season, because he had heard many things of him; and he hoped to have seen some miracle done by him. ⁹Then he questioned with him in many words; but he answered him nothing. ¹⁰And the chief priests and scribes stood and vehemently accused him. ¹¹And Herod with his men of war set him at nought, and mocked him, and arrayed him in a gorgeous robe, and sent him again to Pilate.

¹²And the same day Pilate and Herod were made friends together; for before they were at enmity between themselves.

¹³And Pilate, when he had called together the chief priests and the rulers and the people, ¹⁴said unto them, 'Ye have brought this man unto me, as one that perverteth the people: and, behold, I, having examined him before you, have found no fault in this man touching those things whereof ye accuse

him. [15]No, nor yet Herod: for I sent you to him; and, lo, nothing worthy of death is done unto him. [16]I will therefore chastise him, and release him.' [17](For of necessity he must release one unto them at the feast.)

[18]And they cried out all at once, saying, 'Away with this man, and release unto us Barabbas' [19](who for a certain sedition made in the city, and for murder, was cast into prison). [20]Pilate therefore, willing to release Jesus, spake again to them. [21]But they cried, saying, 'Crucify him, crucify him.' [22]And he said unto them the third time, 'Why, what evil hath he done? I have found no cause of death in him: I will therefore chastise him, and let him go.' [23]And they were instant with loud voices, requiring that he might be crucified. And the voices of them and of the chief priests prevailed. [24]And Pilate gave sentence that it should be as they required. [25]And he released unto them him that for sedition and murder was cast into prison, whom they had desired; but he delivered Jesus to their will. [26]And as they led him away, they laid hold upon one Simon, a Cyrenian, coming out of the country, and on him they laid the cross, that he might bear it after Jesus.

[27]And there followed him a great company of people, and of women, which also bewailed and lamented him. [28]But Jesus turning unto them said, 'Daughters of Jerusalem, weep not for me, but weep for yourselves, and for your children. [29]For, behold, the days are coming, in the which they shall say, "Blessed are the barren, and the wombs that never bore, and the paps which never gave suck." [30]Then shall they begin to say to the mountains, "Fall on us," and to the hills, "Cover us." [31]For if they do these things in a green tree, what shall be done in the dry?' [32]And there were also two

other, malefactors, led with him to be put to death. ³³And when they were come to the place, which is called Calvary, there they crucified him, and the malefactors, one on the right hand, and the other on the left.

³⁴Then said Jesus, 'Father, forgive them; for they know not what they do.' And they parted his raiment, and cast lots. ³⁵And the people stood beholding. And the rulers also with them derided him, saying, 'He saved others; let him save himself, if he be Christ, the chosen of God.' ³⁶And the soldiers also mocked him, coming to him, and offering him vinegar, ³⁷and saying, 'If thou be the king of the Jews, save thyself.' ³⁸And a superscription also was written over him in letters of Greek, and Latin, and Hebrew, 'THIS IS THE KING OF THE JEWS.'

³⁹And one of the malefactors which were hanged railed on him, saying, 'If thou be Christ, save thyself and us.' ⁴⁰But the other answering rebuked him, saying, 'Dost not thou fear God, seeing thou art in the same condemnation? ⁴¹And we indeed justly; for we receive the due reward of our deeds: but this man hath done nothing amiss.' ⁴²And he said unto Jesus, 'Lord, remember me when thou comest into thy kingdom.' ⁴³And Jesus said unto him, 'Verily I say unto thee, today shalt thou be with me in paradise.'

⁴⁴And it was about the sixth hour, and there was a darkness over all the earth until the ninth hour. ⁴⁵And the sun was darkened, and the veil of the temple was rent in the midst.

⁴⁶And when Jesus had cried with a loud voice, he said, 'Father, into thy hands I commend my spirit,' and having said thus, he gave up the ghost. ⁴⁷Now when the centurion saw what was done, he glorified God, saying, 'Certainly this

was a righteous man.' ⁴⁸And all the people that came together to that sight, beholding the things which were done, smote their breasts, and returned. ⁴⁹And all his acquaintance, and the women that followed him from Galilee, stood afar off, beholding these things.

⁵⁰And, behold, there was a man named Joseph, a counsellor; and he was a good man, and a just. ⁵¹(The same had not consented to the counsel and deed of them.) He was of Arimathæa, a city of the Jews, who also himself waited for the kingdom of God. ⁵²This man went unto Pilate, and begged the body of Jesus. ⁵³And he took it down, and wrapped it in linen, and laid it in a sepulchre that was hewn in stone, wherein never man before was laid. ⁵⁴And that day was the preparation, and the sabbath drew on. ⁵⁵And the women also, which came with him from Galilee, followed after, and beheld the sepulchre, and how his body was laid. ⁵⁶And they returned, and prepared spices and ointments; and rested the sabbath day according to the commandment.

24 Now upon the first day of the week, very early in the morning, they came unto the sepulchre, bringing the spices which they had prepared, and certain others with them. ²And they found the stone rolled away from the sepulchre. ³And they entered in, and found not the body of the Lord Jesus. ⁴And it came to pass, as they were much perplexed thereabout, behold, two men stood by them in shining garments. ⁵And as they were afraid, and bowed down their faces to the earth, they said unto them, 'Why seek ye the living among the dead? ⁶He is not here, but is risen. Remember how he spake unto you when he was yet in Galilee, ⁷saying,

"The Son of man must be delivered into the hands of sinful men, and be crucified, and the third day rise again."' ⁸And they remembered his words, ⁹and returned from the sepulchre, and told all these things unto the eleven, and to all the rest. ¹⁰It was Mary Magdalene, and Joanna, and Mary the mother of James, and other women that were with them, which told these things unto the apostles. ¹¹And their words seemed to them as idle tales, and they believed them not. ¹²Then arose Peter, and ran unto the sepulchre, and stooping down, he beheld the linen clothes laid by themselves, and departed, wondering in himself at that which was come to pass.

¹³And, behold, two of them went that same day to a village called Emmaus, which was from Jerusalem about three-score furlongs. ¹⁴And they talked together of all these things which had happened. ¹⁵And it came to pass, that, while they communed together and reasoned, Jesus himself drew near, and went with them. ¹⁶But their eyes were holden that they should not know him. ¹⁷And he said unto them, 'What manner of communications are these that ye have one to another, as ye walk, and are sad?' ¹⁸And the one of them, whose name was Cleopas, answering said unto him, 'Art thou only a stranger in Jerusalem, and hast not known the things which are come to pass there in these days?' ¹⁹And he said unto them, 'What things?' And they said unto him, 'Concerning Jesus of Nazareth, which was a prophet mighty in deed and word before God and all the people; ²⁰and how the chief priests and our rulers delivered him to be condemned to death, and have crucified him. ²¹But we trusted that it had been he which should have redeemed Israel; and beside all this, today is the third day since these things were done. ²²Yea, and certain

women also of our company made us astonished, which were early at the sepulchre; ²³and when they found not his body, they came, saying that they had also seen a vision of angels, which said that he was alive. ²⁴And certain of them which were with us went to the sepulchre, and found it even so as the women had said; but him they saw not.' ²⁵Then he said unto them, 'O fools, and slow of heart to believe all that the prophets have spoken. ²⁶Ought not Christ to have suffered these things, and to enter into his glory?' ²⁷And beginning at Moses and all the prophets, he expounded unto them in all the scriptures the things concerning himself. ²⁸And they drew nigh unto the village, whither they went; and he made as though he would have gone further. ²⁹But they constrained him, saying, 'Abide with us; for it is toward evening, and the day is far spent.' And he went in to tarry with them. ³⁰And it came to pass, as he sat at meat with them, he took bread, and blessed it, and brake, and gave to them. ³¹And their eyes were opened, and they knew him; and he vanished out of their sight. ³²And they said one to another, 'Did not our heart burn within us, while he talked with us by the way, and while he opened to us the scriptures?' ³³And they rose up the same hour, and returned to Jerusalem, and found the eleven gathered together, and them that were with them, ³⁴saying, 'The Lord is risen indeed, and hath appeared to Simon.' ³⁵And they told what things were done in the way, and how he was known of them in breaking of bread.

³⁶And as they thus spake, Jesus himself stood in the midst of them, and saith unto them, 'Peace be unto you.' ³⁷But they were terrified and affrighted, and supposed that they had seen a spirit. ³⁸And he said unto them, 'Why are ye troubled?

And why do thoughts arise in your hearts? ³⁹Behold my hands and my feet, that it is I myself: handle me, and see; for a spirit hath no flesh and bones, as ye see me have.' ⁴⁰And when he had thus spoken, he shewed them his hands and his feet. ⁴¹And while they yet believed not for joy, and wondered, he said unto them, 'Have ye here any meat?' ⁴²And they gave him a piece of a broiled fish, and of an honeycomb. ⁴³And he took it, and did eat before them. ⁴⁴And he said unto them, 'These are the words which I spake unto you, while I was yet with you, that all things must be fulfilled, which were written in the law of Moses, and in the prophets, and in the psalms, concerning me.' ⁴⁵Then opened he their understanding, that they might understand the scriptures, ⁴⁶and said unto them, 'Thus it is written, and thus it behoved Christ to suffer, and to rise from the dead the third day; ⁴⁷and that repentance and remission of sins should be preached in his name among all nations, beginning at Jerusalem. ⁴⁸And ye are witnesses of these things.

⁴⁹'And, behold, I send the promise of my Father upon you; but tarry ye in the city of Jerusalem, until ye be endued with power from on high.'

⁵⁰And he led them out as far as to Bethany, and he lifted up his hands, and blessed them. ⁵¹And it came to pass, while he blessed them, he was parted from them, and carried up into heaven. ⁵²And they worshipped him, and returned to Jerusalem with great joy; ⁵³and were continually in the temple, praising and blessing God. Amen.

john

introduction by blake morrison

From the age of eight to fifteen, I spent every Sunday morning in the choirstalls of an English village church. To be in the choir didn't require singing talent. You just turned up each week and stood there, like something out of Thomas Hardy, raising a song in praise of God, to the accompaniment of a wheezing organ. Our predecessors in the graveyard had done the same. The dusty black cassocks and white surplices waiting for us on pegs in the vestry – they had worn them, too. The choir was small, just six or eight, all children, most of them present under parental duress. With me, it was different: my father was an atheist, my mother an Irish Catholic, and I'd had to fight to join up. It was not that I had a sense of calling. It was simply a way of getting to see my friends on Sunday. We weren't always well-behaved. Gum was surreptitiously chewed during prayers, then deposited in sticky balls and left to harden. Cruel names were invented for those in the paltry congregation. Whispering and giggling were routine. Still, until confirmation (which for me confirmed doubts, not faith) we kept coming. And though I'm no church-goer now, those Sundays will always be part of me. The touch of cold stone flags on a bended knee; the lovely sound of 'daily bread' and 'trespasses'; the melting nothingness (neither flesh nor manna) of a communion wafer; the head-swoon from a sip of wine; the rotting-body smell from water that stood too long in flower-vases; the whitewash walls, the spread-winged golden-eagle lectern stand, the pale-lemon morning light, the wood of the nave so dark it might have been burned – the hours of boredom have long faded, but the sensuousness has stayed.

The Gospels have stayed, too, the miracles and sayings and Passion. To begin with, I preferred the Old Testament, which read like a boy's adventure story spanning several generations: Noah's flood, David's slingstone, Daniel in the lion's den, Moses in his basket, the parting of the Red Sea. Jesus had adventures, too, but you'd not have known it from the face in the stained-glass windows. He looked wan, frozen and passive, too pious for his own good – someone who'd change wine to water, not the other way about. The only impressive thing about him was that it had taken four men to tell his tale. Matthew, Mark, Luke and John: the names sounded familiar, reassuring, trustworthy, and it didn't seem surprising that their stories should vary – when my friends and I related the same events, didn't our versions vary, too? As years passed in the choir-stalls, I became more interested in the Apostles, and tried to put faces to their names. John was the hardest to visualise. He was said to be the son of Zebedee, 'the beloved disciple', but this didn't help much. All I did dimly perceive was that he was the odd one out.

At fifteen, I swapped the Apostles for another Fab Four, the Beatles, whose John was likewise the outsider. Soon enough, the phrase 'gospel truth' had a hollow ring for me – I was discovering stranger, more various truths through drink, drugs, girls, music, the mystic east. The only lingering affection I felt for the C of E came from thinking of Jesus's story as myth or legend – literary fiction, not monotheistic truth. The idea that the Apostles were contemporaries of Christ, writing factual first-hand reports, seemed ridiculous. But once I thought of them as storytellers, drawing on oral tradition, their gospels became more interesting. They were pedagogues, trying to convince others to follow their faith. But they were also, at least in the Authorised Version, hauntingly imaginative writers, John above all.

The literary status of the gospels, the identity of their authors, the degree of historical truth they impart – these are matters scholars debate to this day. Agreement is rare, but one can glimpse a consensus of sorts on several points.

— A man called Jesus did live and preach in Palestine shortly after the time of King Herod's death; a radical thinker and militant leader, he ran into trouble with the authorities and was put to death.

— Matthew, Mark, Luke and John wrote their gospels late in the first century, perhaps drawing on eye-witness accounts that had been passed down: their names were assigned to the Gospels only around 180 AD, and they probably worked closely with other Christian opinion-formers, in effect as editorial teams.

— Each gospel went through several versions, perhaps as many as five, building up from sayings and sermons through 'pericopes' (teaching or episodic units) to full-blown narratives.

— Their purpose was to proclaim the 'good news' of Jesus's life, through accounts of his story and teachings: 'these are written, that ye might believe that Jesus is the Christ, the Son of God; and that believing ye might have life through his name' (*John* 20:31).

— *Mark* was the first gospel to be composed and *John* is probably the last.

The apparently late composition of John's gospel is one of several reasons why it's often treated as marginal and inferior. Its resemblance to *Mark* (and *Luke*) suggests that, if not directly dependent on them, it drew on the same sources for episodes such as the walk on the lake, the feeding of the 5,000 and the miraculous draught of fishes. The chronology of the first three ('synoptic') gospels coincides to a very large degree, whereas *John* ('the fourth gospel') differs in suggesting that Jesus's ministry lasted over three Passovers, not one, and in putting the scourging of the Temple episode early on. The synoptic gospels are also fairly consistent about the teachings of Jesus, whereas what he preaches in *John* shows the influence of later schools of thought, including the Hellenistic and the Hermetic. Many commentators find the structure of *John* dislocated and suggest an alternative arrangement of the chapters. All in all, as E P Sanders puts it in his study *The Historical Figure of Jesus*, 'The synoptic gospels are to be preferred as our basic source of information about Jesus.'

What claims can be made for *John*, then? First, it is the most *poetic* of the gospels. Compare the various openings. *Matthew* begins with a dull, Old Testament-like genealogical table: 'Abraham begat Isaac; and Isaac begat Jacob; and Jacob begat Judas', etc. *Mark* goes in for skittish anecdotes and dress-notes about John the Baptist: 'John was clothed with camel's hair, and with a girdle of skin'. *Luke* writes in drab bureaucratese to Theophilus, the recipient of his missive: 'Forasmuch as many have taken in hand to set forth in order a declaration of those things which are most surely believed among us …' By contrast, *John* opens with one of the greatest passages of poetic prose in the language, philosophically dense, metaphorically rich and rhythmically lucid at the same time:

> In the beginning was the Word, and the Word was with God, and the Word was God. The same was in the beginning with God. All things were made by him; and without him was not any thing made that was made. In him was life; and the life was the light of men. And the light shineth in darkness; and the darkness comprehended it not … And the Word was made flesh, and dwelt among us (and we beheld his glory, the glory as of the only begotten of the Father), full of grace and truth. (1:1–5, 14)

John is thick with symbols and incantations: light, darkness, bread, water, flesh, word. It's also full of lines that have gone into the language: 'God so loved the world, that he gave his only begotten son …'; 'Rise, take up thy bed, and walk'; 'He that is without sin among you, let him first cast a stone at her'; 'I am the good shepherd'; 'I am the resurrection, and the life'; 'The poor always ye have with you'; 'In my father's house are many mansions'; 'Greater love hath no man than this, that a man lay down his life for his friends';

'Put up thy sword into thy sheath'; 'What I have written I have written'. Part of what makes John special is that *it uses metaphors where the other Gospels use similes*. 'Destroy this temple,' Jesus tells the Jews, speaking not of their temple but his body, 'and I will raise it up' (2:19). 'Whosoever drinketh of this water shalt thirst again,' he tells the woman of Samaria by her well, 'but whosoever drinketh of the water that I shall give him shall never thirst' (3:13–14). 'I have meat to eat that ye know not of,' he tells his disciples, '… my meat is to do the will of him that sent me' (4:32–4). Or again to his disciples: 'I am the bread of life: he that cometh to me shall never hunger …' (6:35). Or again: 'I am the light of the world' (8:12). Or: 'I am the true vine, and my Father is the husbandman' (15:1).

Metaphors aren't always easy to understand. They trouble the literal-minded. Jesus causes this trouble. One of the themes of John's gospel is *the difficulty people have in communicating with one another*. Jesus's protracted metaphor about entering into a sheepfold leaves his listeners baffled: 'they understood not what things they were which he spake unto them' (10:6). Talk of the impossibility of their following him also causes confusion: 'Then said the Jews, "Will he kill himself?" Because he saith, "Whither I go, ye cannot come."' Nicodemus is perplexed by the promise of rebirth: how *can* a man be reborn, he asks, stirring Jesus into new poetry: 'Marvel not that I said unto thee, "Ye must be born again." The wind bloweth where it listeth, and thou hearest the sound thereof, but canst not tell whence it cometh, and whither it goeth: so is everyone that is born of the Spirit.' *John*'s Jesus is more seer-like than the Jesus of the other gospels: a prophet, an enigma, a stranger from heaven. He is in touch with truths that defy easy comprehension. But he's also self-aware enough to realise his listeners sometimes find him hard-going: 'I have yet many things to say unto you, but ye cannot bear them now.' He doesn't bear listening to in part because he's gnomic. Or if not gnomic, Gnostic. He speaks an alien language, the poetry of God.

John's *characterisation of Jesus* is another reason why this Gospel stands out. Far from being meek and mild, Jesus here is self-assured, pushy, and somewhat dislikeable. It may not have been the author's intention, but we see why he caused such anger and resentment, and understand his enemies' wish to have him dead and out of the way. When he's not speaking in riddles, he's argumentative. He hectors. He harangues. He throws out insults and reproaches. He pulls rank, advertising his credentials as Son of God, Son of Man, Messiah, more divine than human, just passing through: 'Ye are from beneath; I am from above: ye are of this world; I am not of this world (8:23). There is a ferocious existentialist 'I am' about him. Desperate to defeat the doubters, he is not averse to using signs to establish his authority ('Except ye see signs and wonders, ye will not believe'), which the Jesus of Mark's gospel refuses to do, implying it would be a stunt, a piece of cheap magic ('Verily I say unto you, there shall no sign be given unto this generation'). One of the greatest commentators on the fourth gospel, Rudolf Bultmann, has said that 'Jesus as the Revealer of God reveals nothing but that he is the Revealer.' If this makes him sound like some latter-day

introduction   249 cultist, prone to mystification and Me-ism, it should also be said that he's robust and resourceful, a cartoon character who keeps getting out of impossible scrapes: 'They took up stones to cast at him: but Jesus hid himself, and went out of the temple, going through the midst of them, and so passed by' (8:59). 'They sought again to take him: but he escaped out of their hand, and went away again beyond Jordan ...' (10:39–40). These escapes continue even after the crucifixion, first when Pilate's soldiers fail to carry out an order to break his legs, then when he disappears from the sepulchre in death as well as life, he constantly outwits his enemies.

The Jesus of John's Apostle is often described as mystic. But *he is worldly as well as otherworldly*. When he scourges the temple moneychangers, it's his physical strength that John emphasises: 'and when he had made a scourge of small cords, he drove them all out of the temple, and the sheep, and the oxen; and poured out the changers' money, and overthrew the tables'. There's more physical immediacy when Jesus spits on the ground, 'and made clay of the spittle', to heal a blind man. And there's Martha's pungent reaction when Jesus proposes to raise her brother Lazarus: 'Lord, by this time he stinketh: for he hath been dead four days.' However highflown some of the passages in *John*, we never lose sight of fleshly realities. Nor is there any skimping on political realities. Because the ruling powers in Palestine enjoy only limited independence from Rome, they see Jesus as a dangerous rebel, a threat to the status quo: if a popular uprising is sparked by his teaching, 'the Romans shall come and take away both our place and nation' (11:48).

John is also arguably *the most economical of the gospels*: *Mark* is shorter, with 16 chapters to *John*'s 21. But the fourth gospel includes and develops a number of episodes not to be found in the synoptic gospels: for example, the wedding feast at Cana, the raising of Lazarus, and the conversations with Nicodemus and the Woman of Samaria. As a result, its first half, up to Passover, seems to move with extraordinary speed. There is tension from the outset, with the threat to Jesus established as early as chapter 5 ('And therefore did the Jews persecute Jesus and sought to slay him') and the fact that Judas Iscariot will eventually betray him revealed in chapter 6. There's also a feeling of awful inevitability, as in Shakespearian tragedy: beauty and truth are going to pass from the earth because men love darkness rather than light. Despite the prayer and teaching threaded through it, the narrative never slackens in pace. With the crucifixion and resurrection especially, small details do the work of whole paragraphs: the sponge of vinegar put in Christ's mouth, for example, or the empty linen cloths found in his tomb. At the very end, John acknowledges the conciseness of his method: 'And there are also many other things which Jesus did, the which, if they should be written every one, I suppose that even the world itself could not contain the books that should be written.'

This is the kind of sign-off often found in fairytales and fables, gesturing at riches left out. Heresy though it is to say so, the *Gospel of John* has the quality of a fairytale. It has theological and philosophical aspirations too, of course: as one commentator, John Ashton, has put it, 'It is like finding Hans

Christian Andersen hand in hand with Soren Kierkegaard.' But in a secular age, when many people will be left cold by its more didactic passages, the narrative power of the fourth gospel is what redeems it. In Robert Browning's poem 'A Death in the Desert', a dying John foresees a day when readers will ask: 'Was John at all, and did he say he saw?' But whether John was or wasn't, his gospel is not yet redundant. Some will take it as literal truth, and others embrace its imaginative truth. But there's also what Jesus calls 'the truth [that] shall make you free' (8:32). For John, this is what matters most: the possibility that by reading his gospel we will in some way – emotionally, aesthetically, intellectually, spiritually – be liberated.

Liberation wasn't the sensation I got from it as a rustic choirboy. But re-reading it again lately, I felt a story I'd half-forgotten open up again and carry me back to the place where I first heard it. The rhythms of John's gospel can be inspiring and sensuous in that way. He is an enigmatic guide, the odd one out among the Apostles. But he's also a poet through and through.

the gospel according to st john

In the beginning was the Word, and the Word was with God, and the Word was God. [2] The same was in the beginning with God. [3] All things were made by him; and without him was not any thing made that was made. [4] In him was life; and the life was the light of men. [5] And the light shineth in darkness; and the darkness comprehended it not.

[6] There was a man sent from God, whose name was John. [7] The same came for a witness, to bear witness of the Light, that all men through him might believe. [8] He was not that Light, but was sent to bear witness of that Light. [9] That was the true Light, which lighteth every man that cometh into the world. [10] He was in the world, and the world was made by him, and the world knew him not. [11] He came unto his own, and his own received him not. [12] But as many as received him, to them gave he power to become the sons of God, even to them that believe on his name, [13] which were born, not of blood, nor of the will of the flesh, nor of the will of man, but of God. [14] And the Word was made flesh, and dwelt among us (and we beheld his glory, the glory as of the only begotten of the Father), full of grace and truth.

[15] John bare witness of him, and cried, saying, 'This was he of whom I spake, "He that cometh after me is preferred before me, for he was before me."' [16] And of his fulness have

all we received, and grace for grace. ¹⁷For the law was given by Moses, but grace and truth came by Jesus Christ. ¹⁸No man hath seen God at any time; the only begotten Son, which is in the bosom of the Father, he hath declared him.

¹⁹And this is the record of John, when the Jews sent priests and Levites from Jerusalem to ask him, 'Who art thou?' ²⁰And he confessed, and denied not; but confessed, 'I am not the Christ.' ²¹And they asked him, 'What then? Art thou Elias?' And he saith, 'I am not.' 'Art thou that prophet?' And he answered, 'No.' ²²Then said they unto him, 'Who art thou? That we may give an answer to them that sent us. What sayest thou of thyself?' ²³He said, 'I am the voice of one crying in the wilderness, "Make straight the way of the Lord,"' as said the prophet Esaias. ²⁴And they which were sent were of the Pharisees. ²⁵And they asked him, and said unto him, 'Why baptizest thou then, if thou be not that Christ, nor Elias, neither that prophet?' ²⁶John answered them, saying, 'I baptize with water, but there standeth one among you, whom ye know not. ²⁷He it is, who coming after me is preferred before me, whose shoe's latchet I am not worthy to unloose.' ²⁸These things were done in Bethabara beyond Jordan, where John was baptizing.

²⁹The next day John seeth Jesus coming unto him, and saith, 'Behold the Lamb of God, which taketh away the sin of the world. ³⁰This is he of whom I said, "After me cometh a man which is preferred before me: for he was before me." ³¹And I knew him not: but that he should be made manifest to Israel, therefore am I come baptizing with water.' ³²And John bare record, saying, 'I saw the Spirit descending from

heaven like a dove, and it abode upon him. [33]And I knew him not: but he that sent me to baptize with water, the same said unto me, "Upon whom thou shalt see the Spirit descending, and remaining on him, the same is he which baptizeth with the Holy Ghost." [34]And I saw, and bare record that this is the Son of God.'

[35]Again the next day after John stood, and two of his disciples; [36]and looking upon Jesus as he walked, he saith, 'Behold the Lamb of God!' [37]And the two disciples heard him speak, and they followed Jesus. [38]Then Jesus turned, and saw them following, and saith unto them, 'What seek ye?' They said unto him, 'Rabbi (which is to say, being interpreted, Master), where dwellest thou?' [39]He saith unto them, 'Come and see. They came and saw where he dwelt, and abode with him that day, for it was about the tenth hour.' [40]One of the two which heard John speak, and followed him, was Andrew, Simon Peter's brother. [41]He first findeth his own brother Simon, and saith unto him, 'We have found the Messias, which is, being interpreted, the Christ.' [42]And he brought him to Jesus. And when Jesus beheld him, he said, 'Thou art Simon the son of Jona: thou shalt be called Cephas, which is by interpretation, a stone.'

[43]The day following Jesus would go forth into Galilee, and findeth Philip, and saith unto him, 'Follow me.' [44]Now Philip was of Bethsaida, the city of Andrew and Peter. [45]Philip findeth Nathanael, and saith unto him, 'We have found him, of whom Moses in the law, and the prophets, did write: Jesus of Nazareth, the son of Joseph.' [46]And Nathanael said unto him, 'Can there any good thing come out of Nazareth?' Philip

saith unto him, 'Come and see.' [47] Jesus saw Nathanael coming to him, and saith of him, 'Behold an Israelite indeed, in whom is no guile!' [48] Nathanael saith unto him, 'Whence knowest thou me?' Jesus answered and said unto him, 'Before that Philip called thee, when thou wast under the fig tree, I saw thee.' [49] Nathanael answered and saith unto him, 'Rabbi, thou art the Son of God; thou art the King of Israel.' [50] Jesus answered and said unto him, 'Because I said unto thee, I saw thee under the fig tree, believest thou? Thou shalt see greater things than these.' [51] And he saith unto him, 'Verily, verily, I say unto you, hereafter ye shall see heaven open, and the angels of God ascending and descending upon the Son of man.'

2 And the third day there was a marriage in Cana of Galilee; and the mother of Jesus was there, [2] and both Jesus was called, and his disciples, to the marriage. [3] And when they wanted wine, the mother of Jesus saith unto him, 'They have no wine.' [4] Jesus saith unto her, 'Woman, what have I to do with thee? Mine hour is not yet come.' [5] His mother saith unto the servants, 'Whatsoever he saith unto you, do it.' [6] And there were set there six waterpots of stone, after the manner of the purifying of the Jews, containing two or three firkins apiece. [7] Jesus saith unto them, 'Fill the waterpots with water.' And they filled them up to the brim. [8] And he saith unto them, 'Draw out now, and bear unto the governor of the feast.' And they bare it. [9] When the ruler of the feast had tasted the water that was made wine, and knew not whence it was (but the servants which drew the water knew), the governor of the feast called the bridegroom, [10] and saith

unto him, 'Every man at the beginning doth set forth good wine; and when men have well drunk, then that which is worse: but thou hast kept the good wine until now.' ¹¹ This beginning of miracles did Jesus in Cana of Galilee, and manifested forth his glory; and his disciples believed on him.

¹²After this he went down to Capernaum, he, and his mother, and his brethren, and his disciples, and they continued there not many days.

¹³And the Jews' passover was at hand, and Jesus went up to Jerusalem, ¹⁴ and found in the temple those that sold oxen and sheep and doves, and the changers of money sitting: ¹⁵ and when he had made a scourge of small cords, he drove them all out of the temple, and the sheep, and the oxen; and poured out the changers' money, and overthrew the tables; ¹⁶ and said unto them that sold doves, 'Take these things hence; make not my Father's house an house of merchandise.' ¹⁷And his disciples remembered that it was written, 'The zeal of thine house hath eaten me up.'

¹⁸ Then answered the Jews and said unto him, 'What sign shewest thou unto us, seeing that thou doest these things?' ¹⁹ Jesus answered and said unto them, 'Destroy this temple, and in three days I will raise it up.' ²⁰ Then said the Jews, 'Forty and six years was this temple in building, and wilt thou rear it up in three days?' ²¹ But he spake of the temple of his body. ²² When therefore he was risen from the dead, his disciples remembered that he had said this unto them; and they believed the scripture, and the word which Jesus had said.

²³ Now when he was in Jerusalem at the passover, in the feast day, many believed in his name, when they saw the

miracles which he did. ²⁴But Jesus did not commit himself unto them, because he knew all men, ²⁵and needed not that any should testify of man, for he knew what was in man.

3 There was a man of the Pharisees, named Nicodemus, a ruler of the Jews. ²The same came to Jesus by night, and said unto him, 'Rabbi, we know that thou art a teacher come from God, for no man can do these miracles that thou doest, except God be with him.' ³Jesus answered and said unto him, 'Verily, verily, I say unto thee, except a man be born again, he cannot see the kingdom of God.' ⁴Nicodemus saith unto him, 'How can a man be born when he is old? Can he enter the second time into his mother's womb, and be born?' ⁵Jesus answered, 'Verily, verily, I say unto thee, except a man be born of water and of the Spirit, he cannot enter into the kingdom of God. ⁶That which is born of the flesh is flesh; and that which is born of the Spirit is spirit. ⁷Marvel not that I said unto thee, ye must be born again.' ⁸The wind bloweth where it listeth, and thou hearest the sound thereof, but canst not tell whence it cometh, and whither it goeth: so is every one that is born of the Spirit.' ⁹Nicodemus answered and said unto him, 'How can these things be?' ¹⁰Jesus answered and said unto him, 'Art thou a master of Israel, and knowest not these things? ¹¹Verily, verily, I say unto thee, we speak that we do know, and testify that we have seen; and ye receive not our witness. ¹²If I have told you earthly things, and ye believe not, how shall ye believe, if I tell you of heavenly things? ¹³And no man hath ascended up to heaven, but he that came down from heaven, even the Son of man which is in heaven.

¹⁴ 'And as Moses lifted up the serpent in the wilderness, even so must the Son of man be lifted up: ¹⁵ that whosoever believeth in him should not perish, but have eternal life.

¹⁶ 'For God so loved the world, that he gave his only begotten Son, that whosoever believeth in him should not perish, but have everlasting life. ¹⁷ For God sent not his Son into the world to condemn the world; but that the world through him might be saved.

¹⁸ 'He that believeth on him is not condemned: but he that believeth not is condemned already, because he hath not believed in the name of the only begotten Son of God. ¹⁹ And this is the condemnation, that light is come into the world, and men loved darkness rather than light, because their deeds were evil. ²⁰ For every one that doeth evil hateth the light, neither cometh to the light, lest his deeds should be reproved. ²¹ But he that doeth truth cometh to the light, that his deeds may be made manifest, that they are wrought in God.'

²² After these things came Jesus and his disciples into the land of Judæa; and there he tarried with them, and baptized.

²³ And John also was baptizing in Ænon near to Salim, because there was much water there, and they came, and were baptized. ²⁴ For John was not yet cast into prison.

²⁵ Then there arose a question between some of John's disciples and the Jews about purifying. ²⁶ And they came unto John, and said unto him, 'Rabbi, he that was with thee beyond Jordan, to whom thou barest witness, behold, the same baptizeth, and all men come to him.' ²⁷ John answered and said, 'A man can receive nothing, except it be given him from heaven. ²⁸ Ye yourselves bear me witness, that I said, "I am

not the Christ," but that I am sent before him. ²⁹ He that hath the bride is the bridegroom, but the friend of the bridegroom, which standeth and heareth him, rejoiceth greatly because of the bridegroom's voice: this my joy therefore is fulfilled. ³⁰ He must increase, but I must decrease. ³¹ He that cometh from above is above all; he that is of the earth is earthly, and speaketh of the earth; he that cometh from heaven is above all. ³² And what he hath seen and heard, that he testifieth; and no man receiveth his testimony. ³³ He that hath received his testimony hath set to his seal that God is true. ³⁴ For he whom God hath sent speaketh the words of God, for God giveth not the Spirit by measure unto him. ³⁵ The Father loveth the Son, and hath given all things into his hand. ³⁶ He that believeth on the Son hath everlasting life, and he that believeth not the Son shall not see life; but the wrath of God abideth on him.'

4 When therefore the Lord knew how the Pharisees had heard that Jesus made and baptized more disciples than John ²(though Jesus himself baptized not, but his disciples), ³ he left Judæa, and departed again into Galilee. ⁴ And he must needs go through Samaria. ⁵ Then cometh he to a city of Samaria, which is called Sychar, near to the parcel of ground that Jacob gave to his son Joseph. ⁶ Now Jacob's well was there. Jesus therefore, being wearied with his journey, sat thus on the well, and it was about the sixth hour. ⁷ There cometh a woman of Samaria to draw water. Jesus saith unto her, 'Give me to drink.' ⁸(For his disciples were gone away unto the city to buy meat.) ⁹ Then saith the woman of Samaria unto him,

'How is it that thou, being a Jew, askest drink of me, which am a woman of Samaria?' For the Jews have no dealings with the Samaritans. ¹⁰ Jesus answered and said unto her, 'If thou knewest the gift of God, and who it is that saith to thee, "Give me to drink," thou wouldest have asked of him, and he would have given thee living water.' ¹¹ The woman saith unto him, 'Sir, thou hast nothing to draw with, and the well is deep; from whence then hast thou that living water? ¹² Art thou greater than our father Jacob, which gave us the well, and drank thereof himself, and his children, and his cattle?' ¹³ Jesus answered and said unto her, 'Whosoever drinketh of this water shall thirst again: ¹⁴ but whosoever drinketh of the water that I shall give him shall never thirst; but the water that I shall give him shall be in him a well of water springing up into everlasting life.' ¹⁵ The woman saith unto him, 'Sir, give me this water, that I thirst not, neither come hither to draw.' ¹⁶ Jesus saith unto her, 'Go, call thy husband, and come hither.' ¹⁷ The woman answered and said, 'I have no husband.' Jesus said unto her, 'Thou hast well said, "I have no husband," ¹⁸ for thou hast had five husbands; and he whom thou now hast is not thy husband; in that saidst thou truly.' ¹⁹ The woman saith unto him, 'Sir, I perceive that thou art a prophet. ²⁰ Our fathers worshipped in this mountain; and ye say, that in Jerusalem is the place where men ought to worship.' ²¹ Jesus saith unto her, 'Woman, believe me, the hour cometh, when ye shall neither in this mountain, nor yet at Jerusalem, worship the Father. ²² Ye worship ye know not what: we know what we worship, for salvation is of the Jews. ²³ But the hour cometh, and now is, when the true worshippers shall worship the Father in spirit and in truth, for the Father seeketh such to worship him. ²⁴God is a Spirit, and they that worship him must worship him in spirit and in truth.' ²⁵The woman saith unto him, 'I know that Messias cometh, which is called Christ: when he is come, he will tell us all things.' ²⁶Jesus saith unto her, 'I that speak unto thee am he.'

²⁷And upon this came his disciples, and marvelled that he talked with the woman; yet no man said, 'What seekest thou?' or 'Why talkest thou with her?' ²⁸The woman then left her waterpot, and went her way into the city, and saith to the men, ²⁹'Come, see a man, which told me all things that ever I did: is not this the Christ?' ³⁰Then they went out of the city, and came unto him.

³¹In the mean while his disciples prayed him, saying, 'Master, eat.' ³²But he said unto them, 'I have meat to eat that ye know not of.' ³³Therefore said the disciples one to another, 'Hath any man brought him ought to eat?' ³⁴Jesus saith unto them, 'My meat is to do the will of him that sent me, and to finish his work. ³⁵Say not ye, "There are yet four months, and then cometh harvest"? Behold, I say unto you, lift up your eyes, and look on the fields: for they are white already to harvest. ³⁶And he that reapeth receiveth wages, and gathereth fruit unto life eternal, that both he that soweth and he that reapeth may rejoice together. ³⁷And herein is that saying true, "One soweth, and another reapeth." ³⁸I sent you to reap that whereon ye bestowed no labour; other men laboured, and ye are entered into their labours.'

³⁹And many of the Samaritans of that city believed on him for the saying of the woman, which testified, 'He told

me all that ever I did.' ⁴⁰ So when the Samaritans were come unto him, they besought him that he would tarry with them, and he abode there two days. ⁴¹And many more believed because of his own word; ⁴²and said unto the woman, 'Now we believe, not because of thy saying, for we have heard him ourselves, and know that this is indeed the Christ, the Saviour of the world.'

⁴³ Now after two days he departed thence, and went into Galilee. ⁴⁴ For Jesus himself testified that a prophet hath no honour in his own country. ⁴⁵ Then when he was come into Galilee, the Galilæans received him, having seen all the things that he did at Jerusalem at the feast, for they also went unto the feast. ⁴⁶ So Jesus came again into Cana of Galilee, where he made the water wine. And there was a certain nobleman, whose son was sick at Capernaum. ⁴⁷ When he heard that Jesus was come out of Judæa into Galilee, he went unto him, and besought him that he would come down, and heal his son, for he was at the point of death. ⁴⁸ Then said Jesus unto him, 'Except ye see signs and wonders, ye will not believe.' ⁴⁹ The nobleman saith unto him, 'Sir, come down ere my child die.' ⁵⁰ Jesus saith unto him, 'Go thy way; thy son liveth.' And the man believed the word that Jesus had spoken unto him, and he went his way. ⁵¹And as he was now going down, his servants met him, and told him, saying, 'Thy son liveth.' ⁵² Then enquired he of them the hour when he began to amend. And they said unto him, 'Yesterday at the seventh hour the fever left him.' ⁵³ So the father knew that it was at the same hour, in the which Jesus said unto him, 'Thy son liveth,' and himself believed, and his

whole house. ⁵⁴This is again the second miracle that Jesus did, when he was come out of Judæa into Galilee.

5 After this there was a feast of the Jews; and Jesus went up to Jerusalem. ²Now there is at Jerusalem by the sheep market a pool, which is called in the Hebrew tongue Bethesda, having five porches. ³In these lay a great multitude of impotent folk, of blind, halt, withered, waiting for the moving of the water. ⁴For an angel went down at a certain season into the pool, and troubled the water: whosoever then first after the troubling of the water stepped in was made whole of whatsoever disease he had. ⁵And a certain man was there, which had an infirmity thirty and eight years. ⁶When Jesus saw him lie, and knew that he had been now a long time in that case, he saith unto him, 'Wilt thou be made whole?' ⁷The impotent man answered him, 'Sir, I have no man, when the water is troubled, to put me into the pool: but while I am coming, another steppeth down before me.' ⁸Jesus saith unto him, 'Rise, take up thy bed, and walk.' ⁹And immediately the man was made whole, and took up his bed, and walked; and on the same day was the sabbath.

¹⁰The Jews therefore said unto him that was cured, 'It is the sabbath day: it is not lawful for thee to carry thy bed.' ¹¹He answered them, 'He that made me whole, the same said unto me, "Take up thy bed, and walk."' ¹²Then asked they him, 'What man is that which said unto thee, "Take up thy bed, and walk?"' ¹³And he that was healed wist not who it was, for Jesus had conveyed himself away, a multitude being in that place. ¹⁴Afterward Jesus findeth him in the temple,

and said unto him, 'Behold, thou art made whole; sin no more, lest a worse thing come unto thee.' ¹⁵ The man departed, and told the Jews that it was Jesus, which had made him whole. ¹⁶ And therefore did the Jews persecute Jesus, and sought to slay him, because he had done these things on the sabbath day.

¹⁷ But Jesus answered them, 'My Father worketh hitherto, and I work.' ¹⁸ Therefore the Jews sought the more to kill him, because he not only had broken the sabbath, but said also that God was his Father, making himself equal with God. ¹⁹ Then answered Jesus and said unto them, 'Verily, verily, I say unto you, the Son can do nothing of himself, but what he seeth the Father do: for what things soever he doeth, these also doeth the Son likewise. ²⁰ For the Father loveth the Son, and sheweth him all things that himself doeth, and he will shew him greater works than these, that ye may marvel. ²¹ For as the Father raiseth up the dead, and quickeneth them; even so the Son quickeneth whom he will. ²² For the Father judgeth no man, but hath committed all judgment unto the Son, ²³ that all men should honour the Son, even as they honour the Father. He that honoureth not the Son honoureth not the Father which hath sent him. ²⁴ Verily, verily, I say unto you, he that heareth my word, and believeth on him that sent me, hath everlasting life, and shall not come into condemnation; but is passed from death unto life. ²⁵ Verily, verily, I say unto you, the hour is coming, and now is, when the dead shall hear the voice of the Son of God, and they that hear shall live. ²⁶ For as the Father hath life in himself; so hath he given to the Son to have life in himself; ²⁷ and hath

given him authority to execute judgment also, because he is the Son of man. ²⁸Marvel not at this, for the hour is coming, in the which all that are in the graves shall hear his voice, ²⁹and shall come forth; they that have done good, unto the resurrection of life; and they that have done evil, unto the resurrection of damnation. ³⁰I can of mine own self do nothing: as I hear, I judge, and my judgment is just; because I seek not mine own will, but the will of the Father which hath sent me. ³¹If I bear witness of myself, my witness is not true.

³²'There is another that beareth witness of me; and I know that the witness which he witnesseth of me is true. ³³Ye sent unto John, and he bare witness unto the truth. ³⁴But I receive not testimony from man: but these things I say, that ye might be saved. ³⁵He was a burning and a shining light, and ye were willing for a season to rejoice in his light.

³⁶'But I have greater witness than that of John: for the works which the Father hath given me to finish, the same works that I do, bear witness of me, that the Father hath sent me. ³⁷And the Father himself, which hath sent me, hath borne witness of me. Ye have neither heard his voice at any time, nor seen his shape. ³⁸And ye have not his word abiding in you: for whom he hath sent, him ye believe not.

³⁹'Search the scriptures, for in them ye think ye have eternal life: and they are they which testify of me. ⁴⁰And ye will not come to me, that ye might have life. ⁴¹I receive not honour from men. ⁴²But I know you, that ye have not the love of God in you. ⁴³I am come in my Father's name, and ye receive me not; if another shall come in his own name, him ye will receive. ⁴⁴How can ye believe, which receive honour one of

another, and seek not the honour that cometh from God only? ⁴⁵ Do not think that I will accuse you to the Father: there is one that accuseth you, even Moses, in whom ye trust. ⁴⁶ For had ye believed Moses, ye would have believed me: for he wrote of me. ⁴⁷ But if ye believe not his writings, how shall ye believe my words?'

6 After these things Jesus went over the sea of Galilee, which is the sea of Tiberias. ²And a great multitude followed him, because they saw his miracles which he did on them that were diseased. ³And Jesus went up into a mountain, and there he sat with his disciples. ⁴And the passover, a feast of the Jews, was nigh.

⁵ When Jesus then lifted up his eyes, and saw a great company come unto him, he saith unto Philip, 'Whence shall we buy bread, that these may eat?' ⁶And this he said to prove him, for he himself knew what he would do. ⁷Philip answered him, 'Two hundred pennyworth of bread is not sufficient for them, that every one of them may take a little.' ⁸One of his disciples, Andrew, Simon Peter's brother, saith unto him, ⁹ 'There is a lad here, which hath five barley loaves, and two small fishes, but what are they among so many?' ¹⁰And Jesus said, 'Make the men sit down.' Now there was much grass in the place. So the men sat down, in number about five thousand. ¹¹And Jesus took the loaves; and when he had given thanks, he distributed to the disciples, and the disciples to them that were set down; and likewise of the fishes as much as they would. ¹²When they were filled, he said unto his disciples, 'Gather up the fragments that remain, that nothing be

lost.' ¹³ Therefore they gathered them together, and filled twelve baskets with the fragments of the five barley loaves, which remained over and above unto them that had eaten. ¹⁴ Then those men, when they had seen the miracle that Jesus did, said, 'This is of a truth that prophet that should come into the world.'

¹⁵ When Jesus therefore perceived that they would come and take him by force, to make him a king, he departed again into a mountain himself alone. ¹⁶ And when even was now come, his disciples went down unto the sea, ¹⁷ and entered into a ship, and went over the sea toward Capernaum. And it was now dark, and Jesus was not come to them. ¹⁸ And the sea arose by reason of a great wind that blew. ¹⁹ So when they had rowed about five and twenty or thirty furlongs, they see Jesus walking on the sea, and drawing nigh unto the ship, and they were afraid. ²⁰ But he saith unto them, 'It is I; be not afraid.' ²¹ Then they willingly received him into the ship, and immediately the ship was at the land whither they went.

²² The day following, when the people which stood on the other side of the sea saw that there was none other boat there, save that one whereinto his disciples were entered, and that Jesus went not with his disciples into the boat, but that his disciples were gone away alone. ²³ (Howbeit there came other boats from Tiberias nigh unto the place where they did eat bread, after that the Lord had given thanks.) ²⁴ When the people therefore saw that Jesus was not there, neither his disciples, they also took shipping, and came to Capernaum, seeking for Jesus. ²⁵ And when they had found him on the other side of the sea, they said unto him, 'Rabbi,

when camest thou hither?' ²⁶ Jesus answered them and said, 'Verily, verily, I say unto you, ye seek me, not because ye saw the miracles, but because ye did eat of the loaves, and were filled. ²⁷ Labour not for the meat which perisheth, but for that meat which endureth unto everlasting life, which the Son of man shall give unto you: for him hath God the Father sealed.' ²⁸ Then said they unto him, 'What shall we do, that we might work the works of God?' ²⁹ Jesus answered and said unto them, 'This is the work of God, that ye believe on him whom he hath sent.' ³⁰ They said therefore unto him, 'What sign shewest thou then, that we may see, and believe thee? What dost thou work? ³¹ Our fathers did eat manna in the desert; as it is written, "He gave them bread from heaven to eat."' ³² Then Jesus said unto them, 'Verily, verily, I say unto you, Moses gave you not that bread from heaven; but my Father giveth you the true bread from heaven. ³³ For the bread of God is he which cometh down from heaven, and giveth life unto the world.' ³⁴ Then said they unto him, 'Lord, evermore give us this bread.' ³⁵ And Jesus said unto them, 'I am the bread of life: he that cometh to me shall never hunger; and he that believeth on me shall never thirst. ³⁶ But I said unto you that ye also have seen me, and believe not. ³⁷ All that the Father giveth me shall come to me; and him that cometh to me I will in no wise cast out. ³⁸ For I came down from heaven, not to do mine own will, but the will of him that sent me. ³⁹ And this is the Father's will which hath sent me: that of all which he hath given me I should lose nothing, but should raise it up again at the last day. ⁴⁰ And this is the will of him that sent me: that every one which seeth the Son, and believeth on him, may have everlasting life, and I will raise him up at the last day.' ⁴¹The Jews then murmured at him, because he said, 'I am the bread which came down from heaven.' ⁴²And they said, 'Is not this Jesus, the son of Joseph, whose father and mother we know? How is it then that he saith, "I came down from heaven"?' ⁴³Jesus therefore answered and said unto them, 'Murmur not among yourselves. ⁴⁴No man can come to me, except the Father which hath sent me draw him, and I will raise him up at the last day. ⁴⁵It is written in the prophets, "And they shall be all taught of God." Every man therefore that hath heard, and hath learned of the Father, cometh unto me. ⁴⁶Not that any man hath seen the Father, save he which is of God, he hath seen the Father. ⁴⁷Verily, verily, I say unto you, he that believeth on me hath everlasting life. ⁴⁸I am that bread of life. ⁴⁹Your fathers did eat manna in the wilderness, and are dead. ⁵⁰This is the bread which cometh down from heaven, that a man may eat thereof, and not die. ⁵¹I am the living bread which came down from heaven: if any man eat of this bread, he shall live for ever; and the bread that I will give is my flesh, which I will give for the life of the world.' ⁵²The Jews therefore strove among themselves, saying, 'How can this man give us his flesh to eat?' ⁵³Then Jesus said unto them, 'Verily, verily, I say unto you, except ye eat the flesh of the Son of man, and drink his blood, ye have no life in you. ⁵⁴Whoso eateth my flesh, and drinketh my blood, hath eternal life; and I will raise him up at the last day. ⁵⁵For my flesh is meat indeed, and my blood is drink indeed. ⁵⁶He that eateth my flesh, and drinketh my blood, dwelleth in me, and I in him. ⁵⁷As the living Father hath sent me, and I live by the Father, so he that eateth me, even he shall live by me. ⁵⁸ This is that bread which came down from heaven: not as your fathers did eat manna, and are dead. He that eateth of this bread shall live for ever.' ⁵⁹ These things said he in the synagogue, as he taught in Capernaum. ⁶⁰ Many therefore of his disciples, when they had heard this, said, 'This is an hard saying; who can hear it?' ⁶¹ When Jesus knew in himself that his disciples murmured at it, he said unto them, 'Doth this offend you? ⁶² What and if ye shall see the Son of man ascend up where he was before? ⁶³ It is the spirit that quickeneth; the flesh profiteth nothing; the words that I speak unto you, they are spirit, and they are life. ⁶⁴ But there are some of you that believe not.' For Jesus knew from the beginning who they were that believed not, and who should betray him. ⁶⁵ And he said, 'Therefore said I unto you, that no man can come unto me, except it were given unto him of my Father.'

⁶⁶ From that time many of his disciples went back, and walked no more with him. ⁶⁷ Then said Jesus unto the twelve, 'Will ye also go away?' ⁶⁸ Then Simon Peter answered him, 'Lord, to whom shall we go? Thou hast the words of eternal life. ⁶⁹ And we believe and are sure that thou art that Christ, the Son of the living God.' ⁷⁰ Jesus answered them, 'Have not I chosen you twelve, and one of you is a devil?' ⁷¹ He spake of Judas Iscariot the son of Simon: for he it was that should betray him, being one of the twelve.

7 After these things Jesus walked in Galilee: for he would not walk in Jewry, because the Jews sought to kill him.

²Now the Jews' feast of tabernacles was at hand. ³His brethren therefore said unto him, 'Depart hence, and go into Judæa, that thy disciples also may see the works that thou doest. ⁴For there is no man that doeth any thing in secret, and he himself seeketh to be known openly. If thou do these things, shew thyself to the world.' ⁵For neither did his brethren believe in him. ⁶Then Jesus said unto them, 'My time is not yet come, but your time is alway ready. ⁷The world cannot hate you; but me it hateth, because I testify of it, that the works thereof are evil. ⁸Go ye up unto this feast. I go not up yet unto this feast; for my time is not yet full come.' ⁹When he had said these words unto them, he abode still in Galilee.

¹⁰But when his brethren were gone up, then went he also up unto the feast, not openly, but as it were in secret. ¹¹Then the Jews sought him at the feast, and said, 'Where is he?' ¹²And there was much murmuring among the people concerning him, for some said, 'He is a good man,' others said, 'Nay; but he deceiveth the people.' ¹³Howbeit no man spake openly of him for fear of the Jews.

¹⁴Now about the midst of the feast Jesus went up into the temple, and taught. ¹⁵And the Jews marvelled, saying, 'How knoweth this man letters, having never learned?' ¹⁶Jesus answered them, and said, 'My doctrine is not mine, but his that sent me. ¹⁷If any man will do his will, he shall know of the doctrine, whether it be of God, or whether I speak of myself. ¹⁸He that speaketh of himself seeketh his own glory: but he that seeketh his glory that sent him, the same is true, and no unrighteousness is in him. ¹⁹Did not Moses give you the law, and yet none of you keepeth the law? Why go ye

about to kill me?' ²⁰ The people answered and said, 'Thou hast a devil. Who goeth about to kill thee?' ²¹ Jesus answered and said unto them, 'I have done one work, and ye all marvel. ²² Moses therefore gave unto you circumcision (not because it is of Moses, but of the fathers), and ye on the sabbath day circumcise a man. ²³ If a man on the sabbath day receive circumcision, that the law of Moses should not be broken; are ye angry at me, because I have made a man every whit whole on the sabbath day? ²⁴ Judge not according to the appearance, but judge righteous judgment.' ²⁵ Then said some of them of Jerusalem, 'Is not this he, whom they seek to kill? ²⁶ But, lo, he speaketh boldly, and they say nothing unto him. Do the rulers know indeed that this is the very Christ? ²⁷ Howbeit we know this man whence he is, but when Christ cometh, no man knoweth whence he is.' ²⁸ Then cried Jesus in the temple as he taught, saying, 'Ye both know me, and ye know whence I am; and I am not come of myself, but he that sent me is true, whom ye know not. ²⁹ But I know him, for I am from him, and he hath sent me.' ³⁰ Then they sought to take him: but no man laid hands on him, because his hour was not yet come. ³¹ And many of the people believed on him, and said, 'When Christ cometh, will he do more miracles than these which this man hath done?'

³² The Pharisees heard that the people murmured such things concerning him; and the Pharisees and the chief priests sent officers to take him. ³³ Then said Jesus unto them, 'Yet a little while am I with you, and then I go unto him that sent me. ³⁴ Ye shall seek me, and shall not find me, and where I am, thither ye cannot come.' ³⁵ Then said the Jews among

themselves, 'Whither will he go, that we shall not find him? Will he go unto the dispersed among the Gentiles, and teach the Gentiles? ³⁶What manner of saying is this that he said, "Ye shall seek me, and shall not find me, and where I am, thither ye cannot come"?' ³⁷In the last day, that great day of the feast, Jesus stood and cried, saying, 'If any man thirst, let him come unto me, and drink. ³⁸He that believeth on me, as the scripture hath said, out of his belly shall flow rivers of living water.' ³⁹(But this spake he of the Spirit, which they that believe on him should receive: for the Holy Ghost was not yet given; because that Jesus was not yet glorified.)

⁴⁰Many of the people therefore, when they heard this saying, said, 'Of a truth this is the Prophet.' ⁴¹Others said, 'This is the Christ.' But some said, 'Shall Christ come out of Galilee? ⁴²Hath not the scripture said that Christ cometh of the seed of David, and out of the town of Bethlehem, where David was?' ⁴³So there was a division among the people because of him. ⁴⁴And some of them would have taken him; but no man laid hands on him.

⁴⁵Then came the officers to the chief priests and Pharisees; and they said unto them, 'Why have ye not brought him?' ⁴⁶The officers answered, 'Never man spake like this man.' ⁴⁷Then answered them the Pharisees, 'Are ye also deceived? ⁴⁸Have any of the rulers or of the Pharisees believed on him? ⁴⁹But this people who knoweth not the law are cursed.' ⁵⁰Nicodemus saith unto them (he that came to Jesus by night, being one of them), ⁵¹'Doth our law judge any man, before it hear him, and know what he doeth?' ⁵²They answered and said unto him, 'Art thou also of Galilee? Search, and look: for

out of Galilee ariseth no prophet.' ⁵³And every man went unto his own house.

8 Jesus went unto the mount of Olives. ²And early in the morning he came again into the temple, and all the people came unto him; and he sat down, and taught them. ³And the scribes and Pharisees brought unto him a woman taken in adultery; and when they had set her in the midst, ⁴they say unto him, 'Master, this woman was taken in adultery, in the very act. ⁵Now Moses in the law commanded us, that such should be stoned, but what sayest thou?' ⁶This they said, tempting him, that they might have to accuse him. But Jesus stooped down, and with his finger wrote on the ground, as though he heard them not. ⁷So when they continued asking him, he lifted up himself, and said unto them, 'He that is without sin among you, let him first cast a stone at her.' ⁸And again he stooped down, and wrote on the ground. ⁹And they which heard it, being convicted by their own conscience, went out one by one, beginning at the eldest, even unto the last, and Jesus was left alone, and the woman standing in the midst. ¹⁰When Jesus had lifted up himself, and saw none but the woman, he said unto her, 'Woman, where are those thine accusers? Hath no man condemned thee?' ¹¹She said, 'No man, Lord.' And Jesus said unto her, 'Neither do I condemn thee: go, and sin no more.'

¹²Then spake Jesus again unto them, saying, 'I am the light of the world: he that followeth me shall not walk in darkness, but shall have the light of life.' ¹³The Pharisees therefore said unto him, 'Thou bearest record of thyself; thy

record is not true.' ¹⁴Jesus answered and said unto them, 'Though I bear record of myself, yet my record is true, for I know whence I came, and whither I go; but ye cannot tell whence I come, and whither I go. ¹⁵Ye judge after the flesh; I judge no man. ¹⁶And yet if I judge, my judgment is true, for I am not alone, but I and the Father that sent me. ¹⁷It is also written in your law, that the testimony of two men is true. ¹⁸I am one that bear witness of myself, and the Father that sent me beareth witness of me.' ¹⁹Then said they unto him, 'Where is thy Father?' Jesus answered, 'Ye neither know me, nor my Father. If ye had known me, ye should have known my Father also.' ²⁰These words spake Jesus in the treasury, as he taught in the temple, and no man laid hands on him; for his hour was not yet come. ²¹Then said Jesus again unto them, 'I go my way, and ye shall seek me, and shall die in your sins. Whither I go, ye cannot come.' ²²Then said the Jews, 'Will he kill himself?' because he saith, 'Whither I go, ye cannot come.' ²³And he said unto them, 'Ye are from beneath; I am from above: ye are of this world; I am not of this world. ²⁴I said therefore unto you, that ye shall die in your sins: for if ye believe not that I am he, ye shall die in your sins.' ²⁵Then said they unto him, 'Who art thou?' And Jesus saith unto them, 'Even the same that I said unto you from the beginning. ²⁶I have many things to say and to judge of you, but he that sent me is true; and I speak to the world those things which I have heard of him.' ²⁷They understood not that he spake to them of the Father. ²⁸Then said Jesus unto them, 'When ye have lifted up the Son of man, then shall ye know that I am he, and that I do nothing of myself; but as my Father hath taught me, I speak these things. ²⁹And he that sent me is with me: the Father hath not left me alone, for I do always those things that please him.' ³⁰As he spake these words, many believed on him. ³¹Then said Jesus to those Jews which believed on him, 'If ye continue in my word, then are ye my disciples indeed; ³²and ye shall know the truth, and the truth shall make you free.'

³³They answered him, 'We be Abraham's seed, and were never in bondage to any man. How sayest thou, "Ye shall be made free"?' ³⁴Jesus answered them, 'Verily, verily, I say unto you, whosoever committeth sin is the servant of sin. ³⁵And the servant abideth not in the house for ever, but the Son abideth ever. ³⁶If the Son therefore shall make you free, ye shall be free indeed. ³⁷I know that ye are Abraham's seed; but ye seek to kill me, because my word hath no place in you. ³⁸I speak that which I have seen with my Father, and ye do that which ye have seen with your father.' ³⁹They answered and said unto him, 'Abraham is our father.' Jesus saith unto them, 'If ye were Abraham's children, ye would do the works of Abraham. ⁴⁰But now ye seek to kill me, a man that hath told you the truth, which I have heard of God: this did not Abraham. ⁴¹Ye do the deeds of your father.' Then said they to him, 'We be not born of fornication; we have one Father, even God.' ⁴²Jesus said unto them, 'If God were your Father, ye would love me: for I proceeded forth and came from God; neither came I of myself, but he sent me. ⁴³Why do ye not understand my speech? Even because ye cannot hear my word. ⁴⁴Ye are of your father the devil, and the lusts of your father ye will do. He was a murderer from the beginning,

and abode not in the truth, because there is no truth in him. When he speaketh a lie, he speaketh of his own: for he is a liar, and the father of it. ⁴⁵And because I tell you the truth, ye believe me not. ⁴⁶Which of you convinceth me of sin? And if I say the truth, why do ye not believe me? ⁴⁷He that is of God heareth God's words: ye therefore hear them not, because ye are not of God.' ⁴⁸Then answered the Jews, and said unto him, 'Say we not well that thou art a Samaritan, and hast a devil?' ⁴⁹Jesus answered, 'I have not a devil; but I honour my Father, and ye do dishonour me. ⁵⁰And I seek not mine own glory: there is one that seeketh and judgeth. ⁵¹Verily, verily, I say unto you, if a man keep my saying, he shall never see death.' ⁵²Then said the Jews unto him, 'Now we know that thou hast a devil. Abraham is dead, and the prophets; and thou sayest, "If a man keep my saying, he shall never taste of death." ⁵³Art thou greater than our father Abraham, which is dead? And the prophets are dead. Whom makest thou thyself?' ⁵⁴Jesus answered, 'If I honour myself, my honour is nothing: it is my Father that honoureth me; of whom ye say, that he is your God; ⁵⁵yet ye have not known him; but I know him, and if I should say, "I know him not" I shall be a liar like unto you; but I know him, and keep his saying. ⁵⁶Your father Abraham rejoiced to see my day, and he saw it, and was glad.' ⁵⁷Then said the Jews unto him, 'Thou art not yet fifty years old, and hast thou seen Abraham?' ⁵⁸Jesus said unto them, 'Verily, verily, I say unto you, before Abraham was, I am.' ⁵⁹Then took they up stones to cast at him: but Jesus hid himself, and went out of the temple, going through the midst of them, and so passed by.

9 And as Jesus passed by, he saw a man which was blind from his birth. ²And his disciples asked him, saying, 'Master, who did sin, this man, or his parents, that he was born blind?' ³Jesus answered, 'Neither hath this man sinned, nor his parents, but that the works of God should be made manifest in him. ⁴I must work the works of him that sent me, while it is day; the night cometh, when no man can work. ⁵As long as I am in the world, I am the light of the world.' ⁶When he had thus spoken, he spat on the ground, and made clay of the spittle, and he anointed the eyes of the blind man with the clay, ⁷and said unto him, 'Go, wash in the pool of Siloam' (which is by interpretation, Sent). He went his way therefore, and washed, and came seeing.

⁸The neighbours therefore, and they which before had seen him that he was blind, said, 'Is not this he that sat and begged?' ⁹Some said, 'This is he,' others said, 'He is like him,' but he said, 'I am he.' ¹⁰Therefore said they unto him, 'How were thine eyes opened?' ¹¹He answered and said, 'A man that is called Jesus made clay, and anointed mine eyes, and said unto me, "Go to the pool of Siloam, and wash," and I went and washed, and I received sight.' ¹²Then said they unto him, 'Where is he?' He said, 'I know not.'

¹³They brought to the Pharisees him that aforetime was blind. ¹⁴And it was the sabbath day when Jesus made the clay, and opened his eyes. ¹⁵Then again the Pharisees also asked him how he had received his sight. He said unto them, 'He put clay upon mine eyes, and I washed, and do see.' ¹⁶Therefore said some of the Pharisees, 'This man is not of God, because he keepeth not the sabbath day.' Others said, 'How

can a man that is a sinner do such miracles?' And there was a division among them. [17] They say unto the blind man again, 'What sayest thou of him, that he hath opened thine eyes?' He said, 'He is a prophet.' [18] But the Jews did not believe concerning him, that he had been blind, and received his sight, until they called the parents of him that had received his sight. [19] And they asked them, saying, 'Is this your son, who ye say was born blind? How then doth he now see?' [20] His parents answered them and said, 'We know that this is our son, and that he was born blind [21] but by what means he now seeth, we know not; or who hath opened his eyes, we know not. He is of age; ask him: he shall speak for himself.' [22] These words spake his parents, because they feared the Jews: for the Jews had agreed already, that if any man did confess that he was Christ, he should be put out of the synagogue. [23] Therefore said his parents, 'He is of age; ask him.' [24] Then again called they the man that was blind, and said unto him, 'Give God the praise; we know that this man is a sinner.' [25] He answered and said, 'Whether he be a sinner or no, I know not; one thing I know, that, whereas I was blind, now I see.' [26] Then said they to him again, 'What did he to thee? How opened he thine eyes?' [27] He answered them, 'I have told you already, and ye did not hear: wherefore would ye hear it again? Will ye also be his disciples?' [28] Then they reviled him, and said, 'Thou art his disciple; but we are Moses' disciples. [29] We know that God spake unto Moses; as for this fellow, we know not from whence he is.' [30] The man answered and said unto them, 'Why herein is a marvellous thing, that ye know not from whence he is, and yet he hath opened mine eyes. ³¹Now we know that God heareth not sinners, but if any man be a worshipper of God, and doeth his will, him he heareth. ³²Since the world began was it not heard that any man opened the eyes of one that was born blind. ³³If this man were not of God, he could do nothing.' ³⁴They answered and said unto him, 'Thou wast altogether born in sins, and dost thou teach us?' And they cast him out. ³⁵Jesus heard that they had cast him out; and when he had found him, he said unto him, 'Dost thou believe on the Son of God?' ³⁶He answered and said, 'Who is he, Lord, that I might believe on him?' ³⁷And Jesus said unto him, 'Thou hast both seen him, and it is he that talketh with thee.' ³⁸And he said, 'Lord, I believe.' And he worshipped him.

³⁹And Jesus said, 'For judgment I am come into this world, that they which see not might see; and that they which see might be made blind.' ⁴⁰And some of the Pharisees which were with him heard these words, and said unto him, 'Are we blind also?' ⁴¹Jesus said unto them, 'If ye were blind, ye should have no sin, but now ye say, "We see"; therefore your sin remaineth.'

10 'Verily, verily, I say unto you, he that entereth not by the door into the sheepfold, but climbeth up some other way, the same is a thief and a robber. ²But he that entereth in by the door is the shepherd of the sheep. ³To him the porter openeth; and the sheep hear his voice, and he calleth his own sheep by name, and leadeth them out. ⁴And when he putteth forth his own sheep, he goeth before them, and the sheep follow him, for they know his voice. ⁵And a stranger

will they not follow, but will flee from him, for they know not the voice of strangers.' ⁶ This parable spake Jesus unto them, but they understood not what things they were which he spake unto them. ⁷ Then said Jesus unto them again, 'Verily, verily, I say unto you, I am the door of the sheep. ⁸ All that ever came before me are thieves and robbers, but the sheep did not hear them. ⁹ I am the door: by me if any man enter in, he shall be saved, and shall go in and out, and find pasture. ¹⁰ The thief cometh not, but for to steal, and to kill, and to destroy: I am come that they might have life, and that they might have it more abundantly. ¹¹ I am the good shepherd: the good shepherd giveth his life for the sheep. ¹² But he that is an hireling, and not the shepherd, whose own the sheep are not, seeth the wolf coming, and leaveth the sheep, and fleeth, and the wolf catcheth them, and scattereth the sheep. ¹³ The hireling fleeth, because he is an hireling, and careth not for the sheep. ¹⁴ I am the good shepherd, and know my sheep, and am known of mine. ¹⁵ As the Father knoweth me, even so know I the Father, and I lay down my life for the sheep. ¹⁶ And other sheep I have, which are not of this fold: them also I must bring, and they shall hear my voice; and there shall be one fold: and one shepherd. ¹⁷ Therefore doth my Father love me, because I lay down my life, that I might take it again. ¹⁸ No man taketh it from me, but I lay it down of myself. I have power to lay it down, and I have power to take it again. This commandment have I received of my Father.'

¹⁹ There was a division therefore again among the Jews for these sayings. ²⁰ And many of them said, 'He hath a devil, and is mad; why hear ye him?' ²¹ Others said, 'These are not

the words of him that hath a devil. Can a devil open the eyes of the blind?'

²²And it was at Jerusalem the feast of the dedication, and it was winter. ²³And Jesus walked in the temple in Solomon's porch. ²⁴Then came the Jews round about him, and said unto him, 'How long dost thou make us to doubt? If thou be the Christ, tell us plainly.' ²⁵Jesus answered them, 'I told you, and ye believed not: the works that I do in my Father's name, they bear witness of me. ²⁶But ye believe not, because ye are not of my sheep, as I said unto you. ²⁷My sheep hear my voice, and I know them, and they follow me, ²⁸and I give unto them eternal life; and they shall never perish, neither shall any man pluck them out of my hand. ²⁹My Father, which gave them me, is greater than all; and no man is able to pluck them out of my Father's hand. ³⁰I and my Father are one.' ³¹Then the Jews took up stones again to stone him. ³²Jesus answered them, 'Many good works have I shewed you from my Father; for which of those works do ye stone me?' ³³The Jews answered him, saying, 'For a good work we stone thee not; but for blasphemy; and because that thou, being a man, makest thyself God.' ³⁴Jesus answered them, 'Is it not written in your law, "I said, ye are gods"? ³⁵If he called them gods, unto whom the word of God came, and the scripture cannot be broken; ³⁶say ye of him, whom the Father hath sanctified, and sent into the world, "Thou blasphemest," because I said, "I am the Son of God"? ³⁷If I do not the works of my Father, believe me not. ³⁸But if I do, though ye believe not me, believe the works: that ye may know, and believe, that the Father is in me, and I in him.' ³⁹Therefore they sought again to take

him: but he escaped out of their hand, [40] and went away again beyond Jordan into the place where John at first baptized; and there he abode. [41] And many resorted unto him, and said, 'John did no miracle, but all things that John spake of this man were true.' [42] And many believed on him there.

11 Now a certain man was sick, named Lazarus, of Bethany, the town of Mary and her sister Martha. [2] (It was that Mary which anointed the Lord with ointment, and wiped his feet with her hair, whose brother Lazarus was sick.) [3] Therefore his sisters sent unto him, saying, 'Lord, behold, he whom thou lovest is sick.' [4] When Jesus heard that, he said, 'This sickness is not unto death, but for the glory of God, that the Son of God might be glorified thereby.' [5] Now Jesus loved Martha, and her sister, and Lazarus. [6] When he had heard therefore that he was sick, he abode two days still in the same place where he was. [7] Then after that saith he to his disciples, 'Let us go into Judæa again.' [8] His disciples say unto him, 'Master, the Jews of late sought to stone thee; and goest thou thither again?' [9] Jesus answered, 'Are there not twelve hours in the day? If any man walk in the day, he stumbleth not, because he seeth the light of this world. [10] But if a man walk in the night, he stumbleth, because there is no light in him.' [11] These things said he, and after that he saith unto them, 'Our friend Lazarus sleepeth; but I go, that I may awake him out of sleep.' [12] Then said his disciples, 'Lord, if he sleep, he shall do well.' [13] Howbeit Jesus spake of his death, but they thought that he had spoken of taking of rest in sleep. [14] Then said Jesus unto them plainly, 'Lazarus is dead. [15] And I am

glad for your sakes that I was not there, to the intent ye may believe; nevertheless let us go unto him.' ¹⁶ Then said Thomas, which is called Didymus, unto his fellowdisciples, 'Let us also go, that we may die with him.' ¹⁷ Then when Jesus came, he found that he had lain in the grave four days already. ¹⁸ Now Bethany was nigh unto Jerusalem, about fifteen furlongs off, ¹⁹ and many of the Jews came to Martha and Mary, to comfort them concerning their brother. ²⁰ Then Martha, as soon as she heard that Jesus was coming, went and met him, but Mary sat still in the house. ²¹ Then said Martha unto Jesus, 'Lord, if thou hadst been here, my brother had not died. ²² But I know, that even now, whatsoever thou wilt ask of God, God will give it thee.' ²³ Jesus saith unto her, 'Thy brother shall rise again.' ²⁴ Martha saith unto him, 'I know that he shall rise again in the resurrection at the last day.' ²⁵ Jesus said unto her, 'I am the resurrection, and the life: he that believeth in me, though he were dead, yet shall he live, ²⁶ and whosoever liveth and believeth in me shall never die. Believest thou this?' ²⁷ She saith unto him, 'Yea, Lord, I believe that thou art the Christ, the Son of God, which should come into the world.' ²⁸ And when she had so said, she went her way, and called Mary her sister secretly, saying, 'The Master is come, and calleth for thee.' ²⁹ As soon as she heard that, she arose quickly, and came unto him. ³⁰ Now Jesus was not yet come into the town, but was in that place where Martha met him. ³¹ The Jews then which were with her in the house, and comforted her, when they saw Mary, that she rose up hastily and went out, followed her, saying, 'She goeth unto the grave to weep there.' ³² Then when Mary was come where Jesus was, and saw him, she fell down at his feet, saying unto him, 'Lord, if thou hadst been here, my brother had not died.' ³³ When Jesus therefore saw her weeping, and the Jews also weeping which came with her, he groaned in the spirit, and was troubled, ³⁴ and said, 'Where have ye laid him?' They said unto him, 'Lord, come and see.' ³⁵ Jesus wept. ³⁶ Then said the Jews, 'Behold how he loved him!' ³⁷And some of them said, 'Could not this man, which opened the eyes of the blind, have caused that even this man should not have died?' ³⁸ Jesus therefore again groaning in himself cometh to the grave. It was a cave, and a stone lay upon it. ³⁹ Jesus said, 'Take ye away the stone.' Martha, the sister of him that was dead, saith unto him, 'Lord, by this time he stinketh, for he hath been dead four days.' ⁴⁰ Jesus saith unto her, 'Said I not unto thee, that, if thou wouldest believe, thou shouldest see the glory of God?' ⁴¹Then they took away the stone from the place where the dead was laid. And Jesus lifted up his eyes, and said, 'Father, I thank thee that thou hast heard me. ⁴²And I knew that thou hearest me always, but because of the people which stand by I said it, that they may believe that thou hast sent me.' ⁴³And when he thus had spoken, he cried with a loud voice, 'Lazarus, come forth.' ⁴⁴And he that was dead came forth, bound hand and foot with graveclothes, and his face was bound about with a napkin. Jesus saith unto them, 'Loose him, and let him go.' ⁴⁵ Then many of the Jews which came to Mary, and had seen the things which Jesus did, believed on him. ⁴⁶ But some of them went their ways to the Pharisees, and told them what things Jesus had done.

⁴⁷ Then gathered the chief priests and the Pharisees a

council, and said, 'What do we? For this man doeth many miracles. ⁴⁸ If we let him thus alone, all men will believe on him, and the Romans shall come and take away both our place and nation.' ⁴⁹And one of them, named Caiaphas, being the high priest that same year, said unto them, 'Ye know nothing at all, ⁵⁰ nor consider that it is expedient for us, that one man should die for the people, and that the whole nation perish not.' ⁵¹And this spake he not of himself, but being high priest that year, he prophesied that Jesus should die for that nation; ⁵² and not for that nation only, but that also he should gather together in one the children of God that were scattered abroad. ⁵³ Then from that day forth they took counsel together for to put him to death. ⁵⁴ Jesus therefore walked no more openly among the Jews; but went thence unto a country near to the wilderness, into a city called Ephraim, and there continued with his disciples.

⁵⁵And the Jews' passover was nigh at hand, and many went out of the country up to Jerusalem before the passover, to purify themselves. ⁵⁶ Then sought they for Jesus, and spake among themselves, as they stood in the temple, 'What think ye, that he will not come to the feast?' ⁵⁷ Now both the chief priests and the Pharisees had given a commandment, that, if any man knew where he were, he should shew it, that they might take him.

12 Then Jesus six days before the passover came to Bethany, where Lazarus was which had been dead, whom he raised from the dead. ² There they made him a supper, and Martha served, but Lazarus was one of them that sat at

the table with him. ³ Then took Mary a pound of ointment of spikenard, very costly, and anointed the feet of Jesus, and wiped his feet with her hair, and the house was filled with the odour of the ointment. ⁴ Then saith one of his disciples, Judas Iscariot, Simon's son, which should betray him, ⁵ 'Why was not this ointment sold for three hundred pence, and given to the poor?' ⁶ This he said, not that he cared for the poor; but because he was a thief, and had the bag, and bare what was put therein. ⁷ Then said Jesus, 'Let her alone: against the day of my burying hath she kept this. ⁸ For the poor always ye have with you; but me ye have not always.' ⁹ Much people of the Jews therefore knew that he was there, and they came not for Jesus' sake only, but that they might see Lazarus also, whom he had raised from the dead.

¹⁰ But the chief priests consulted that they might put Lazarus also to death; ¹¹ because that by reason of him many of the Jews went away, and believed on Jesus.

¹² On the next day much people that were come to the feast, when they heard that Jesus was coming to Jerusalem, ¹³ took branches of palm trees, and went forth to meet him, and cried, 'Hosanna: blessed is the King of Israel that cometh in the name of the Lord.' ¹⁴ And Jesus, when he had found a young ass, sat thereon; as it is written, ¹⁵ 'Fear not, daughter of Sion: behold, thy King cometh, sitting on an ass's colt.' ¹⁶ These things understood not his disciples at the first, but when Jesus was glorified, then remembered they that these things were written of him, and that they had done these things unto him. ¹⁷ The people therefore that was with him when he called Lazarus out of his grave, and raised him from

the dead, bare record. ¹⁸For this cause the people also met him, for that they heard that he had done this miracle. ¹⁹The Pharisees therefore said among themselves, 'Perceive ye how ye prevail nothing? Behold, the world is gone after him.'

²⁰And there were certain Greeks among them that came up to worship at the feast. ²¹The same came therefore to Philip, which was of Bethsaida of Galilee, and desired him, saying, 'Sir, we would see Jesus.' ²²Philip cometh and telleth Andrew, and again Andrew and Philip tell Jesus.

²³And Jesus answered them, saying, 'The hour is come, that the Son of man should be glorified. ²⁴Verily, verily, I say unto you, except a corn of wheat fall into the ground and die, it abideth alone, but if it die, it bringeth forth much fruit. ²⁵He that loveth his life shall lose it; and he that hateth his life in this world shall keep it unto life eternal. ²⁶If any man serve me, let him follow me; and where I am, there shall also my servant be: if any man serve me, him will my Father honour. ²⁷Now is my soul troubled; and what shall I say? "Father, save me from this hour." But for this cause came I unto this hour. ²⁸Father, glorify thy name.' Then came there a voice from heaven, saying, 'I have both glorified it, and will glorify it again.' ²⁹The people therefore, that stood by, and heard it, said that it thundered; others said, 'An angel spake to him.' ³⁰Jesus answered and said, 'This voice came not because of me, but for your sakes. ³¹Now is the judgment of this world: now shall the prince of this world be cast out. ³²And I, if I be lifted up from the earth, will draw all men unto me.' ³³This he said, signifying what death he should die. ³⁴The people answered him, 'We have heard out of the law that

Christ abideth for ever, and how sayest thou the Son of man must be lifted up? Who is this Son of man?' ³⁵ Then Jesus said unto them, 'Yet a little while is the light with you. Walk while ye have the light, lest darkness come upon you: for he that walketh in darkness knoweth not whither he goeth. ³⁶ While ye have light, believe in the light, that ye may be the children of light.' These things spake Jesus, and departed, and did hide himself from them.

³⁷ But though he had done so many miracles before them, yet they believed not on him, ³⁸ that the saying of Esaias the prophet might be fulfilled, which he spake, 'Lord, who hath believed our report? And to whom hath the arm of the Lord been revealed?' ³⁹ Therefore they could not believe, because that Esaias said again, ⁴⁰ 'He hath blinded their eyes, and hardened their heart; that they should not see with their eyes, nor understand with their heart, and be converted, and I should heal them.' ⁴¹ These things said Esaias, when he saw his glory, and spake of him.

⁴² Nevertheless among the chief rulers also many believed on him; but because of the Pharisees they did not confess him, lest they should be put out of the synagogue, ⁴³ for they loved the praise of men more than the praise of God.

⁴⁴ Jesus cried and said, 'He that believeth on me, believeth not on me, but on him that sent me. ⁴⁵ And he that seeth me seeth him that sent me. ⁴⁶ I am come a light into the world, that whosoever believeth on me should not abide in darkness. ⁴⁷ And if any man hear my words, and believe not, I judge him not: for I came not to judge the world, but to save the world. ⁴⁸ He that rejecteth me, and receiveth not my

words, hath one that judgeth him: the word that I have spoken, the same shall judge him in the last day. [49] For I have not spoken of myself; but the Father which sent me, he gave me a commandment, what I should say, and what I should speak. [50] And I know that his commandment is life everlasting: whatsoever I speak therefore, even as the Father said unto me, so I speak.'

13 Now before the feast of the passover, when Jesus knew that his hour was come that he should depart out of this world unto the Father, having loved his own which were in the world, he loved them unto the end. [2] And supper being ended, the devil having now put into the heart of Judas Iscariot, Simon's son, to betray him; [3] Jesus knowing that the Father had given all things into his hands, and that he was come from God, and went to God; [4] he riseth from supper, and laid aside his garments; and took a towel, and girded himself. [5] After that he poureth water into a bason, and began to wash the disciples' feet, and to wipe them with the towel wherewith he was girded. [6] Then cometh he to Simon Peter, and Peter saith unto him, 'Lord, dost thou wash my feet?' [7] Jesus answered and said unto him, 'What I do thou knowest not now; but thou shalt know hereafter.' [8] Peter saith unto him, 'Thou shalt never wash my feet.' Jesus answered him, 'If I wash thee not, thou hast no part with me.' [9] Simon Peter saith unto him, 'Lord, not my feet only, but also my hands and my head.' [10] Jesus saith to him, 'He that is washed needeth not save to wash his feet, but is clean every whit: and ye are clean, but not all.' [11] For he knew who should betray

him; therefore said he, 'Ye are not all clean.' ¹²So after he had washed their feet, and had taken his garments, and was set down again, he said unto them, 'Know ye what I have done to you? ¹³Ye call me "Master" and "Lord", and ye say well; for so I am. ¹⁴If I then, your Lord and Master, have washed your feet, ye also ought to wash one another's feet. ¹⁵For I have given you an example, that ye should do as I have done to you. ¹⁶Verily, verily, I say unto you, the servant is not greater than his lord; neither he that is sent greater than he that sent him. ¹⁷If ye know these things, happy are ye if ye do them.

¹⁸'I speak not of you all; I know whom I have chosen: but that the scripture may be fulfilled. He that eateth bread with me hath lifted up his heel against me. ¹⁹Now I tell you before it come, that, when it is come to pass, ye may believe that I am he. ²⁰Verily, verily, I say unto you, he that receiveth whomsoever I send receiveth me; and he that receiveth me receiveth him that sent me.' ²¹When Jesus had thus said, he was troubled in spirit, and testified, and said, 'Verily, verily, I say unto you, that one of you shall betray me.' ²²Then the disciples looked one on another, doubting of whom he spake. ²³Now there was leaning on Jesus' bosom one of his disciples, whom Jesus loved. ²⁴Simon Peter therefore beckoned to him, that he should ask who it should be of whom he spake. ²⁵He then lying on Jesus' breast saith unto him, 'Lord, who is it?' ²⁶Jesus answered, 'He it is, to whom I shall give a sop, when I have dipped it.' And when he had dipped the sop, he gave it to Judas Iscariot, the son of Simon. ²⁷And after the sop Satan entered into him. Then said Jesus unto him, 'That thou doest, do quickly.' ²⁸Now no man at the table

knew for what intent he spake this unto him. ²⁹ For some of them thought, because Judas had the bag, that Jesus had said unto him, 'Buy those things that we have need of against the feast,' or, that he should give something to the poor. ³⁰ He then having received the sop went immediately out, and it was night.

³¹ Therefore, when he was gone out, Jesus said, 'Now is the Son of man glorified, and God is glorified in him. ³² If God be glorified in him, God shall also glorify him in himself, and shall straightway glorify him. ³³ Little children, yet a little while I am with you. Ye shall seek me, and as I said unto the Jews, "Whither I go, ye cannot come"; so now I say to you. ³⁴ A new commandment I give unto you, that ye love one another; as I have loved you, that ye also love one another. ³⁵ By this shall all men know that ye are my disciples, if ye have love one to another.'

³⁶ Simon Peter said unto him, 'Lord, whither goest thou?' Jesus answered him, 'Whither I go, thou canst not follow me now; but thou shalt follow me afterwards.' ³⁷ Peter said unto him, 'Lord, why cannot I follow thee now? I will lay down my life for thy sake.' ³⁸ Jesus answered him, 'Wilt thou lay down thy life for my sake? Verily, verily, I say unto thee, the cock shall not crow, till thou hast denied me thrice.

14 'Let not your heart be troubled: ye believe in God, believe also in me. ² In my Father's house are many mansions: if it were not so, I would have told you. I go to prepare a place for you. ³ And if I go and prepare a place for you, I will come again, and receive you unto myself; that

where I am, there ye may be also. ⁴And whither I go ye know, and the way ye know.' ⁵Thomas saith unto him, 'Lord, we know not whither thou goest; and how can we know the way?' ⁶Jesus saith unto him, 'I am the way, the truth, and the life: no man cometh unto the Father, but by me. ⁷If ye had known me, ye should have known my Father also: and from henceforth ye know him, and have seen him.' ⁸Philip saith unto him, 'Lord, shew us the Father, and it sufficeth us.' ⁹Jesus saith unto him, 'Have I been so long time with you, and yet hast thou not known me, Philip? He that hath seen me hath seen the Father; and how sayest thou then, "Shew us the Father"? ¹⁰Believest thou not that I am in the Father, and the Father in me? The words that I speak unto you I speak not of myself; but the Father that dwelleth in me, he doeth the works. ¹¹Believe me that I am in the Father, and the Father in me, or else believe me for the very works' sake. ¹²Verily, verily, I say unto you, he that believeth on me, the works that I do shall he do also; and greater works than these shall he do; because I go unto my Father. ¹³And whatsoever ye shall ask in my name, that will I do, that the Father may be glorified in the Son. ¹⁴If ye shall ask any thing in my name, I will do it.

¹⁵'If ye love me, keep my commandments. ¹⁶And I will pray the Father, and he shall give you another Comforter, that he may abide with you for ever; ¹⁷even the Spirit of truth; whom the world cannot receive, because it seeth him not, neither knoweth him, but ye know him; for he dwelleth with you, and shall be in you. ¹⁸I will not leave you comfortless; I will come to you. ¹⁹Yet a little while, and the world seeth me no more; but ye see me: because I live, ye shall live

also. ²⁰At that day ye shall know that I am in my Father, and ye in me, and I in you. ²¹He that hath my commandments, and keepeth them, he it is that loveth me: and he that loveth me shall be loved of my Father, and I will love him, and will manifest myself to him.' ²²Judas saith unto him, not Iscariot, 'Lord, how is it that thou wilt manifest thyself unto us, and not unto the world?' ²³Jesus answered and said unto him, 'If a man love me, he will keep my words: and my Father will love him, and we will come unto him, and make our abode with him. ²⁴He that loveth me not keepeth not my sayings, and the word which ye hear is not mine, but the Father's which sent me. ²⁵These things have I spoken unto you, being yet present with you. ²⁶But the Comforter, which is the Holy Ghost, whom the Father will send in my name, he shall teach you all things, and bring all things to your remembrance, whatsoever I have said unto you. ²⁷Peace I leave with you, my peace I give unto you: not as the world giveth, give I unto you. Let not your heart be troubled, neither let it be afraid. ²⁸Ye have heard how I said unto you, "I go away, and come again unto you." If ye loved me, ye would rejoice, because I said I go unto the Father, for my Father is greater than I. ²⁹And now I have told you before it come to pass, that, when it is come to pass, ye might believe. ³⁰Hereafter I will not talk much with you, for the prince of this world cometh, and hath nothing in me. ³¹But that the world may know that I love the Father; and as the Father gave me commandment, even so I do. Arise, let us go hence.

15

'I am the true vine, and my Father is the husbandman. ²Every branch in me that beareth not fruit he taketh away, and every branch that beareth fruit, he purgeth it, that it may bring forth more fruit. ³Now ye are clean through the word which I have spoken unto you. ⁴Abide in me, and I in you. As the branch cannot bear fruit of itself, except it abide in the vine; no more can ye, except ye abide in me. ⁵I am the vine, ye are the branches. He that abideth in me, and I in him, the same bringeth forth much fruit, for without me ye can do nothing. ⁶If a man abide not in me, he is cast forth as a branch, and is withered; and men gather them, and cast them into the fire, and they are burned. ⁷If ye abide in me, and my words abide in you, ye shall ask what ye will, and it shall be done unto you. ⁸Herein is my Father glorified, that ye bear much fruit; so shall ye be my disciples. ⁹As the Father hath loved me, so have I loved you; continue ye in my love. ¹⁰If ye keep my commandments, ye shall abide in my love; even as I have kept my Father's commandments, and abide in his love. ¹¹These things have I spoken unto you, that my joy might remain in you, and that your joy might be full.

¹²'This is my commandment: that ye love one another, as I have loved you. ¹³Greater love hath no man than this, that a man lay down his life for his friends. ¹⁴Ye are my friends, if ye do whatsoever I command you. ¹⁵Henceforth I call you not servants; for the servant knoweth not what his lord doeth; but I have called you friends, for all things that I have heard of my Father I have made known unto you. ¹⁶Ye have not chosen me, but I have chosen you, and ordained you, that ye should go and bring forth fruit, and that your fruit should

remain: that whatsoever ye shall ask of the Father in my name, he may give it you. [17] These things I command you, that ye love one another.

[18] 'If the world hate you, ye know that it hated me before it hated you. [19] If ye were of the world, the world would love his own: but because ye are not of the world, but I have chosen you out of the world, therefore the world hateth you. [20] Remember the word that I said unto you, "The servant is not greater than his lord." If they have persecuted me, they will also persecute you; if they have kept my saying, they will keep yours also. [21] But all these things will they do unto you for my name's sake, because they know not him that sent me. [22] If I had not come and spoken unto them, they had not had sin: but now they have no cloke for their sin. [23] He that hateth me hateth my Father also. [24] If I had not done among them the works which none other man did, they had not had sin: but now have they both seen and hated both me and my Father. [25] But this cometh to pass, that the word might be fulfilled that is written in their law: "They hated me without a cause."

[26] 'But when the Comforter is come, whom I will send unto you from the Father, even the Spirit of truth, which proceedeth from the Father, he shall testify of me. [27] And ye also shall bear witness, because ye have been with me from the beginning.

16 'These things have I spoken unto you, that ye should not be offended. [2] They shall put you out of the synagogues: yea, the time cometh, that whosoever killeth you will think that he doeth God service. [3] And these things will they

do unto you, because they have not known the Father, nor me. ⁴But these things have I told you, that when the time shall come, ye may remember that I told you of them. And these things I said not unto you at the beginning, because I was with you. ⁵But now I go my way to him that sent me; and none of you asketh me, "Whither goest thou?" ⁶But because I have said these things unto you, sorrow hath filled your heart. ⁷Nevertheless I tell you the truth. It is expedient for you that I go away: for if I go not away, the Comforter will not come unto you; but if I depart, I will send him unto you. ⁸And when he is come, he will reprove the world of sin, and of righteousness, and of judgment: ⁹of sin, because they believe not on me; ¹⁰of righteousness, because I go to my Father, and ye see me no more; ¹¹of judgment, because the prince of this world is judged. ¹²I have yet many things to say unto you, but ye cannot bear them now. ¹³Howbeit when he, the Spirit of truth, is come, he will guide you into all truth, for he shall not speak of himself; but whatsoever he shall hear, that shall he speak, and he will shew you things to come. ¹⁴He shall glorify me, for he shall receive of mine, and shall shew it unto you. ¹⁵All things that the Father hath are mine: therefore said I, that he shall take of mine, and shall shew it unto you.

¹⁶'A little while, and ye shall not see me, and again, a little while, and ye shall see me, because I go to the Father.' ¹⁷Then said some of his disciples among themselves, 'What is this that he saith unto us, "A little while, and ye shall not see me, and again, a little while, and ye shall see me," and, "Because I go to the Father"?' ¹⁸They said therefore, 'What is this that he saith, "A little while?" We cannot tell what he

saith.' ¹⁹ Now Jesus knew that they were desirous to ask him, and said unto them, 'Do ye enquire among yourselves of that I said, "A little while, and ye shall not see me, and again, a little while, and ye shall see me"? ²⁰ Verily, verily, I say unto you that ye shall weep and lament, but the world shall rejoice; and ye shall be sorrowful, but your sorrow shall be turned into joy. ²¹ A woman when she is in travail hath sorrow, because her hour is come, but as soon as she is delivered of the child, she remembereth no more the anguish, for joy that a man is born into the world. ²² And ye now therefore have sorrow, but I will see you again, and your heart shall rejoice, and your joy no man taketh from you. ²³ And in that day ye shall ask me nothing. Verily, verily, I say unto you, whatsoever ye shall ask the Father in my name, he will give it you. ²⁴ Hitherto have ye asked nothing in my name: ask, and ye shall receive, that your joy may be full.

²⁵ 'These things have I spoken unto you in proverbs, but the time cometh, when I shall no more speak unto you in proverbs, but I shall shew you plainly of the Father. ²⁶ At that day ye shall ask in my name, and I say not unto you that I will pray the Father for you, ²⁷ for the Father himself loveth you, because ye have loved me, and have believed that I came out from God. ²⁸ I came forth from the Father, and am come into the world; again, I leave the world, and go to the Father.'

²⁹ His disciples said unto him, 'Lo, now speakest thou plainly, and speakest no proverb. ³⁰ Now are we sure that thou knowest all things, and needest not that any man should ask thee: by this we believe that thou camest forth from God.' ³¹ Jesus answered them, 'Do ye now believe? ³² Behold, the

hour cometh, yea, is now come, that ye shall be scattered, every man to his own, and shall leave me alone, and yet I am not alone; because the Father is with me. ³³ These things I have spoken unto you, that in me ye might have peace. In the world ye shall have tribulation: but be of good cheer; I have overcome the world.'

17 These words spake Jesus, and lifted up his eyes to heaven, and said, 'Father, the hour is come; glorify thy Son, that thy Son also may glorify thee. ²As thou hast given him power over all flesh, that he should give eternal life to as many as thou hast given him. ³And this is life eternal, that they might know thee the only true God, and Jesus Christ, whom thou hast sent. ⁴I have glorified thee on the earth: I have finished the work which thou gavest me to do. ⁵And now, O Father, glorify thou me with thine own self with the glory which I had with thee before the world was.

⁶ 'I have manifested thy name unto the men which thou gavest me out of the world: thine they were, and thou gavest them me; and they have kept thy word. ⁷Now they have known that all things whatsoever thou hast given me are of thee. ⁸For I have given unto them the words which thou gavest me; and they have received them, and have known surely that I came out from thee, and they have believed that thou didst send me. ⁹I pray for them: I pray not for the world, but for them which thou hast given me; for they are thine. ¹⁰And all mine are thine, and thine are mine; and I am glorified in them. ¹¹And now I am no more in the world, but these are in the world, and I come to thee. Holy Father, keep

through thine own name those whom thou hast given me, that they may be one, as we are. [12] While I was with them in the world, I kept them in thy name; those that thou gavest me I have kept, and none of them is lost, but the son of perdition; that the scripture might be fulfilled. [13] And now come I to thee; and these things I speak in the world, that they might have my joy fulfilled in themselves. [14] I have given them thy word; and the world hath hated them, because they are not of the world, even as I am not of the world. [15] I pray not that thou shouldest take them out of the world, but that thou shouldest keep them from the evil. [16] They are not of the world, even as I am not of the world. [17] Sanctify them through thy truth: thy word is truth. [18] As thou hast sent me into the world, even so have I also sent them into the world. [19] And for their sakes I sanctify myself, that they also might be sanctified through the truth.

[20] 'Neither pray I for these alone, but for them also which shall believe on me through their word; [21] that they all may be one; as thou, Father, art in me, and I in thee, that they also may be one in us: that the world may believe that thou hast sent me. [22] And the glory which thou gavest me I have given them; that they may be one, even as we are one: [23] I in them, and thou in me, that they may be made perfect in one; and that the world may know that thou hast sent me, and hast loved them, as thou hast loved me. [24] Father, I will that they also, whom thou hast given me, be with me where I am; that they may behold my glory, which thou hast given me, for thou lovedst me before the foundation of the world.

[25] 'O righteous Father, the world hath not known thee,

but I have known thee, and these have known that thou hast sent me. ²⁶And I have declared unto them thy name, and will declare it, that the love wherewith thou hast loved me may be in them, and I in them.'

18 When Jesus had spoken these words, he went forth with his disciples over the brook Cedron, where was a garden, into the which he entered, and his disciples. ²And Judas also, which betrayed him, knew the place, for Jesus ofttimes resorted thither with his disciples. ³Judas then, having received a band of men and officers from the chief priests and Pharisees, cometh thither with lanterns and torches and weapons. ⁴Jesus therefore, knowing all things that should come upon him, went forth, and said unto them, 'Whom seek ye?' ⁵They answered him, 'Jesus of Nazareth.' Jesus saith unto them, 'I am he.' And Judas also, which betrayed him, stood with them. ⁶As soon then as he had said unto them, 'I am he,' they went backward, and fell to the ground. ⁷Then asked he them again, 'Whom seek ye?' And they said, 'Jesus of Nazareth.' ⁸Jesus answered, 'I have told you that I am he: if therefore ye seek me, let these go their way,' ⁹that the saying might be fulfilled, which he spake: 'Of them which thou gavest me have I lost none.' ¹⁰Then Simon Peter having a sword drew it, and smote the high priest's servant, and cut off his right ear. The servant's name was Malchus. ¹¹Then said Jesus unto Peter, 'Put up thy sword into the sheath; the cup which my Father hath given me, shall I not drink it?' ¹²Then the band and the captain and officers of the Jews took Jesus, and bound him, ¹³and led him away to Annas first; for he was father-in-law to Caiaphas, which was the high priest that same year. [14] Now Caiaphas was he, which gave counsel to the Jews, that it was expedient that one man should die for the people.

[15] And Simon Peter followed Jesus, and so did another disciple; that disciple was known unto the high priest, and went in with Jesus into the palace of the high priest. [16] But Peter stood at the door without. Then went out that other disciple, which was known unto the high priest, and spake unto her that kept the door, and brought in Peter. [17] Then saith the damsel that kept the door unto Peter, 'Art not thou also one of this man's disciples?' He saith, 'I am not.' [18] And the servants and officers stood there, who had made a fire of coals, for it was cold, and they warmed themselves, and Peter stood with them, and warmed himself.

[19] The high priest then asked Jesus of his disciples, and of his doctrine. [20] Jesus answered him, 'I spake openly to the world; I ever taught in the synagogue, and in the temple, whither the Jews always resort; and in secret have I said nothing. [21] Why askest thou me? Ask them which heard me, what I have said unto them; behold, they know what I said.' [22] And when he had thus spoken, one of the officers which stood by struck Jesus with the palm of his hand, saying, 'Answerest thou the high priest so?' [23] Jesus answered him, 'If I have spoken evil, bear witness of the evil, but if well, why smitest thou me?' [24] Now Annas had sent him bound unto Caiaphas the high priest. [25] And Simon Peter stood and warmed himself. They said therefore unto him, 'Art not thou also one of his disciples?' He denied it, and said, 'I am not.'

²⁶ One of the servants of the high priest, being his kinsman whose ear Peter cut off, saith, 'Did not I see thee in the garden with him?' ²⁷ Peter then denied again, and immediately the cock crew.

²⁸ Then led they Jesus from Caiaphas unto the hall of judgment, and it was early; and they themselves went not into the judgment hall, lest they should be defiled; but that they might eat the passover. ²⁹ Pilate then went out unto them, and said, 'What accusation bring ye against this man?' ³⁰ They answered and said unto him, 'If he were not a malefactor, we would not have delivered him up unto thee.' ³¹ Then said Pilate unto them, 'Take ye him, and judge him according to your law.' The Jews therefore said unto him, 'It is not lawful for us to put any man to death,' ³² that the saying of Jesus might be fulfilled, which he spake, signifying what death he should die. ³³ Then Pilate entered into the judgment hall again, and called Jesus, and said unto him, 'Art thou the King of the Jews?' ³⁴ Jesus answered him, 'Sayest thou this thing of thyself, or did others tell it thee of me?' ³⁵ Pilate answered, 'Am I a Jew? Thine own nation and the chief priests have delivered thee unto me; what hast thou done?' ³⁶ Jesus answered, 'My kingdom is not of this world: if my kingdom were of this world, then would my servants fight, that I should not be delivered to the Jews, but now is my kingdom not from hence.' ³⁷ Pilate therefore said unto him, 'Art thou a king then?' Jesus answered, 'Thou sayest that I am a king. To this end was I born, and for this cause came I into the world, that I should bear witness unto the truth. Every one that is of the truth heareth my voice.' ³⁸ Pilate saith unto him, 'What is

truth?' And when he had said this, he went out again unto the Jews, and saith unto them, 'I find in him no fault at all. ³⁹ But ye have a custom, that I should release unto you one at the passover: will ye therefore that I release unto you the King of the Jews?' ⁴⁰ Then cried they all again, saying, 'Not this man, but Barabbas.' Now Barabbas was a robber.

19 Then Pilate therefore took Jesus, and scourged him. ²And the soldiers platted a crown of thorns, and put it on his head, and they put on him a purple robe, ³and said, 'Hail, King of the Jews!' and they smote him with their hands. ⁴Pilate therefore went forth again, and saith unto them, 'Behold, I bring him forth to you, that ye may know that I find no fault in him.' ⁵Then came Jesus forth, wearing the crown of thorns, and the purple robe. And Pilate saith unto them, 'Behold the man!' ⁶When the chief priests therefore and officers saw him, they cried out, saying, 'Crucify him, crucify him.' Pilate saith unto them, 'Take ye him, and crucify him, for I find no fault in him.' ⁷The Jews answered him, 'We have a law, and by our law he ought to die, because he made himself the Son of God.'

⁸When Pilate therefore heard that saying, he was the more afraid, ⁹and went again into the judgment hall, and saith unto Jesus, 'Whence art thou?' But Jesus gave him no answer. ¹⁰Then saith Pilate unto him, 'Speakest thou not unto me? Knowest thou not that I have power to crucify thee, and have power to release thee?' ¹¹Jesus answered, 'Thou couldest have no power at all against me, except it were given thee from above: therefore he that delivered me unto thee

hath the greater sin.' [12]And from thenceforth Pilate sought to release him, but the Jews cried out, saying, 'If thou let this man go, thou art not Cæsar's friend; whosoever maketh himself a king speaketh against Cæsar.'

[13] When Pilate therefore heard that saying, he brought Jesus forth, and sat down in the judgment seat in a place that is called the Pavement, but in the Hebrew, Gabbatha. [14]And it was the preparation of the passover, and about the sixth hour, and he saith unto the Jews, 'Behold your King!' [15]But they cried out, 'Away with him, away with him, crucify him.' Pilate saith unto them, 'Shall I crucify your King?' The chief priests answered, 'We have no king but Cæsar.' [16] Then delivered he him therefore unto them to be crucified. And they took Jesus, and led him away. [17]And he bearing his cross went forth into a place called the place of a skull, which is called in the Hebrew Golgotha, [18] where they crucified him, and two other with him, on either side one, and Jesus in the midst.

[19]And Pilate wrote a title, and put it on the cross. And the writing was, 'Jesus of Nazareth the King of the Jews.' [20] This title then read many of the Jews, for the place where Jesus was crucified was nigh to the city, and it was written in Hebrew, and Greek, and Latin. [21] Then said the chief priests of the Jews to Pilate, 'Write not, "The King of the Jews", but that he said, "I am King of the Jews."' [22] Pilate answered, 'What I have written I have written.'

[23] Then the soldiers, when they had crucified Jesus, took his garments, and made four parts, to every soldier a part; and also his coat. Now the coat was without seam, woven from the top throughout. [24] They said therefore among themselves,

'Let us not rend it, but cast lots for it, whose it shall be,' that the scripture might be fulfilled, which saith, 'They parted my raiment among them, and for my vesture they did cast lots.' These things therefore the soldiers did. ²⁵ Now there stood by the cross of Jesus his mother, and his mother's sister, Mary the wife of Cleophas, and Mary Magdalene. ²⁶ When Jesus therefore saw his mother, and the disciple standing by, whom he loved, he saith unto his mother, 'Woman, behold thy son!' ²⁷ Then saith he to the disciple, 'Behold thy mother!' And from that hour that disciple took her unto his own home.

²⁸After this, Jesus knowing that all things were now accomplished, that the scripture might be fulfilled, saith, 'I thirst.' ²⁹ Now there was set a vessel full of vinegar, and they filled a spunge with vinegar, and put it upon hyssop, and put it to his mouth. ³⁰ When Jesus therefore had received the vinegar, he said, 'It is finished,' and he bowed his head, and gave up the ghost. ³¹ The Jews therefore, because it was the preparation, that the bodies should not remain upon the cross on the sabbath day (for that sabbath day was an high day), besought Pilate that their legs might be broken, and that they might be taken away. ³² Then came the soldiers, and brake the legs of the first, and of the other which was crucified with him. ³³ But when they came to Jesus, and saw that he was dead already, they brake not his legs, ³⁴ but one of the soldiers with a spear pierced his side, and forthwith came there out blood and water. ³⁵And he that saw it bare record, and his record is true, and he knoweth that he saith true, that ye might believe. ³⁶ For these things were done,

that the scripture should be fulfilled: 'A bone of him shall not be broken.' ³⁷And again another scripture saith, 'They shall look on him whom they pierced.'

³⁸And after this Joseph of Arimathæa, being a disciple of Jesus, but secretly for fear of the Jews, besought Pilate that he might take away the body of Jesus, and Pilate gave him leave. He came therefore, and took the body of Jesus. ³⁹And there came also Nicodemus, which at the first came to Jesus by night, and brought a mixture of myrrh and aloes, about an hundred pound weight. ⁴⁰Then took they the body of Jesus, and wound it in linen clothes with the spices, as the manner of the Jews is to bury. ⁴¹Now in the place where he was crucified there was a garden; and in the garden a new sepulchre, wherein was never man yet laid. ⁴²There laid they Jesus therefore because of the Jews' preparation day, for the sepulchre was nigh at hand.

20 The first day of the week cometh Mary Magdalene early, when it was yet dark, unto the sepulchre, and seeth the stone taken away from the sepulchre. ²Then she runneth, and cometh to Simon Peter, and to the other disciple, whom Jesus loved, and saith unto them, 'They have taken away the Lord out of the sepulchre, and we know not where they have laid him.' ³Peter therefore went forth, and that other disciple, and came to the sepulchre. ⁴So they ran both together, and the other disciple did outrun Peter, and came first to the sepulchre. ⁵And he stooping down, and looking in, saw the linen clothes lying; yet went he not in. ⁶Then cometh Simon Peter following him, and went into the sepulchre, and seeth

the linen clothes lie, [7]and the napkin, that was about his head, not lying with the linen clothes, but wrapped together in a place by itself. [8]Then went in also that other disciple, which came first to the sepulchre, and he saw, and believed. [9]For as yet they knew not the scripture, that he must rise again from the dead. [10]Then the disciples went away again unto their own home.

[11]But Mary stood without at the sepulchre weeping, and as she wept, she stooped down, and looked into the sepulchre, [12]and seeth two angels in white sitting, the one at the head, and the other at the feet, where the body of Jesus had lain. [13]And they say unto her, 'Woman, why weepest thou?' She saith unto them, 'Because they have taken away my Lord, and I know not where they have laid him.' [14]And when she had thus said, she turned herself back, and saw Jesus standing, and knew not that it was Jesus. [15]Jesus saith unto her, 'Woman, why weepest thou? Whom seekest thou?' She, supposing him to be the gardener, saith unto him, 'Sir, if thou have borne him hence, tell me where thou hast laid him, and I will take him away.' [16]Jesus saith unto her, 'Mary.' She turned herself, and saith unto him, 'Rabboni,' which is to say, 'Master'. [17]Jesus saith unto her, 'Touch me not, for I am not yet ascended to my Father, but go to my brethren, and say unto them, "I ascend unto my Father, and your Father; and to my God, and your God."' [18]Mary Magdalene came and told the disciples that she had seen the Lord, and that he had spoken these things unto her.

[19]Then the same day at evening, being the first day of the week, when the doors were shut where the disciples were

assembled for fear of the Jews, came Jesus and stood in the midst, and saith unto them, 'Peace be unto you.' [20] And when he had so said, he shewed unto them his hands and his side. Then were the disciples glad, when they saw the Lord. [21] Then said Jesus to them again, 'Peace be unto you: as my Father hath sent me, even so send I you.' [22] And when he had said this, he breathed on them, and saith unto them, 'Receive ye the Holy Ghost. [23] Whose soever sins ye remit, they are remitted unto them; and whose soever sins ye retain, they are retained.'

[24] But Thomas, one of the twelve, called Didymus, was not with them when Jesus came. [25] The other disciples therefore said unto him, 'We have seen the Lord.' But he said unto them, 'Except I shall see in his hands the print of the nails, and put my finger into the print of the nails, and thrust my hand into his side, I will not believe.'

[26] And after eight days again his disciples were within, and Thomas with them; then came Jesus, the doors being shut, and stood in the midst, and said, 'Peace be unto you.' [27] Then saith he to Thomas, 'Reach hither thy finger, and behold my hands; and reach hither thy hand, and thrust it into my side; and be not faithless, but believing.' [28] And Thomas answered and said unto him, 'My Lord and my God.' [29] Jesus saith unto him, 'Thomas, because thou hast seen me, thou hast believed: blessed are they that have not seen, and yet have believed.'

[30] And many other signs truly did Jesus in the presence of his disciples, which are not written in this book: [31] but these are written, that ye might believe that Jesus is the Christ, the Son of God; and that believing ye might have life through his name.

john

21 After these things Jesus shewed himself again to the disciples at the sea of Tiberias; and on this wise shewed he himself. ²There were together Simon Peter, and Thomas called Didymus, and Nathanael of Cana in Galilee, and the sons of Zebedee, and two other of his disciples. ³Simon Peter saith unto them, 'I go a fishing.' They say unto him, 'We also go with thee.' They went forth, and entered into a ship immediately; and that night they caught nothing. ⁴But when the morning was now come, Jesus stood on the shore, but the disciples knew not that it was Jesus. ⁵Then Jesus saith unto them, 'Children, have ye any meat?' They answered him, 'No.' ⁶And he said unto them, 'Cast the net on the right side of the ship, and ye shall find.' They cast therefore, and now they were not able to draw it for the multitude of fishes. ⁷Therefore that disciple whom Jesus loved saith unto Peter, 'It is the Lord.' Now when Simon Peter heard that it was the Lord, he girt his fisher's coat unto him (for he was naked), and did cast himself into the sea. ⁸And the other disciples came in a little ship (for they were not far from land, but as it were two hundred cubits), dragging the net with fishes. ⁹As soon then as they were come to land, they saw a fire of coals there, and fish laid thereon, and bread. ¹⁰Jesus saith unto them, 'Bring of the fish which ye have now caught.' ¹¹Simon Peter went up, and drew the net to land full of great fishes, an hundred and fifty and three, and for all there were so many, yet was not the net broken. ¹²Jesus saith unto them, 'Come and dine.' And none of the disciples durst ask him, 'Who art thou?' knowing that it was the Lord. ¹³Jesus then cometh, and taketh bread, and giveth them, and fish

likewise. ¹⁴ This is now the third time that Jesus shewed himself to his disciples, after that he was risen from the dead.

¹⁵ So when they had dined, Jesus saith to Simon Peter, 'Simon, son of Jonas, lovest thou me more than these?' He saith unto him, 'Yea, Lord; thou knowest that I love thee.' He saith unto him, 'Feed my lambs.' ¹⁶ He saith to him again the second time, 'Simon, son of Jonas, lovest thou me?' He saith unto him, 'Yea, Lord; thou knowest that I love thee.' He saith unto him, 'Feed my sheep.' ¹⁷ He saith unto him the third time, 'Simon, son of Jonas, lovest thou me?' Peter was grieved because he said unto him the third time, 'Lovest thou me?' And he said unto him, 'Lord, thou knowest all things; thou knowest that I love thee.' Jesus saith unto him, 'Feed my sheep.' ¹⁸ Verily, verily, I say unto thee, 'When thou wast young, thou girdedst thyself, and walkedst whither thou wouldest, but when thou shalt be old, thou shalt stretch forth thy hands, and another shall gird thee, and carry thee whither thou wouldest not.' ¹⁹ This spake he, signifying by what death he should glorify God. And when he had spoken this, he saith unto him, 'Follow me.' ²⁰ Then Peter, turning about, seeth the disciple whom Jesus loved following, which also leaned on his breast at supper, and said, 'Lord, which is he that betrayeth thee?' ²¹ Peter seeing him saith to Jesus, 'Lord, and what shall this man do?' ²² Jesus saith unto him, 'If I will that he tarry till I come, what is that to thee? Follow thou me.' ²³ Then went this saying abroad among the brethren, that that disciple should not die; yet Jesus said not unto him, 'He shall not die,' but, 'If I will that he tarry till I come, what is that to thee?' ²⁴ This is the disciple which testifieth of

these things, and wrote these things, and we know that his testimony is true. [25]And there are also many other things which Jesus did, the which, if they should be written every one, I suppose that even the world itself could not contain the books that should be written. Amen.

Also available from Canongate:

REVELATIONS
Personal Responses to the Books of the Bible

With an Introduction by Richard Holloway

**A unique anthology that collects the Introductions to the bestselling
Pocket Canons into one volume**

'It's worth the cover price just to see such an extraordinary collection of names gathered
on the same contents page. Nowhere else will you find Nick Cave rubbing shoulders
with the Dalai Lama, or Bono and Joanna Trollope, Mordecai Richler, Peter Ackroyd,
Will Self, Ruth Rendell and many others . . . Overwhelmingly, these introductions kindle
a desire to look at the original texts with fresh eyes.' *Observer*

'Like the best conversation: intellectually rigorous and controversial, yet always alert
to the profound and enduring significance of these ancient stories for today's more
fractured, dislocated humanity.' *Metro*

£8.99

ISBN 978 1 84195 748 7

BETWEEN THE MONSTER AND THE SAINT
Reflections on the Human Condition

RICHARD HOLLOWAY

'Vigorously argued . . . Richard Holloway brilliantly illuminates
the divided spirit of man.' *Observer*

Being human isn't easy. We might think that consciousness and free will give us control
over our lives, but our minds are dangerous and unpredictable places. We are susceptible
to forces we don't understand. We are capable of inflicting immense cruelty on one
another, and yet we also have the capacity to be tender, to empathise, to feel.

'Fresh and illuminating . . . arresting and profound.' John Gray

'An eloquent disquisition on humankind's self-division between our finer and our baser
inclinations.' Salley Vickers, *Independent on Sunday*

£7.99

ISBN 978 1 84767 254 4

Also available:

EBook
£7.99
ISBN 978 1 84767 397 8

THE GOOD MAN JESUS AND THE SCOUNDREL CHRIST

PHILIP PULLMAN

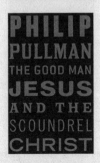

Philip Pullman retells the story of Jesus in this explosive addition to Canongate's *Myths* series

In this ingenious and spell-binding retelling of the life of Jesus, Philip Pullman revisits the most influential story ever told.

Charged with mystery, compassion and enormous power, *The Good Man Jesus and the Scoundrel Christ* throws fresh light on who Jesus was and asks the reader questions that will continue to resonate long after the final page is turned. Above all, this book is about how stories become stories.

£14.99

ISBN 978 1 84767 825 6

Also available:

Audio Book
£16.99
ISBN 978 1 84767 827 0

EBook
£12.99
ISBN 978 1 84767 828 7

THE DEATH OF BUNNY MUNRO

NICK CAVE

A darkly funny and very moving father–son story from the world-famous musician

Bunny Munro sells beauty products and the dream of hope to lonely housewives along the south coast of England. Set adrift by his wife's sudden death and struggling to keep a grip on reality, he does the only thing he can think of – with his young son in tow, he hits the road.

An account of one man's judgement and death, *The Death of Bunny Munro* is also a tender portrait of the relationship between father and son.

'A filthy, rollicking tale of one man's seedy descent into hell . . . Accessible, thrilling and gloriously impolite, it's a morality tale with all the fire, brimstone and humanity that Nick Cave is known for.' *Daily Telegraph*

'Told with verve, studded with scalding humour . . . What lingers are the linguistic fireworks.' *Observer*

'You will blanch with horror, recoil with distress and then, most unexpectedly of all, feel some sort of twisted sympathy for his anarchistic antichrist of a hero.' *Irish Independent*

£16.99

ISBN 978 1 84767 376 3

Also available:

Audio Book
£30.00
ISBN 978 1 84767 547 7

EBook
£16.99
ISBN 978 1 84767 548 4